occasionally, for the author is dealing largely with the upper regions of the range and, as he expresses it, tries to avoid sliding down into the foothills.

In addition to his consecutive account of what has taken place in the Sierra since its discovery, Mr. Farquhar thoroughly re-examines the events and the characters of those who participated in them; he corrects numerous errors and reappraises such figures as John C. Frémont, Josiah Dwight Whitney, and Clarence King. John Muir is shown to be the true champion of the Sierra, a leader unexcelled in the interpretation of its features and the conservation of its values.

The book is illustrated by drawings, original photographs, and maps specially drawn to assist the reader. The end of each chapter has amplifying notes and references for those interested in further pursuit of a subject.

HISTORY OF THE SIERRA NEVADA

Lyell Fork of the Tuolumne River.

HISTORY
OF THE SIERRA NEVADA

BY

FRANCIS P. FARQUHAR

PUBLISHED BY
UNIVERSITY OF CALIFORNIA PRESS
BERKELEY AND LOS ANGELES
IN COLLABORATION WITH
THE SIERRA CLUB
1966

THIS BOOK IS LOVINGLY DEDICATED

TO MY WIFE

MARJORY BRIDGE FARQUHAR

WHO HAS SHARED WITH ME SO MANY HAPPY EXPERIENCES

IN YOSEMITE AND THE HIGH SIERRA

TABLE OF CONTENTS

LIST OF ILLUSTRATIONS

AAJ   *American Alpine Journal*, American Alpine Club, New York

Bancroft, *California*   Hubert Howe Bancroft, *History of California*, 7 vols., 1884-1890

Bancroft, *Chronicles*   Hubert Howe Bancroft, *Chronicles of the Builders of the Commonwealth*, 7 vols., 1891-1892

Brewer Journal   Up and Down California in 1860-1864: The Journal of William H. Brewer, New Haven: Yale University Press; new edition, Berkeley and Los Angeles: University of California Press, 1949

CHS   California Historical Society, San Francisco

CHSQ   California Historical Society Quarterly

CSL   California State Library, Sacramento

Farquhar   Francis P. Farquhar, *Yosemite, the Big Trees, and the High Sierra: A Selective Bibliography*, Berkeley and Los Angeles: University of California Press, 1948. (Lists and describes 25 titles of historical interest.)

HSSCA   Historical Society of Southern California Annual

PHR   Pacific Historical Review, Berkeley and Los Angeles: University of California Press

SCB   Sierra Club Bulletin, Sierra Club, San Francisco

Wagner-Camp   Henry R. Wagner and Charles L. Camp, *The Plains and the Rockies: A Bibliography of Original Narratives of Travel and Adventure, 1800-1865*, San Francisco: Grabhorn Press, 1937; new edition, Columbus, Ohio: Long's College Book Company, 1953. (Contains a numbered list of 429 titles.)

Wheat   Carl I. Wheat, *Mapping the Transmississippi West*, 5 vols. (the last in two parts), San Francisco: Institute of Historical Cartography, 1957-1963. (Contains a numbered list of 1,302 maps, dated from 1540 to 1884, many of them reproduced.)

YNN   Yosemite Nature Notes, Yosemite National Park, 1922-1961

PREFACE

This history deals with human experiences in the Sierra Nevada from the time the Spaniards first saw it in the latter part of the eighteenth century to the present, when its economic and recreational uses serve several million people. For the earlier part of this period records are scarce and incomplete and every advantage has been taken of those that are available; in the latter part the records are so voluminous that it has been necessary sometimes to make a selection in order to keep the story in balance. Thus, in the condensation, the reader may find his favorite topic neglected or omitted altogether. Nevertheless, the book will, I believe, be found on the whole to be in proper perspective. It will be observed that this history deals primarily with the High Sierra. The foothills and the mining towns have been dealt with by others in great detail, so I have resisted the temptation, save in a few instances that seemed relevant, to leave the mountains and slide downhill toward the lowlands.

One general observation I should like to make about the men and women who appear in this story. Almost all of them were young, in their twenties or early thirties, at the time we meet them. They were strong, vigorous, and eager. They faced the unknown barrier of the Sierra and overcame it. In later days they explored every canyon and peak and turned their energies into preserving a fair share of the high country in its natural condition so that others might find health and inspiration there.

In assembling the facts that form the basis of this narrative I have gone to original sources as much as possible. In some instances this has resulted in a revision of hitherto generally accepted accounts. Should there be any doubts in the reader's mind, the references at the end of each chapter will guide him to the sources of information. These references are also available for those who wish to examine the precise text of quotations. I have taken the liberty to depart from these texts now and then in order to provide smoother reading, but in no way to distort the meaning. For example, I have occasionally omitted words, even whole sentences, without using the conventional signs of omission, and I have changed spelling and punctuation to conform to current usage. I believe the general reader will profit by this practice and the scholar will lose nothing of importance.

This book has been prepared over a good many years. Some of the material has been published in the *Sierra Club Bulletin* and other periodicals, but the final revision and writing of the present text has been the work of the past two years. In all of this I have been helped immeasurably by my friends, who have read chapters as the work progressed and have made valuable suggestions. Among those to whom I am especially indebted are George P. Hammond, Director of the Bancroft Library, and Dale L. Morgan, Robert H. Becker, and Barr Tompkins, of the Bancroft staff; also Charles L. Camp, Robert F. Heizer, and George R. Stewart, of the University of California; John B. Condliffe and Chancellor Franklin Murphy, patient and generous campmates at the Bohemian Grove; Emanuel Fritz, also a companion in the Grove and expert forester; Allan R. Ottley, of the California State Library; Stewart Mitchell, of Sacramento, authority on Sierra roads; Douglass Hubbard, of Yosemite; Dave Brower and George Marshall, of the Sierra Club; Ansel Adams for his counsel and for the use of his beautiful photographs; and finally, those candid critics, my son Peter and my wife Marjory. There are many others to whom I am indebted, but I cannot name them all here. There is one, however, to whom I give special thanks—D. Hanson Grubb, friend of many years, a devoted lover of the Sierra, who has never ceased to encourage me and stimulate me to keep my promise to write this book. In the final stages of its production, Lawton Kennedy for his designing, and Lloyd Lyman, Conrad Mollath, and Grace Buzaljko, of the University of California Press, have been most helpful and cooperative, and I am glad to take this opportunity to express my thanks.

FRANCIS P. FARQUHAR

Berkeley, California
July, 1965

HISTORY OF THE SIERRA NEVADA

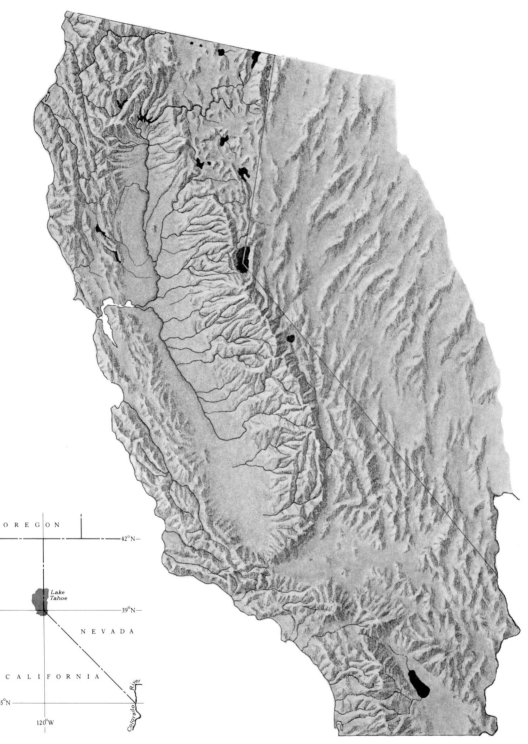

The Sierra Nevada in relation to the Central Valley of California.
(The detailed maps are at the end of the book.)

I

THE SIERRA NEVADA

The Sierra Nevada is defined as "limited on the north by the gap south of Lassen Peak, and on the south by Tehachapi Pass." It is about four hundred miles long and varies in breadth from forty to eighty miles. Save for a small angle of the state of Nevada that penetrates Lake Tahoe, it lies entirely in California. To the geologist the Sierra Nevada "constitutes a magnificent unit, one of the finest examples on the face of the globe of a single range, the type of its class."[1]

To the geographer it is of equal interest. In more than one sense it constitutes a barrier—a barrier to human migration, and a barrier to the winds and storms that press upon it. As a barrier to weather the range has a beneficial effect. In winter the storm clouds deposit their watery burden in successive layers of snow, which in due time give birth to streams that merge into rivers and bring life to the land below.

Water, in all its forms, is indeed the crowning glory of the Sierra. The crystalline snows harden beneath the rocky peaks and crests into perpetual snowfields, disclosing here and there beds of blue ice, reminders of the vaster glaciers that ages ago sculptured the cirques and canyons. The cirques now enfold little lakes, sapphire and emerald in hue; sometimes half-frozen, even in summer. Here, in these granite heights, all is silent—silent and undisturbed. But from below comes the tinkling sound of running water; then a murmuring and a splashing as the newborn streams glide into pools irradiated by beams of sunlight. Now comes the great drama of the Sierra. The streams gather volume and begin a boisterous journey, plunging to the depths of canyons in leaping and twisting cascades. In Yosemite, heart of the Sierra, the forms of water attain their most exciting expression. There the great waterfalls leap from lofty cliffs in magnificent variety. In contrast, there are throughout the range hundreds of quiet lakes, lapped in rock basins, bordered by pines and alders. Whether in motion or at rest, the waters of the Sierra are a constant joy to the beholder. Above all, they are the Sierra's greatest contribution to human welfare.

The Sierra Nevada is generally considered by geologists to be a portion of the earth's crust that has been detached and uplifted on its eastern margin so as to be tilted to the west in a long moderate slope, segmented laterally by deep canyons. The eastern profile is more complicated. Along much of its length there is a precipitous escarpment, but toward the north this abruptness disappears and the rise to the main crest is more gradual, though sometimes tortuous. At the midway point the crest is so flattened that an interior range has sometimes been mistaken for the summit until more closely examined. Conversely, farther north, at Lake Tahoe, the main crest is separated from the adjacent valley by a trough that contains the lake, with a subordinate range to the east.

The fundamental basis of this great tilted block is igneous rock—granite in varied forms and textures. This granitic bedrock is exposed in large areas of serrated ridges and peaks, in domes and bosses, in perpendicular cliffs, and the clean-swept flanks of canyons. There are glaciated surfaces polished smooth as glass and there are surfaces roughened by ages of weathering. The granite is found in exfoliated slabs and in massive rectangular blocks, in broken talus, and in the boulders and gravel of streambeds. Yet even the casual observer must notice that all is not granite in the Sierra. There are red mountains and there are black ones, such as Mount Dana and Red Slate Peak, Mount Lyell and Mount Goddard, and the Kaweah Peaks. Geologists tell us that these are the remains of an ancient range of metamorphic rock that stood on top of the granite before the uplift. Most of this was eroded away long ago, but substantial portions remain to give variety to the landscape. Another geologic agency, vulcanism, has enhanced the variety. Although there are no huge volcanic cones as in the Cascades, there is ample evidence of enormous eruptions in some early period. The famous Table Mountain and the curious Dardanelles in the Stanislaus region indicate that the land was once flooded with lava. Smaller and more recent volcanic remnants are found in a number of places. The most remarkable is the Devil's Postpile,[2] rivaling in the perfection of its geometric forms the Giant's Causeway in Ireland and Fingal's Cave on the Scottish island of Staffa. In the higher regions of the Sierra metals occur, but only sparsely. A few copper claims have been worked, but no appreciable amount of ore has ever been taken out. Silver has been found, but the hoped-for bonanzas never materialized. The story of gold belongs largely to the western foothills, and with the exception of Gold Lake and Mariposa (to be touched upon later) is purposely excluded from this history lest it obscure all other subjects.

On the long western slope is the unique forest belt that distinguishes the Sierra Nevada, unique in its relatively restricted area and in the variety and quality of its trees. The conifers, which are the dominant feature, are among the finest specimens of their kind in the world, towering to heights rarely excelled, beautiful in their proportions and in the texture of their bark and foliage. Famous above all others is the Big Tree, the *Sequoia gigantea*, found in its natural state only in the Sierra Nevada of California. More extensive, and quite as much to be admired, are the two great pines, the Yellow Pine

Ansel Adams

Sugar Pine cones.

and the Sugar Pine. These are the trees that the lumbermen seek for their massive beams and their broad, clear boards. Of the Sugar Pine John Muir wrote: "This is the noblest pine yet discovered, surpassing all others not merely in size but also in its kingly beauty and majesty. The trunk is a smooth, round, delicately tapered shaft, mostly without limbs, and colored rich purplish-brown, usually enlivened with tufts of yellow lichen. At the top of this magnificent bole, long curving branches sweep gracefully outward and downward. The needles are about three inches long, finely tempered and arranged in rather loose tassels at the end of slender branchlets that close the long, outsweeping limbs. How well they sing in the wind, and how strikingly harmonious an effect is made by the immense cylindrical cones that depend loosely from the ends of the main branches!"[3]

Above and below the two great pines are other varieties, less valuable commercially, yet not to be overlooked. As one ascends from the bare foothills to the forest belt one encounters the Digger Pine with its long needles and big hook-encrusted cones. It is worthless for lumber, but makes good firewood. At higher altitudes is the Lodgepole, also known as the Tamrac Pine. It is the characteristic tree of the Tuolumne Meadows and other frequented camp-grounds and is remembered by campers for the little cones, the last of which can never quite be found and removed from underneath the sleeping bag. In the southern part of the Sierra, in the plateau region near Mount Whitney, the Foxtail Pine commands attention for its sturdy weather-beaten trunk and its branchlets rounded with needles in a form that suggests its name. Still higher is the Whitebark Pine, the timberline tree of the Sierra. Sometimes it is found solitary, standing straight and slim, but more often it grows in clumps, flattened by storms, barely higher than a man's shoulder. Nothing can com-pare with it for a high-mountain bivouac—a bed of soft needles beneath a weatherproof covering of closely knit branches. A smoldering bit of pitchy wood outside the nest completes the comfort and happiness of the mountain-eer. The Pinyon, although a dominant tree in the Southwest, is a novelty in the Sierra. It is found scattered along the eastern wall, rarely west of the main crest. It has but one needle to a socket, instead of the two, three, or five of other pines. The nuts, hard-won from the compact cones, when cracked open present a small kernel, highly esteemed as a delicacy.

One might continue to dwell among the pines, but there are other trees to consider. There are the Douglas Fir (which is not a fir at all, but is *sui gen-eris*), the graceful Mountain Hemlock, the Western White Pine, and the handsome Incense Cedar. And there are the true firs, the White Fir and the Red Fir, which constitute a large part of the forest belt. On rocky slopes and high plateaus stands the Juniper, an uncompromising individualist. There is unlimited variety in its stocky trunks, strong limbs, and crowns of massed foliage—dark green, laced with clusters of turquoise-blue berries. A Juniper that stands above the South Fork of the Stanislaus, the "Bennett Tree," is claimed as a rival of the Sequoia and the Bristlecone Pine for the honor of being "the oldest living thing."[4]

In autumn, at one of the passes, Ebbetts perhaps, or Carson, the landscape is illuminated by a sea of golden Aspen, tying the Sierra to similar scenes in the Rockies and the Appalachians; for the Aspen is almost the only tree that is common throughout the land. Maples and Birches, local varieties, add color to canyon walls. In the spring the Dogwood lights up the forest with its large white flowers. Great Oaks adorn the floors of canyons, and smaller Live Oaks ornament the ledges of the canyon walls.

It is but a step from forest to chaparral. Manzanita, though at times almost a tree, is ordinarily only a few feet high, sometimes even trailing on the ground. In whatever form, its smooth red stems and bright green leaves at-tract the eye. Little clusters of delicate pink flowers, which later turn to

berries (*manzanitas*=little apples) belie the hostility of the bush to any pene-
tration of its territory. Other forms of chaparral are equally attractive and
equally defensive—Buckthorn, Chinquapin, and the fragrant, blossoming
Ceanothus.

In early summer, and at high altitudes all summer long, the Sierra is one
great garden of flowers. There is no massed color, and one is hardly aware
of them from an automobile. One has to approach on foot, lovingly, and with
time to enjoy their beauty. On entering Yosemite Valley early in summer
one is greeted by the Azalea. The white sweet-smelling flowers hang over
the Merced like the "bower of roses by Bendemeer's stream," and like the roses
not to be forgotten. Nor will one forget the bright yellow Evening Primroses
that adorn Yosemite's meadows. In the forest belt the Snow Plant raises its
scarlet spike while patches of snow still lie round about. Lovelier by far is
the Mariposa Lily, varying in color from nearly white to pale lavender to
pale rose, each petal marked by a red-brown eyespot. Above the forest belt
are hanging gardens, where little streams trickle down through moss and
grass, adorned with brilliant spots of color—scarlet Pentstemon and Columbine, bright blue Larkspur and Monkshood, yellow Mimulus, the orange
Leopard Lily, and the lavender-pink blossoms of the Wild Onion. The hanging gardens are the home of the White Violet and the Rein Orchis, the latter
a spiral of miniature white flowers. Nearby in open alpine meadows are the
red-and-yellow Paintbrush, the blue Gentian, and a galaxy of pink Shooting
Stars. Higher still are rock gardens trimmed with the Sierra Primrose and the
Scarlet Gilia. Here are the alpine heathers—the rose-purple Bryanthus and
the little white bells of Cassiope. All around are carpets of Phlox and Pussy
Paws and the minutiae of mosses and lichens. For one who climbs to the high
passes or ventures out upon granite ledges there is a supreme reward, the
fragrant cerulean blue flower clusters of the Polemonium. On the return to
lower levels one is accompanied all the way by Lupine, varying from little
blue-and-white mats near the peaks to many-branched leafy bushes below,
in all shades of blue and yellow.

There are said to be ten thousand kinds of insects in the Sierra Nevada.
But let us leave them to the entomologists and the fishermen—all, that is, save
the butterflies. Of these there are any number of spectacular ones to enliven
the scene, floating and dancing in glade and meadow. And there are some
rare ones, such as Behr's Sulfur, to rejoice the collector—if he can get them.
The herpetologist will find amphibians and reptiles in abundance, all harmless except one, the Rattlesnake. However, he is most considerate and gives
fair warning not to come too near. Casualties are rare.[5]

The birds of the Sierra are numerous, beautiful, and interesting. Although
all are worthy of notice, three stand out as distinctive examples of their kind,
the Water Ouzel, the Clark Nutcracker, and the Rosy Finch. John Muir, in

one of the most delightful of bird biographies, describes the Ouzel: "He is a singularly joyous and loveable little fellow, about the size of a robin, clad in a plain waterproof suit of bluish gray, with a tinge of chocolate on the head and shoulders. In form he is about as smoothly plump as a pebble that has been whirled in a pot-hole, the flowing contour of his body being interrupted only by his strong feet and bill, the crisp wing-tips, and the up-slanted wren-like tail."[6] The Ouzel is never far from water, usually in its most turbulent form. He flies behind waterfalls and dives into racing rapids. His song is as exquisite as the lark's. The Nutcracker, on the other hand, is a raucous, caw-ing bird, related to the jays. He lives in the open upper reaches of the timber and is often seen restlessly flying from one dead treetop to another, conspicu-ous in his mantle of contrasting white and black feathers. He is a great des-troyer of pine cones, extracting their seeds with blows of his sharp, powerful beak. Despite his uncouth manner, his harsh voice, and solitary aloofness, the Clark Nutcracker has a place all his own in the nostalgic memory of high-mountain campers.

The Rosy Finch, the third representative of bird life of the Sierra, has little of voice or plumage to commend him. His tuneless chirp is beguiling to no one save the climber of mountain peaks. To him it is a cheerful, companion-able sound, for the Rosy Finch, as he flutters out on the snowfields to pick up frost-deadened insects, is often the only sign of life.

The larger animals have never been as conspicuous in the Sierra Nevada as in the Rocky Mountains and the Northwest, although once they were more numerous than they are now. The Grizzly Bear, largest and most ferocious animal of the region, was once common in the forest belt and canyons of the Sierra, but his mode of life was incompatible with that of civilized man, and he was doomed to extinction. Pioneer literature is full of encounters with Grizzlies. Most picturesque of all is the story of "Grizzly Adams." He had a way with animals and was able to tame even Grizzlies. He captured several not far from Yosemite Valley and took them, together with other animals, to San Francisco, where he displayed them during the late 1850's in what he called a "Mountaineer Museum." There he attracted the attention of Theo-dore Hittell, who wrote newspaper articles about him, and eventually a book.[7] In the spring of 1860 Adams took his menagerie around the Horn to New York and entered into a contract with P. T. Barnum for a traveling exhibit. It did not last long, for after a few weeks Adams died of an old injury. Barnum in his *Autobiography* quotes the dying hunter: "I have attended preaching every day, Sundays and all, for the last six years. Sometimes an old grizzly gave me the sermon, sometimes it was a panther; often it was the thunder and lightning, the tempest, or the hurricane on the peaks of the Sierra Nevada; but whatever preached to me, it always taught me the majesty of the Creator, and revealed to me the undying and unchanging love of our kind Father in heaven." Not one California Grizzly remains alive today; the last record of one is dated 1924.

The Black Bear, however, is common enough, especially in tourist centers and campgrounds—harmless, amusing, frequently a nuisance. One hears of "Cinnamon Bears" or "Brown Bears," but they are merely color phases of the Black Bear, even occasionally of the same litter.

The "panther" mentioned by Adams was the Mountain Lion (Puma or Cougar), still an inhabitant of the Sierra despite many years of his attempted suppression as a predator. For a long time there was a bounty on his head, but that has been removed, for it is now realized that he is not a menace to human society, but only to deer, his principal diet. There are many reports of hearing the "scream" of a Mountain Lion, but rarely has there been any substantiation that would connect it with the Mountain Lion. According to naturalists he is a singularly silent animal, and the "scream" probably comes from an owl or perhaps a wildcat. The Wildcat (Bobcat or Lynx) is shy and when seen is usually bounding away for cover. The Red Fox, too, is a wary animal and keeps out of sight as much as possible. The only truly savage animals in the Sierra are the members of the weasel family—the Wolverine, the Fisher, the Otter, the Mink, the Pine Marten, and the little Weasel himself, and they are savage only to other small animals. All except the Wolverine. He is powerful and fearless and never retreats and is not to be trifled with. The Wolverine is a nocturnal hunter, except in winter, and so is seldom seen by man.

Wolves are mentioned in travelers' accounts, but it is doubtful if Wolves ever inhabited the Sierra Nevada, except for an occasional "stray" from farther east. In most instances it is the big Mountain Coyote that is mistaken for a Wolf. The Coyote, at a distance, may look like a Wolf, but he has a voice that is unmistakably his own. One naturalist describes his high-pitched howls: "Sometimes a single animal will call, at other times there will be a chorus, seemingly joined in from every direction. It is a weird wild sound sufficient to chill the blood of the inexperienced camper, but always a thrill to those who love the wilderness and its inhabitants."[8]

There is an abundance of lesser folk in the Sierra—the Marmot, the Badger, the Cony or Pika, the Snowshoe Rabbit, the Belding Ground Squirrel and the Golden-Mantled Ground Squirrel, and many others, including the Chickaree or Douglas Squirrel, subject of another of John Muir's essays.[9] Of hoofed animals there are two kinds in the Sierra, the Mule Deer and the Mountain Sheep. The Mule Deer outnumbers all the other larger mammals. He is protected by refuge in the National Parks and by state game laws; but in open season many a buck falls before the marksmanship of the intrepid sportsman. The Deer population shows no sign of diminishing. Not so with the Mountain Sheep (Bighorn), which have almost reached the point of extinction. Once there were many bands along the crest of the Sierra, but during years of excessive grazing by domestic flocks they were crowded out in all save a very few places.[10] The surviving bands may increase with protection and management, or they may be wiped out.

In the Sierra Nevada *fish* and *trout* are synonymous. There are two kinds of native trout, the Cutthroat and the Rainbow, with their several subdivisions. Of the former, the Lake Tahoe Trout and the Royal Silver reach their maximum development in Lake Tahoe. At one time, years ago, they were caught commercially in enormous quantities and, before the days of "limits," sportsmen vied with each other for records both in size and numbers, hastening the species toward extinction. Happily these practices were curbed, and the big fish of Lake Tahoe now seem assured of survival. The Rainbow varieties are more widely distributed and have not been subjected to such avarice and plunder. The Golden Trout, originally found in small streams of the upper Kern, not only has survived in its natural habitat but has been transplanted in many other streams and lakes, which have proved hospitable.[11] It has all the refinements of its species and in addition distinctive colors that rival those of the exotic fishes of tropical seas. Other varieties of Trout and Char have been introduced—the Mackinaw in the Tahoe region, and the Brown Trout and Eastern Brook Trout all through the Sierra—so that if one gets far enough away from the odor of gasoline he may count on a plentiful catch for the evening meal.[12]

NOTES AND REFERENCES

This chapter is based partly on personal observation, of a nontechnical character, and more particularly on the following books and papers of competent scientists.

GENERAL

Tracy I. Storer and Robert L. Usinger, *Sierra Nevada Natural History: An Illustrated Handbook*, Berkeley and Los Angeles: University of California Press, 1963.

GEOLOGY

Henry W. Turner, "The Rocks of the Sierra Nevada," *Fourteenth Annual Report of the United States Geological Survey, 1892–'93.*
———, "Further Contributions to the Geology of the Sierra Nevada," *Seventeenth Annual Report of the United States Geological Survey, 1895–'96.*
Waldemar Lindgren, "The Tertiary Gravels of the Sierra Nevada of California," *United States Geological Survey Professional Paper 73*, 1911.
François E. Matthes, "Geologic History of the Yosemite Valley," *United States Geological Survey Professional Paper 160*, 1930.
———, *The Incomparable Valley*, Berkeley and Los Angeles: University of California Press, 1950.
Fritiof Fryxell (ed.), *François Matthes and the Marks of Time*, San Francisco: Sierra Club, 1962.

TREES

Willis Linn Jepson, *The Silva of California*, Berkeley: University of California Press, 1910.

Howard E. McMinn and Evelyn Maino, *An Illustrated Manual of Pacific Coast Trees*, Berkeley: University of California Press, 2nd ed., 1937.

FLOWERS

Harvey Monroe Hall and Carlotta Case Hall, *A Yosemite Flora*, San Francisco: Paul Elder, 1912.

Willis Linn Jepson, *A Manual of the Flowering Plants of California*, Berkeley: Associated Students Store, 1925.

BUTTERFLIES

Vernon L. Kellogg, "Butterflies of the Mountain Summits," *SCB*, June, 1913, 9:2.

Fordyce Grinnell, Jr., "A Butterfly of the High Sierra Nevada—Behr's Alpine Sulphur," *SCB*, June, 1913, 9:2.

Laurence Ilsley Hewes, "Butterflies—Try and Get Them," *SCB*, February, 1933, 18:1.

BIRDS AND MAMMALS

Joseph Grinnell and Tracy Irwin Storer, *Animal Life in the Yosemite*, Berkeley: University of California Press, 1924.

Joseph Grinnell, Joseph S. Dixon, and Jean M. Linsdale, *Fur-Bearing Mammals of California*, Berkeley: University of California Press, 1937.

Robert T. Orr, *Mammals of Lake Tahoe*, San Francisco: California Academy of Sciences, 1949.

Lowell Sumner and Joseph S. Dixon, *Birds and Mammals of the Sierra Nevada*, Berkeley and Los Angeles: University of California Press, 1953.

Tracy I. Storer and Lloyd P. Tevis, Jr., *California Grizzly*, Berkeley and Los Angeles: University of California Press, 1955.

FISHES

Barton Warren Evermann, "The Golden Trout of the Southern High Sierras," *Bulletin of the Bureau of Fisheries, 1905*, vol. 25, Washington, D. C., 1906.

Barton Warren Evermann and Harold C. Bryant, "California Trout," *California Fish and Game*, July, 1919, 5:3.

1. Andrew C. Lawson, "The Sierra Nevada," *University of California Chronicle*, April, 1891, 23:2.

2. François E. Matthes, "The Devil's Postpile and Its Strange Setting," *SCB*, February 1930, 15:1; reprinted in Fritiof Fryxell, *François Matthes and the Marks of Time*, San Francisco: Sierra Club, 1962.

3. John Muir, *The Mountains of California*, New York, Century Company, 1894. (Originally published in *Scribner's Monthly*, September, 1881.)

4. Clarence K. Bennett, "The Largest Juniper," *SCB*, February 1933, 18:1; *The Pony Express*, Sonora, December, 1962, and January and October, 1963.

5. Sixteen Eagle Scouts on a trip to the Kern River country one time were told by the Scoutmaster what to do in case of rattlesnakes. "Thus we learned our first lesson," wrote one of the Scouts in his diary, "in how to take care of ourselves in a dense rattlesnake country." The density proved rather less than expected. No

tourniquets were required. John R. Locke, Jr., *Trip of the Sequoia Eagles to the Summit of Mount Whitney*, Dinuba, 1926 (copy in BL).

6. John Muir, *The Mountains of California*. (Origially published in *Scribner's Monthly*, February, 1878.)

7. Theodore H. Hittell, *The Adventures of James Capen Adams, Mountaineer and Grizzly Bear Hunter, of California*, San Francisco, 1860. Francis P. Farquhar, "The Grizzly Bear Hunter of California," *Essays for Henry R. Wagner*, San Francisco: Grabhorn Press, 1947.

8. Robert T. Orr, *Mammals of Lake Tahoe*.

9. John Muir, *The Mountains of California*. (Originally published in *Scribner's Monthly*, December, 1878.)

10. Fred L. Jones, "A Survey of the Sierra Nevada Bighorn," *SCB*, June 1950, 35:6.

11. Evermann and Bryant, "California Trout," *California Fish and Game*, July, 1919, 5:3.

12. Charles McDermand, *Waters of the Golden Trout Country*, New York: Putnam, 1946; and his *Yosemite and Kings Canyon Trout*, New York, 1947.

II

INDIANS OF THE SIERRA NEVADA

Long before any white men arrived on the scene there were Indians living on both sides of the Sierra. How long they had been there is uncertain, but it was evidently a very long time, long enough for them to develop their own characteristics, quite different from those of any other western Indians. The Indians of the Sierra were not all of the same tribal or linguistic stock, but in other respects they had much in common. Nowhere was there anything resembling civilization as we conceive of it—no permanent buildings, no cultivated fields, no pasturing of tame animals, and only the simplest type of government. The gathering and preparation of food required most of their time.

There were five distinct groups of Indians, three on the western side of the Sierra, two on the eastern. Each had its own territory and hunting grounds, though there was some overlapping of the latter. On the west the most numerous were the Yokuts, whose villages, in the foothills and along the lower courses of the rivers, ranged from the head of the San Joaquin Valley as far north as the Fresno River. At one time their territory extended a little farther north, but by the time the Americans came their numbers had declined and their territory was correspondingly reduced. The Yokuts were the first Indians of the Sierra to have contact with white men, when Spanish missionaries and explorers visited their villages in the 1770's. From the Fresno north to the American River lived the Miwok; and north of that, the Maidu. It was the Maidu and the Miwok with whom the American immigrants and gold-seekers came into hostile contact. East of the Sierra, along the upper reaches of the Truckee, Carson, and Walker rivers, were the Washo. Their summer range extended to Lake Tahoe and over the crest a little way down the Stanislaus River. South of the Washo were the Mono, a Paiute people, with a considerably wider range. They even crossed the mountains, and a group known as the Monache occupied territory adjoining the Yokuts. This was done the more easily as the Yokuts were an easygoing, peaceable people, not particularly hard-pressed for subsistence.

The mode of life of all these people was much the same, except that in the arid country east of the Sierra they were more mobile. In the west their villages were in long-established locations. Their dwellings, brush and bark wickiups, could be moved from one site to another. Sources of subsistence were limited in variety, though plentiful enough in season. In the west the basic diet consisted of meal ground from acorns and leached of the bitter tannin, often combined with such delicacies as dried grasshoppers and cater-pillars. There were also plant bulbs, berries, and fish, augmented occasionally by the meat of deer or of small animals. East of the Sierra the diet was even more limited in variety. Pinyon nuts replaced acorns, spiced by the dried larvae of a little fly prolific on the shores of alkaline lakes. There were also rabbits, lizards, birds, and fish. In all areas cooking was usually done in closely woven baskets or in beds of hot ashes. Clothing was scant or nonexistent, except for robes of squirrel or rabbit skins worn in ceremonials or occa-sionally in winter. There was practically no pottery; on the other hand, basketry was highly developed both in design and workmanship. Bows and arrows and spears, used almost exclusively for hunting, were also skillfully made. The delicately formed arrowpoints, usually of obsidian (volcanic glass), compare favorably with those from other areas.

Although the Indians' permanent residence was in the mild climate of the valleys and foothills of the range, there is ample evidence that the higher country was well known to the tribes on both sides. Escape from summer heat was just as desirable to them as it is to us now, and the high mountain lakes and meadows just as attractive. In summer the villages were virtually abandoned as the cool heights were sought. The sites of the summer *ran-cherías* are still to be found, marked by circles of rocks and by holes in the bedrock for grinding acorns. Little flakes and chips of obsidian scattered about testify to the making of arrowpoints. Now and then a whole point may be uncovered, lost long ago, perhaps in an unsuccessful shot at a bird or an animal. There are other signs of summer occupancy, such as trails worn in the soft ground of the forest, trails not made by modern boots or by horses and mules. One such is the old Mono trail through the forest above Yosemite leading to Mono Pass and Bloody Canyon. This was one of the main trade routes across the mountains. Other known routes were across the other Mono Pass (leading from Owens Valley to the South Fork of the San Joaquin), Taboose Pass, and Kearsarge Pass (both from Owens Valley to the Kings), and Walker Pass into the Kern. Over these trade routes a considerable ex-change of products was carried on. The Yokuts, for instance, supplied skins of deer, antelope, and elk; baskets of willow bark; acorns and shell beads. In return they received pinyon nuts, red paint, and the strong sinew-backed bows that were a specialty of the Paiutes. Farther north the Miwok people supplied acorns, berries, baskets, and arrow shafts, in exchange for pinyon nuts, red and white paint, rabbit skins, and pumice stone. The Mono Craters were the principal source of obsidian for spear and arrowpoints.

This slender but sufficient economy was rudely interrupted by the arrival of the white man. The Spaniards, except as a possible source of epidemics,

Hutchings' Magazine

Indian woman gathering acorns.

brought little disturbance to the foothill Indians. They did, however, add a highly prized variant to the meager Indian diet, namely, horseflesh. Indian raids upon the coastal settlements and the capture of horses were followed by expeditions of soldiers sent to recapture the *caballadas*, but by the time they got there no living animals were to be found, only smoldering heaps of bones. All that was gained by the Spaniards was a little more knowledge of the Sierra foothills and of the Indian character. When at last the Americans came the serenity of the Indians' life was altered drastically. For two centuries, first on the Atlantic coast and then on the western plains, there had been a tradition of hostility between the two races, an attitude that was quite unnecessarily perpetuated in the California mountains. The Americans regarded the Indian as a pest, to be pushed aside ar obliterated. "Miners staked their claims in his territory; cut his acorn-bearing trees for fuel; hunted his game for food; destroyed his bulbous roots in digging for gold; invaded his family, taking young Indian women, willing or not, for servants or wives. Suffering from loss of food and territory the Indians made raids on the whites, taking what they could from the trading posts; stealing horses from the corrals; burning houses; even murdering, then fleeing to the mountains. A deadly hate was engendered; the Indian would drive the last miner from his territory.

The whites determined to subjugate the Indians and kill all of them if necessary."[1]

As time went on and the Indians were subdued, it was discovered that they were not so bad after all. Finally, protected on reservations or living peaceably in small communities, they became useful citizens. In later years intelligent efforts were made to learn more about them, their ways of life, and their myths and legends. Their folklore were found to have considerable imaginative merit, far superior to the white man's inventions that had been attributed to them, especially those in Yosemite guidebooks and sundry poetic fantasies.

A remarkable finale to the story of the primitive Indian occurred in 1911, when Ishi stepped out of the Stone Age past into the modern world. He was the last survivor of the Yahi, a tribe that had lived at the very northern edge of the Sierra, near Mount Lassen, having had little contact with white men. Through kind and understanding treatment, much was learned from him about the ways and thoughts of primitive Indians. His physician and friend, Dr. Saxton Pope, wrote of him at his death in San Francisco: "And so, stoic and unafraid, departed the last wild Indian of America. He closes a chapter in history. He looked upon us as sophisticated children—smart, but not wise. We knew many things, and much that is false. He knew nature, which is always true. His were the qualities of character that last forever. He was kind; he had courage and self-restraint, and though all had been taken from him, there was no bitterness in his heart. His soul was that of a child, his mind that of a philosopher."[2]

NOTES AND REFERENCES

Material for this chapter has been gathered from the following: Robert F. Heizer and M. A. Whipple, *The California Indians: A Source Book*, Berkeley and Los Angeles: University of California Press, 1951; A. L. Kroeber, *Handbook of the Indians of California*, Washington: Bureau of American Ethnology, 1925; Stephen Powers, *Tribes of California*, Washington, 1877; F. F. Latta, *Handbook of Yokuts Indians*, Oildale, Calif.: Bear State Books, 1949; and *Reports of the University of California Survey*: No. 34, James A. Bennyhoff, "An Appraisal of the Archaeological Resources of Yosemite National Park," 1956; No. 51, Albert B. Elsasser, "The Archaeology of the Sierra Nevada in California and Nevada," 1960; No. 54, James T. Davis, "Trade Routes and Economic Exchange Among the Indians of California," 1961; No. 58, M. G. Hindes, "The Archaeology of the Huntington Lake Region in the Southern Sierra Nevada, California," 1962.

1. Mrs. H. J. Taylor, *Yosemite Indians and Other Sketches*, San Francisco: Johnck and Seeger, 1936.
2. Saxton T. Pope, in Theodora Kroeber, *Ishi in Two Worlds*, Berkeley and Los Angeles: University of California Press, 1961.

III

SPANISH DISCOVERY AND EXPLORATION

The first European to sail a ship along the coast of what we now call California was Juan Rodríguez Cabrillo. In November 1542, while close to shore a little south of Monterey, he and his men beheld mountains covered with snow and spoke of them as *las sierras nevadas*, the snowy range.[1] When maps were made a little later, based on accounts of this voyage, the name "Sierra Nevada" appeared at various points along the coast in accordance with the cartographers' interpretations of the descriptions. Cabrillo, however, never saw the mountains *now* known as the Sierra Nevada, nor did any white man set eyes upon them until more than two centuries later. The first overland journey from Mexico to California—"Alta California" as it was then known—was not made until 1769, when Gaspar de Portolá's party discovered San Francisco Bay. In 1772 Captain Pedro Fages reached a point near the junction of the Sacramento and San Joaquin rivers. He was accompanied by a padre, Fray Juan Crespi, who described the scene in his diary as follows: "We made out that these three arms or three large rivers were formed by a very large river, a league in width at least, which descended from some high mountains to the southeast, very far distant."[2] Crespi made a quaint drawing showing the river debouching from the mountains. The year 1772 thus marks the earliest description, written and pictorial, of the Sierra Nevada.

Captain Fages saw the Sierra a little later in the same year from the southern end of the San Joaquin Valley. On a journey from San Diego, by way of Cajon Pass and the Mojave Desert, he reached Buena Vista Lake, at the foot of Tejon Pass. He described the scene as we recognize it today: "The range inland on the other side of the river is very high and its peaks are perpetually covered with snow. Many trees of a variety of species grow in the excellent soil of the foothills."[3] Thus the Sierra Nevada becomes a reality.

Four years later, in 1776, the Franciscan missionaries Francisco Garcés and Pedro Font gave further definition to the range, and Font placed it definitely on a map for the first time.[4] Garcés and Font were members of the Anza expedition that had come overland from Mexico to found a settlement on San Francisco Bay. While Garcés remained in the south, Font came on to the Bay and joined an exploration of its shores. From a hill near the mouth of the Sacramento River he beheld the scene that Crespi had reported. "Looking to the northeast," he wrote in his journal, "we saw an immense treeless plain into

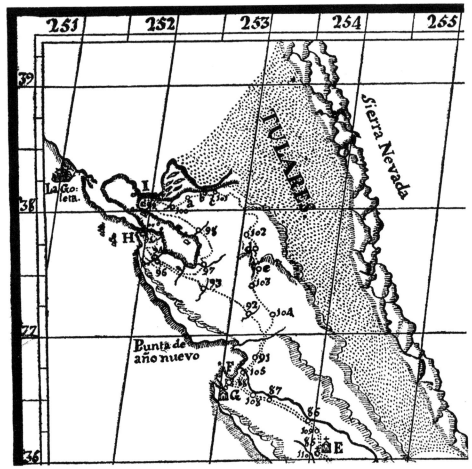

First showing of the "Sierra Nevada": portion of Font map, 1776.

which the water spreads widely, forming several low islets; at the opposite end
of this extensive plain, about forty leagues off, we saw a great snow-covered
range [*una gran sierra nevada*] which seemed to me to run from south-
southeast to north-northwest."[5] In this manner was our Sierra Nevada named,
although at the time the name was merely descriptive, not specific.

At about the same time, Garcés, in the south, was visiting the tulares and
rancherías that had been reported by Fages. From Tehachapi he observed
mountains stretching northeast and north and gave them the name "Sierra de
San Marcos." Shortly afterwards he came to a large river, "whose waters,
crystalline, bountiful, and palatable, flowed on a course from the east through
a straitened channel."[6] He called the river San Felipe, now Kern River.
When Garcés and Font met some time later and compared notes, they concluded that the mountains they had seen were one and the same range.[7]

The descriptions of Font and Garcés appeared to be leading toward a comprehensive knowledge of the interior of California and a delineation of the Sierra Nevada, but such was not the case. There were no more explorations in that direction for the remainder of the century. Not until 1805 was a further contribution made to knowledge of this region. To the Spaniard it presented no attraction. He was neither a fur trapper nor a hunter of game, and he suspected nothing of the golden treasure hidden in the Sierra foothills. If it had not been for the Indians he would have left the region entirely alone.

The presence of the Indians, however, made contact with the interior a necessity. The Indians harbored refugees from the coastal missions, and they stole horses. They had to be pursued by soldiers and punished. The refugees were not easily found, and the horses were never retrieved. Indians stole horses not for use as livestock, but for meat, and once in possession of such tempting flesh they lost little time in consuming it.

As time went on the Franciscan missionaries also visited the interior, searching for mission sites and hoping for wholesale baptisms. Sometimes they went alone but usually they accompanied the military parties. Thus, in 1804, Fray Juan Martín crossed the Coast Range to the nearby interior valley, known to the Spaniards as *los tulares* (the place of reeds), and, in the summer of 1806, Fray José María Zalvidea accompanied a military expedition as far as the mouth of Kern River. Neither trip had important results.[8]

More notable than these visits was one led by Ensign Gabriel Moraga in the fall of 1806.[9] That the route was not unfamiliar to him is intimated by his reference to a journey of the preceding year, in which the San Joaquin and Kings rivers were given the names they now bear. Kings River is a contracted translation of *Rio de los Santos Reyes* (River of the Holy Kings), evidence that Moraga's party camped at the river on January 6, the day of Epiphany, commemorative of the visit of the Magi to the infant Jesus. Moraga's expedition of 1806 added further to the nomenclature of the Sierra. After crossing the San Joaquin his party came to a place which his men called *Las Mariposas* because of the swarms of butterflies (*mariposas*) which flew into their eyes and ears. They discovered and named the Merced River (*Rio de Nuestra Señora de la Merced*), crossed other streams farther north, returned to the San Joaquin, and followed one of the rivers a little way up toward the mountains. They noticed an abundance of Pine and *Palo colorado* (Redwood), but it is most unlikely that they went far enough to have reached any of the Big Tree groves: they probably mistook Cedar for the familiar Redwood of the coast.[10]

At the San Joaquin River they found some Indians who gave them very puzzling information. About twenty years before, they were told, soldiers had come from the other side of the mountains and had killed some of the Indians. Moraga's men presumed that these soldiers had come from New

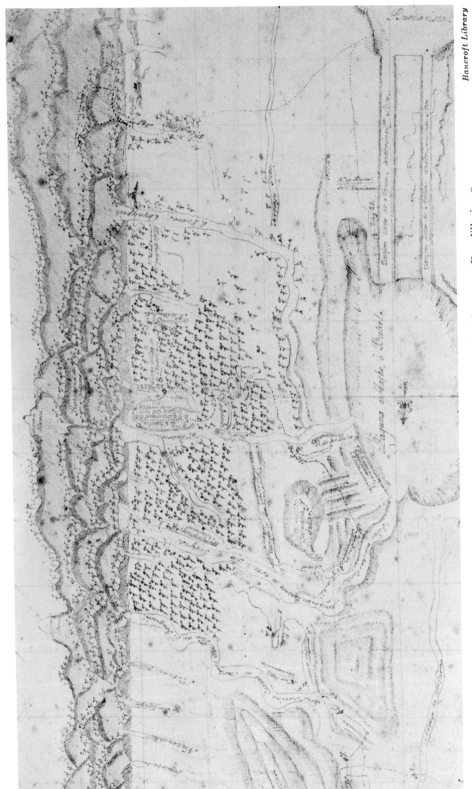

The Sierra from the San Joaquin Valley, as sketched by Lieutenant Estudillo in 1819.

Mexico. There was, of course, scarcely a remote possibility that they had come directly across the Sierra from New Mexico, or from anywhere else. The most likely explanation is that some punitive expedition from the coast, coming from the south along the foothills, appeared to have come out of the mountains. The tale had its effect, however, for it set the Spaniards speculating about what lay beyond the Sierra. At Kings River there was more talk of men from across the mountains, but nothing definite. They camped for several days at the Kaweah River and found the place then, as now, a delightful spot. After crossing the dry beds of Tule River and Pozo Creek they came to the Kern and there found evidence of Zalvidea's visit earlier in the year. For a month Moraga and his diarist, Fray Pedro Muñoz, had been in sight of the Sierra and had become familiar with the lower courses of its rivers. But, although New Mexico might not be far beyond, it was clear that there was no easy way across the mountains.

Having examined the foothills of the Sierra toward the south, Moraga at the next opportunity turned his attention toward the north.[11] Starting from Misión de San José,[12] he crossed the San Joaquin and ascended both the Stanislaus and the Mokelumne rivers some distance toward the mountains. At the Sacramento, which he named, he crossed to the west side and went on at least as far as the present site of Colusa, where he could see the Marysville Buttes.

From this journey it was learned that to the north, as well as to the south, the Sierra placed an eastern limit upon the Spanish occupation of California. Although the Spaniards continued to explore the interior for mission sites, practically nothing was added thereafter to their knowledge of the Sierra, except a few words of description by Father Narciso Durán in 1817.[13] Writing from a point near the site of Sacramento, he says that "looking to the northeast through a gap in the grove of the river bank, we discerned the famous Sierra Nevada. The white part of this Sierra seemed to be all snow, although, as they say, it is also a species of white rock which looks like snow." A little later and farther up the river, Durán writes: "Once the pass of the Sierra is discovered, which the northern end seems to offer, we should be able to ascertain the truth of what the Indians have told us for some years past, that on the other side of the Sierra Nevada there are people like our soldiers. We have never been able to clear up the matter and know whether they are Spanish from New Mexico, or English from the Columbia, or Russians from La Bodega."

These references to foreigners beyond the Sierra remain a perplexity. Certainly the Russians never penetrated very far inland from their settlements at Bodega and Fort Ross, and could not have been on the eastern side of the Sierra at any time. It seems too early for North West Company men or others from the north to have come near enough to cause comment among California Indians. The most plausible explanation seems to be that the reports arose from the presence in the Utah country of Spanish traders and adventurers from New Mexico. Although they came nowhere near the Sierra Nevada, it is not unreasonable to suppose that accounts of the strange white men would travel from tribe to tribe until the matter became a common subject of remark throughout the West.

The character of the Sierra Nevada had by this time begun to take definite shape in the records of civilization, even though no white man had attained its summits or had passed over its crest. It was known to be a massive mountain several hundred miles long, with rivers of considerable volume emerging from unascertained heights to form two principal streams. Extensive forests had been observed above its barren foothills, and higher still there were rocks that looked like snow and summits unmistakably covered with snow. All this is very well summarized in a sketch made in 1819 by Lieutenant José María Estudillo.[14] It shows the debouchements of the San Joaquin, the Kings, the Kaweah, and the Kern, with forests extending high up into the mountains. Two peaks are labeled *sierra blanca* (i.e., white mountain); the northern one might well be a representation of Mount Goddard, the more southerly the Kaweahs.

By this time the genius and energy that had brought the Spaniards over uncharted seas and across deserts and mountains were spent. The vast forests, the deep canyons, the lofty peaks of the Sierra Nevada remained unvisited. A new wave was about to appear on the east, soon to become a flood tide. Toward the end of the year 1826 a band of American "mountain men," fur hunters, led by Jedediah Smith, straggled into the Spanish Mission of San Gabriel—a conjunction of historic portent for California.

NOTES AND REFERENCES

1. Henry R. Wagner, *Spanish Voyages to the Northwest Coast of America in the Sixteenth Century*, CHS, 1929; and Wagner, *Juan Rodríguez Cabrillo, Discoverer of the Coast of California*, CHS, 1941.

2. Herbert Eugene Bolton, *Fray Juan Crespi, Missionary Explorer of the Pacific Coast*, Berkeley: University of California Press, 1927.

3. Translation of a passage in *Report by Fages to Bucareli*, 1775 (in BL); see also Bolton, "In the San Joaquin Ahead of Garcés," *CHSQ*, September, 1931, 10:3; and Herbert Ingram Priestley, *A Historical, Political, and Natural Description of California by Pedro Fages, Soldier of Spain*, Berkeley: University of California Press, 1937.

4. Font made two maps showing the Sierra Nevada (*Wheat* 166 and 169), both reproduced in Irving Bodine Richman, *San Francisco Bay and California in 1776*, Providence, R. I.: John Carter Brown Library, 1911; Bolton, *Font's Complete Diary*, Berkeley: University of California Press, 1931; and Neal Harlow, *The Maps of San Francisco Bay*, San Francisco: Grabhorn Press, 1950.

5. Frederick J. Teggart, "The Anza Expedition of 1775-76: Diary of Pedro Font," *Publications of the Academy of Pacific Coast History*, University of California, 1913, 3:1; Bolton, *Font*.

6. Elliott Coues, *On the Trail of a Spanish Pioneer: The Diary and Itinerary of Francisco Garcés*, New York: Francis P. Harper, 1909.

7. Bolton, *Font*; Teggart, "Anza"; Coues, *Garcés*.

8. Priestley, *Franciscan Explorations in California*, Glendale, Calif.: Arthur H. Clark Co., 1946.

9. Bancroft, *California*, II; also, an unpublished diary of Pedro Muñoz, *Archivo de Santa Barbara, IV* (in BL).

10. Moraga had come to California in 1781 at the age of fourteen and had lived in Branciforte (Santa Cruz), where he must have been familiar with redwood trees. Muñoz, however, was a newcomer and to him cedar and redwood doubtless looked the same.

11. Donald G. Cutter, *The Diary of Ensign Gabriel Moraga's Expedition of Discovery in the Sacramento Valley, 1808*, Los Angeles, 1957.

12. *Misión de San José* is the Spanish name for the Mission; the Americanized name of the locality is now Mission San Jose. It is some twelve miles from the city of San Jose.

13. Charles Edward Chapman, "Expedition on the Sacramento and San Joaquin Rivers in 1817. Diary of Fray Narciso Durán," *Publications of the Academy of Pacific Coast History*, 1911, 2:5.

14. Reproduced in Priestley, *Franciscan Explorations*.

IV

JEDEDIAH SMITH AND
THE FIRST CROSSING OF THE SIERRA

When Jedediah Smith and his band of trappers arrived in California they had come by a route far south of the Sierra. They had struggled up the "Inconstant River" (the Mojave) and had at last reached the haven of San Gabriel Mission in the Spanish settlements. There Father José Bernardo Sánchez welcomed them with kindly hospitality. However, when Governor Echeandia at San Diego learned of their arrival things were different. Instead of granting permission for the Americans to proceed northward by the coast, he ordered the intruders to leave at once by the way they had come. Jedediah, nevertheless, had no intention of abandoning his search for new beaver country. So, although he departed as ordered, instead of going back by the Mojave to the Colorado, he turned northward over the Tehachapi and entered the Central Valley.

Before following his subsequent movements, let us become better acquainted with Jedediah Strong Smith.[1] He was only twenty-seven years old in 1826, yet even then he was one of the most experienced among that extraordinary group of "mountain men" that would include such famous names as Jim Bridger, David Jackson, William Sublette, James Clyman. He was highly respected not alone for his physical prowess, but for a moral character almost unique among his associates. Born in south central New York on January 6, 1799, he received a good education and was especially well grounded in the Bible. At the age of twenty-three he went to St. Louis, metropolis of the fur trade, and enlisted with the Ashley–Henry expedition to the Upper Missouri. During the next few years, until his sadly premature death by Indian arrows on the Cimarron in 1831, he came to know more about the Far West than any of his contemporaries. Most of the mountain men knew the upper reaches of the Missouri, but Jedediah penetrated beyond into the very heart of the Hudson's Bay Company domain; he was a pioneer of South Pass, and was hard on the heels of the discoverers of Great Salt Lake. So, when in 1826, the new firm of Smith, Jackson and Sublette sought new beaver country away from the rivalry of the overworked streams of the Rockies, Smith was clearly the man to lead it. The most likely region seemed to be the unexplored country to the west and south, and in choosing this Jedediah became the first American to lead an overland party from United

States territory to Spanish California. As a consequence he was also the first to cross the barrier of the Sierra Nevada—not from east to west, as might be supposed, but in the opposite direction.

The movements of Smith's party up to the time of leaving San Gabriel Mission in January, 1827, are well documented. Both Smith and his chief lieutenant, Harrison Rogers, kept diaries. Portions of these have survived and have been published;[2] but the parts relating to the approach to the Sierra and to Smith's crossing of it have not been found. For this period we must rely upon other records. Aside from maps, the most important of these is a letter written by Smith after his return to the rendezvous at Bear River, north of Great Salt Lake.[3] It is addressed to General William Clark, Superintendent of Indian Affairs, at St. Louis, himself one of the greatest of American explorers. After describing the first part of his journey and the refusal of Governor Echeandia to allow him to trade up the coast, Smith continues:

"I returned to my party at San Gabriel and purchased such articles as were necessary and went eastward of the Spanish settlements on the route I had come in. I steered my course northwest, keeping from 150 to 200 miles from the seacoast, a very high range of mountains being on the east. After traveling 300 miles in that direction, through a country somewhat fertile, in which there were a great many Indians, mostly naked and destitute of arms, with the exception of bows and arrows, and what is very singular among Indians, they cut their hair to the length of three inches. They proved to be friendly. The manner of living is on fish, roots, acorns, and grass.

"On my arrival at a river which I called the Wim-mel-che (named after a tribe of Indians who reside on it of that name), I found a few Beaver—Elk, Deer, and Antelope in abundance. I here made a small hunt and attempted to take my party across the mountain which I before mentioned, and which I called Mount Joseph, to come on and join my partners at the Great Salt Lake. I found the snow so deep on Mount Joseph that I could not cross my horses, five of which starved to death. I was compelled therefore to return to the valley which I had left, and there leaving my party I started with two men, seven horses, and two mules, which I loaded with hay for the horses and provisions for ourselves, and started on the twentieth of May and succeeded in crossing it in eight days, having lost only two horses and one mule. I found the snow on the top of the mountain from four to eight feet deep, but it was so consolidated by the heat of the sun that my horses only sunk from half a foot to one foot deep.

"After traveling twenty days from the east side of Mount Joseph I struck the southwest corner of the Great Salt Lake, traveling over a country completely barren and destitute of game. When we arrived at the Salt Lake we had but one horse and one mule remaining, which were so poor that they could scarce carry the little camp equipage which I had along. The balance of the horses I was compelled to eat as they gave out."

From this letter it is possible to account for Smith's movements in a general way, but much is left in doubt and it is surprising what a variety of conclusions have been reached by historians, particularly in the nineteenth century. In fact, until recently, they have given very inadequate attention to the achievements of Jedediah Smith and, when it came to tracing his routes, they have invariably been wide of the mark. Thus we find the great Bancroft saying, "There are no means of knowing anything about his route; but I think he is as likely to have crossed the mountains near the present railroad line as elsewhere." In a footnote he goes even farther astray: "Still it is not impossible or unlikely that in this trip or on the return Smith went through Walker Pass, as Warner and others say, or followed the Humboldt or Mary, as Sprague tells us."[5] The Warner and Sprague references cited by Bancroft are so full of errors that they can be dismissed from the historical record.[6]

A letter addressed to Fray Narciso Durán at Misión de San José, written May 19, the day before Smith set out on his successful attempt to cross the mountain, furnishes some additional information. "Reverend Father," Smith writes, "I understand through the medium of one of your Christian Indians, that you are anxious to know who we are, as some of the Indians have been at the Mission and informed you that there were certain white people in the country. We are Americans, on our journey to the River Columbia. We were in at the Mission San Gabriel, in January last. I have made several efforts to cross the mountains, but the snow being so deep, I could not succeed in getting over. I returned to this place, it being the only point to kill meat, to wait a few weeks until the snow melts so that I can go on. The Indians here, also, being friendly, I consider it the most safe point for me to remain until such time as I can cross the mountains with my horses, having lost a great many in attempting to cross ten or fifteen days since. I am a long ways from home, and am anxious to get there as soon as the nature of the case will admit. Our situation is quite unpleasant, being destitute of clothing and most necessities of life, wild meat being our principal subsistence. I am, Reverend Father, your strange, but real friend and Christian, J. S. Smith."[7]

Even this letter failed to guide historians to the base camp from which Smith set out to cross the Sierra. Not until 1918, when Harrison Clifford Dale brought to light the journal of Harrison G. Rogers and other material, did anyone produce a well-founded critical examination of this point. A debate followed that narrowed the field of speculation but did not for some time reach a satisfactory conclusion.[8] All dispute about Smith's base camp was brought to an end in 1934, when Maurice Sullivan published the results of his remarkable researches.[9] He had discovered a transcript of Jedediah Smith's lost diary, which included the period of his return to California in 1827. In it Smith says that his object in returning "was to relieve my party on the Appelamminy and then proceed further in examination of the country beyond Mt. St. Joseph and along the sea coast." He continues to speak of the Appelamminy and states that the Mission of "St. Joseph" was about seventy miles southwest. There is abundant evidence that the Appelamminy and the Stanislaus are the same,[10] and there can be no further doubt that it was on the Stanislaus that Jedediah Smith left his party and started across the Sierra in May, 1827.

The references to the American River which misled the early historians can now be accounted for. When Smith was heading north with his whole party after his return to California in February, 1828, he says in his diary that, at the junction of the American River and the Sacramento, he was within a mile of the place where he had struck the river the preceding April. "The river was quite rapid and the rushing of the water brought fresh to my remembrance the cascades of Mt. Joseph and the unpleasant times I had passed there when surrounded by the snow which continued falling. My horses freezing, my men discouraged and our utmost exertion necessary to keep from freezing to death." It appears, then, that Smith was on the American River in 1827 and that he attempted to cross there, but had to turn back on account of continued snow.[11]

We can now summarize with confidence the story of the first crossing of the Sierra Nevada. In the early spring of 1827 Jedediah Smith and his band of trappers were moving slowly northward through the San Joaquin Valley, probing the tributary streams for beaver. At the Wimmelche River, which we know as the Kings, they attempted to cross the mountains, but the snow was too deep. They kept on trying and at the American River made a major effort. But they were still too early, and high water and freezing temperature forced them to return to the valley. They retraced their steps to the Stanislaus River, which Smith called the Appelamminy. There, Jedediah, accompanied by Silas Gobel and Robert Evans, left the rest of the party and made a determined effort to cross the mountains and get back to the rendezvous beyond Salt Lake. Starting on May 20 from the north bank of the Stanislaus, they veered gradually away from the river and its canyons, climbed up through the foothills to the forests of pine and fir, and eventually reached the granite ridges. By this time the snow was well packed and they were able to make good progress. In a week they reached the main crest of the Sierra not far from the present Ebbetts Pass.[12] Thence they found their way down the eastern slope and into the deserts of Nevada. A High Sierra pass had been crossed for the first time by white men.

NOTES AND REFERENCES

1. Dale L. Morgan, *Jedediah Smith and the Opening of the West*, Indianapolis, 1953, is today the standard biography; but Maurice S. Sullivan, *Jedediah Smith, Trader and Trail Breaker*, New York, Press of the Pioneers, 1936, is still satisfactory; and John G. Neihardt, *Splendid Wayfaring*, New York, 1920, is good for general reading. Neihardt also wrote an epic poem, *The Song of Jed Smith*, New York, 1941. A comprehensive bibliography of sources up to 1926, by A. P. Nasatir, is in *HSSCA*, 1926, 13:8; also Don M. and Doris H. Chase, "Bibliography of Sources Relating to Jedediah Strong Smith," *Pacific Historian*, August and November, 1963, 7:3 and 4; May, 1964, 8:2.

2. Harrison Clifford Dale initiated the modern period of critical study of Smith's travels with *The Ashley-Smith Exploration*, Cleveland: Arthur H. Clark Co., 1918; 2d ed., extensively revised, Glendale, Calif.: Clark, 1941.

3. The original of this letter is believed not to be extant. The text used here, with slight editing for ease of reading, is an early copy in the Indian Office, Department of the Interior (Record Group 75, Letters Received, Miscellaneous). That copy is substantially the same as another early copy in the records of the Kansas State Historical Society. It is the basis of all studies of Smith's far western travels. It was first printed, with some alterations of style but not of meaning, in the St. Louis *Missouri Republican*, Oct. 11, 1827. A translation into French appeared in *Nouvelles Annales des Voyages*, Paris, 1828.

4. What does Smith mean by "Mt. Joseph" or "Mt. St. Joseph"? Undoubtedly, the range of moutains that he crossed. "Mt. St. Joseph" on the Brué map of 1834 (*Wheat* 404) is clearly so intended. But on the Burr map of 1839 (*Wheat* 441) "Mount Joseph" is applied only to the northern part of the Sierra Nevada, far north of Smith's route. On the Wilkes map of 1841 (*Wheat* 458) "Mt. St. Joseph" becomes a single peak at the extreme northern end of the "California Range." The origin of the name has been the subject of considerable speculation. Sullivan (see n. 1) thought that it "may have been suggested by the proximity of Mission San Jose: but if Smith came away from San Gabriel with the same exalting [*sic*] opinion of the character of 'Father Joseph' as that expressed by Harrison Rogers, he may have named the mountain range in honor of the missionary" (Maurice S. Sullivan, *The Travels of Jedediah Smith*, Santa Ana, Calif.: Fine Arts Press, 1934). Dale Morgan goes all out for Father José Sánchez. "The alternative suggestion," he says, "that Jedediah named the Sierra for Mission San Jose is not even remotely plausible" (*Jedediah Smith*). Now, I have the greatest respect for Dale Morgan's scholarship and his fine sense of history, but in this I cannot agree with him. Though Father Sánchez was doubtless a saintly man, it is observed that Smith used the name "Saint Joseph" as well as plain "Joseph" for the mountain. What could have been more natural than that, when one of the Mission Indians was asked the name of the mountain, he should have given almost the only Spanish name he knew, "San José"? I have discussed this repeatedly with my friend Dale Morgan, but so far each stands firmly on his own opinion.

5. Bancroft, *California*, III.

6. Warner's reminiscences, like so many pioneers' recollections written long after the events, are frequently at variance with known facts. ("Reminiscences of Early California from 1831 to 1846," by Col. J. J. Warner, in *HSSCA*, 1907-1908, 7:2-3.) Thomas Sprague, of Genoa, Carson Valley, wrote a letter to Edmund Randolph telling about Smith's alleged discovery of gold—a required subject

among pioneers—and furnishing additional "facts" in connection with Randolph's *Address on the History of California*, San Francisco, September 10, 1860. Sprague's letter was included in the publication of Randolph's address and was also printed in *Hutchings' Magazine*, February, 1861. Among a multitude of other errors, Sprague states that Smith "discovered what is now called Humboldt River. He called it Mary's River, from his Indian wife Mary." Smith didn't discover that river, did not even see it, did not have an Indian wife, didn't have any wife.

7. This letter has been frequently published. The original is not known to be extant. The present text is taken from Dale, *Ashley-Smith*, 1918 edition.

8. Dale argued convincingly that Smith's base camp was on the Stanislaus, but reached his conclusion partly on false premises, for he was confused about the habitat of the Wimmelche Indians: he placed them *north* of Kings River. Dr. C. Hart Merriam ("First Crossing of the Sierra Nevada," *SCB*, 1923, 11:4) corrected Dale, asserting emphatically that they lived *on*, not *north* of the river. He brushed aside Dale's Stanislaus theory and stated positively that Smith "left his party on the American Fork." Merriam accepted at face value the unreliable statements of Warner (*op. cit.*) and the historian Guinn (*HSSCA*, 1896, 3:4). Merriam declared "it may be accepted as an established fact that Smith crossed the Sierra in the neighborhood of the American River." Meanwhile, F. N. Fletcher, of Reno, Nevada, had been studying the question from the point of view of one who knew the eastern side of the Sierra. Relying strongly on the Gallatin map of 1836 (*Wheat* 417), he proceeded to demolish Merriam's fixation about the American River crossing ("Eastbound Route of Jedediah S. Smith—1827," *CHSQ*, January, 1924, 2:4; also, Fletcher, *Early Nevada*, 1929). He agrees with Dale that Smith went up the Stanislaus, and takes him across the mountains in the vicinity of Sonora Pass. Fletcher, however, made the mistake of disputing Merriam on an Indian question. "Possibly further investigations," he ventures, "may disclose that they, the Wimmilche, roamed as far north as the Stanislaus." This drew the wrath of Dr. Merriam. "It is hoped," he thundered, "that no one will ever again attempt to locate the Wimmelche elsewhere than on their own ground on the river named by the Spaniards *Rio de los Reyes*, by Smith the Wimmelche and by the Americans *Kings River*." (*CHSQ*, April, 1924, 3:1). Except for the Indian lore, Fletcher had rather the better of the argument. Dale, in spite of his false premise about the Wimmelche, had come closer to the mark than any of his predecessors. But he spoiled matters by attempting to be too precise. He should have stopped with "he followed the Stanislaus," but he went on to say "he followed up the middle fork of this river." One simply does not go up the steep canyon of the Middle Fork of the Stanislaus.

9. Sullivan, *Travels of Jedediah Smith*. Just before his death in January, 1935, Sullivan completed a popular account, published posthumously, *Jedediah Smith, Trader and Trail Breaker*, New York: Press of the Pioneers, 1936.

10. The Wilkes map of 1841 (*Wheat* 458) correctly shows the Appelamminy as a tributary of the San Joaquin.

11. Confirmation comes from the Burr map of 1839 which Sullivan brought to light after nearly a century of obscurity, *Map of the United States of North America with Parts of the Adjacent Countries*, by David H. Burr (*Wheat* 441). The pertinent portion was reproduced by Sullivan. It is known that Smith made maps of his explorations and both Albert Gallatin and Burr doubtless saw them, or copies. Burr, especially, shows considerable knowledge of Jedediah's routes and indicates some of them. A loop drawn in the American River region coincides

precisely with the testimony of the diary. As if this were not enough, a discovery by Carl Wheat in 1953 puts a final stamp on the matter. He found in the files of the American Geographical Society, New York, a copy of the well-known Frémont map of 1845 (*Wheat* 497) that proved to be of unexpected interest. On it were superimposed certain pen and pencil lines and notations traceable to George Gibbs of Oregon, and Wheat demonstrated that the information came directly from Smith himself. This copy, known as the Frémont-Gibbs-Smith map (*Wheat* 398), is the subject of a monograph entitled *Jedediah Smith and His Maps of the American West*, by Dale L. Morgan and Carl I. Wheat, CHS, San Francisco, 1954, in which the map is reproduced, together with the Gallatin, Burr, and Wilkes maps.

12. Morgan and Wheat, *ibid.*, concur in this conclusion, which I had stated in "Jedediah Smith and the First Crossing of the Sierra," *SCB*, June, 1943, 28:3.

V

JOSEPH WALKER AND ZENAS LEONARD

Soon after Jedediah Smith left California in 1828 by a northerly route, avoiding another passage of the Sierra, other trappers began to converge upon the territory he had struggled so hard to exploit. They were overshooting the mark so far as beaver were concerned; rewards in furs were relatively slight, but as forerunners of American expansion their influence was tremendous. For a while they did not try to force the formidable barrier of the Sierra Nevada, but outflanked it at its northern and southern extremities. In 1829 and 1830 Peter Skene Ogden and Roderick McLeod, Hudson's Bay Company men, found routes by way of Pit River and possibly Feather River.[1]

Meanwhile, from far distant Taos, in New Mexico, a band of American "free trappers" led by Ewing Young arrived at San Gabriel mission. Among them was a young fellow of twenty years, Christopher Carson by name, whose recollections, dictated many years later, give us almost the only personal record of the event. From San Gabriel they crossed to the interior valley. "We had plenty to eat and found grass in abundance for our animals. We found signs of trappers on the San Joaquin. We followed their trail and, in a few days, overtook the party and found them to be of the Hudson Bay Company. They were sixty men strong, commanded by Peter Ogden. We trapped down the San Joaquin and its tributaries and found but little beaver, but game plenty: elk, deer, and antelope in thousands. We traveled near each other until we came to the Sacramento; then we separated, Ogden taking up the Sacramento for Columbia river. We remained during the summer. Not being the season for trapping, we passed our time in hunting." [2]

Kit Carson had many opportunities that summer to become familiar with the region at the western base of the Sierra, and this explains his confidence when several years later he crossed the range with Frémont. On one occasion during the earlier trip he was with a party that pursued some Indian horse thieves "upwards of one hundred miles into the Sierra Nevada." It would be interesting to know where they went, but there is slight chance of finding out. Carson returned to New Mexico with Ewing Young by much the same way they had come.

In the fall and winter of 1832-1833 Young led another party to the interior of California. Not Carson this time, but J. J. Warner, a member of the party, tells us that they trapped the Kings River "up to and some distance into the mountains and then passed on to the San Joaquin River, trapped that river down to canoe navigation in the foothills." Once more, Young's men found themselves in the wake of other trappers, whom they met on the Sacramento. And again they proved to be Hudson's Bay Company men, led this time by Michel La Framboise.[3]

Nothing of importance, either to them or to us, came of these trapping expeditions. Neither the Americans nor the British had among them anyone, except perhaps Ogden, of the quality of Jedediah Smith, and they furnished few maps or recognizable descriptions of the country. We may certainly assume that they did not penetrate very far into the High Sierra or into the great canyons of the Merced and the Kings.

In the year 1833, however, an expedition of quite different character came to California. The whole Rocky Mountain region was at that time burgeoning with seekers for furs. Rival companies and independent trappers were striving to outmaneuver each other, while the shy beaver, so eagerly sought, was becoming harder and harder to find. Meanwhile, Captain B. L. E. Bonneville, U.S.A., whose rather disproportionate fame was soon to be gained through Washington Irving, was trying to make a spectacular coup.[4] On leave from the Army, he had a large force in the Snake River country and in the summer of 1833 made rendezvous on the Green. There he detached a division of more than seventy men in charge of one of his most reliable lieutenants, Joseph Reddeford Walker. The objectives of this detachment have been discussed at length by historians. Washington Irving says that Walker's instructions were to explore the country around Great Salt Lake for beaver. Other sources, however, indicate a different objective, more consistent with what took place. Zenas Leonard, clerk of the expedition, says that Walker "was ordered to steer through an unknown country, towards the Pacific," and that it was because he was anxious to go to the coast that he himself joined the party. Another trapper, George Nidever, stated later that he joined with the express purpose of going to California.[5] At all events, whether the primary intention was to hunt beaver or to explore the country, Walker's expedition opened a new route to California and brought back a great deal of geographical knowledge. Of special interest to us was the crossing of the Sierra Nevada for the first time from east to west and the discovery of two of its most illustrious features.

Walker, thirty-five years old, was already a veteran of the frontier. Irving describes him as "about six feet high, strong built, dark complexioned, brave in spirit, though mild in manners. He had resided for many years in Missouri, on the frontier; had been among the earliest adventurers to Santa Fé, where he went to trap beaver, and was taken by the Spaniards. Being liberated, he engaged with the Spaniards and Sioux Indians in a war against the Pawnees;

then returned to Missouri, and had acted by turns as sheriff, trader, trapper, until he was enlisted as a leader by Captain Bonneville." Leonard said of him that he "was a man well calculated to undertake a business of this kind. He was well hardened to the hardships of the wilderness, understood the character of the Indians very well, and was kind and affable to his men, but at the same time at liberty to command without giving offence." [6]

Zenas Leonard, quite as much as Walker, deserves a place in the portrait gallery of the Sierra. From his home in Clearfield County, Pennsylvania, where he was born in 1809, he came to St. Louis at the age of twenty-one in search of employment in the fur trade. He began as a clerk and was soon on his way to the Rocky Mountains. No word was received from him at home for five years, and he was given up for lost until suddenly in the fall of 1835 he turned up at his father's home. He was warmly welcomed by his family and friends, who were eager to hear about his adventures. To oblige them he gave an account to the local newspaper, which was published serially, and afterwards in book form. The editor and publisher gives the following testimonial of its authenticity:

"Our author kept a minute journal of every incident that occurred, but unfortunately, a part of his narrative was stolen from him by hostile Indians; still, however, he was enabled to replace the most important events, by having access to the journal kept by the commander of the expedition. His character for candour and truth, among his acquaintances, we have never heard suspected; and, indeed, among the many who heard the narrative from his own lips, we have yet to hear the first one say they disbelieve it."

With the earlier experiences of Leonard up to the time of his embarking upon the California expedition we are not concerned. The account of the California expedition in all essentials rings true despite certain almost irreconcilable conflicts in the day by day account and in the description of the country. Let us see if we can follow Zenas Leonard and the Walker party across the Sierra Nevada and satisfy ourselves about the identification of what they saw.

Without difficulty we can follow the party down the general course of the Humboldt River, which they called Barren River, to the Sink of the Humboldt. From that point, on the 10th of October, Leonard says: "We continued our course in the direction of a large mountain, which we could see was covered with snow on the summit. In the evening we camped on the margin of a large lake formed by a river which heads in this mountain. The next day we traveled up this river towards the mountain, where we encamped for the night. This mountain is very high, as the snow extends down the side nearly half way—the mountain runs north and south." We may assume that the party came to Carson Valley. For about a week thereafter they tried to find a way by which they could take their horses over the mountain. The horses were getting weaker and food was giving out. They came to what at first they thought was the top of the mountain. There they encamped, "but without anything to eat for our horses, as the ground was covered with a deep snow."[7]

The account that follows is of more than ordinary interest, for it presents the first description ever given of some of the characteristic features of the High Sierra. Moreover, it describes the first of a long series of desperate efforts to force a passage across the range under wintry conditions. Many another group, including Frémont and the Donners, were to experience similar hardships among these mountains, which can be so delightfully hospitable in summer and so ferocious in winter.

"The next morning it was with no cheerful prospect that each man prepared himself for traveling, as we had nothing to eat worth mentioning. As we advanced, in the hollows sometimes we would encounter prodigious quantities of snow. When we would come to such places, a certain portion of the men would be appointed alternately to go forward and break the road, to enable our horses to get through; and if any of the horses would get swamped, these men were to get them out. In this tedious and tiresome manner we spent the whole day without going more than eight or ten miles. In some of these ravines where the snow is drifted from the peaks, it never entirely melts, and may be found in this season of the year, from ten to one hundred feet deep. From the appearance it never melts on the top, but in warm weather the heap sinks by that part melting which lays next the ground." If Leonard's concept of snow-fields should be challenged, it must be remembered that he was in utterly strange surroundings, entirely without precedent.

They now began to butcher their horses in order to keep themselves alive. The journey continued over hills, rocks, and deep snow. Leonard says that in most of the hollows the snow looked as if it had remained there all summer, as below the surface it was packed close and firm, but on the top it was loose and light as it had fallen only a day or two previously. They encamped at a lake where they found "very indifferent grass." But they had seen nothing yet to encourage the belief that they were nearing the opposite side of the mountain, nor had they found any game. There came a morning when there was less snow and more timber and a number of small lakes. According to Leonard the timber was principally "pine, cedar and red wood, mostly of a scrubby and knotty quality." At this altitude there was, of course, no Redwood as we define it; the trees were probably Juniper.

The narrative continues: "After traveling a few miles, further however than any other day since we had reached the top of the mountain, we again en-camped on the margin of another small lake, where we also had the good fortune to find some pasture for our horses. The next morning several parties were despatched in search of a pass over the mountain, and to make search for game; but they all returned in the evening without finding either. The prospect at this time began to grow somewhat gloomy and threaten us with hard times again. We were at a complete stand. No one was acquainted with the country, nor no person knew how wide the summit of this mountain was. We had traveled for five days since we arrived at what we supposed to be the summit—were now still surrounded with snow and rugged peaks—the vigour of every man almost exhausted—nothing to give our poor horses, which were no longer any assistance to us in traveling, but a burthen, for we had to help the most of them along as we would an old and feeble man."

But in this darkest moment they were approaching a climax; a climax not only in their journey, but in its historic significance. They were about to have a glimpse of one of the wonders of the world.

Elise Gow Jackaline

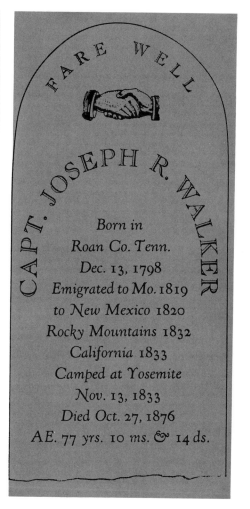

FARE WELL

CAPT. JOSEPH R. WALKER

Born in
Roan Co. Tenn.
Dec. 13, 1798
Emigrated to Mo. 1819
to New Mexico 1820
Rocky Mountains 1832
California 1833
Camped at Yosemite
Nov. 13, 1833
Died Oct. 27, 1876
AE. 77 yrs. 10 ms. & 14 ds.

Joseph Walker's grave, Martinez, California.

"We traveled a few miles every day, still on the top of the mountain, and our course continually obstructed with snow, hills and rocks. Here we began to encounter in our path, many small streams which would shoot out from under these high snow-banks, and after running a short distance in deep chasms which they have through ages cut in the rocks, precipitate themselves from one lofty precipice to another, until they are exhausted in rain below. Some of these precipices appeared to us to be more than a mile high. Some of the men thought that if we could succeed in descending one of these precipices to the bottom, we might thus work our way into the valley below—but on making several attempts we found it utterly impossible for a man to descend, to say nothing of the horses."[8]

Search the whole Sierra and you can find but one spot that would inspire this description—the northern brink of Yosemite Valley. There had been an early snowfall that season, as Leonard said, and this, followed by a few bright days, would have replenished the streams and given new birth to the Yosemite Falls. Here, then, is the record of the *discovery of Yosemite*, written and published years before any other white man could have beheld it. In his later years, Joseph Walker was proud to claim this discovery and requested that it be mentioned on the tombstone over his grave in Contra Costa County, where he spent the last years of his life.

But while Walker, or at least some of his men, undoubtedly *saw* Yosemite and camped near it, they did not camp *in* the Valley; moreover, the date on the stone is definitely wrong if Leonard is correct that they were near tidewater when the famous shower of meteors occurred on November 12, 1833.[9]

Accepting the fact that Walker's party saw Yosemite, we can make a reasonable interpretation of Leonard's narrative of the preceding few weeks. From somewhere west of Tuolumne Meadows the party must have been following the general course of the old Mono Indian trail, in general the route of the present Tioga Road. Before reaching this they had struggled for a number of days through a country of hills, rocks, and snowfields, had found lakes and timberline-type trees. They could not, therefore, have crossed by Bloody Canyon and Mono Pass, nor even Tioga Pass; for if they had, they would not have encountered the rough country described. The answer seems clear. They must have been floundering through the intricate mazes of the northern tributaries of the Tuolumne River. Working backwards, this brings us to the most likely point of crossing the crest, somewhere at the head of East Walker River west of Bridgeport Valley.

If this interpretation is correct, the rest of the journey as described by Zenas Leonard can be located without much difficulty. They kept along the top of the dividing ridge between two of these chasms—Yosemite and the Tuolumne—and were becoming more and more discouraged and desperate when one of the hunter-scouts brought into camp some acorns. The hunter had got them from an Indian, who was apparently on a journey across the mountains and who fled in terror, dropping his basket. "These nuts," says Leonard, "caused no little rejoicing in our camp, not only on account of their value as food, but because they gave us the gratifying evidence that a country mild and salubrious enough to produce acorns was not far distant." They continued their journey in better spirits, and in two or three days "arrived at the brink of the mountain." Here they had a spectacular view of the plain in front of them, but were confronted also with the problem of a precipitous descent. Next morning they found an Indian path, which, although it was extremely steep and difficult, they descended in a zigzag until they were halted at a precipice. They discovered a place where they could let their horses down by ropes one at a time. They had been greatly cheered by the killing of a deer, and after they got down off the rocks, sent hunters out for more game. Two large deer and a black bear were brought in. By this time they had left the region of snow and had reached a timbered country.

We now come to the second historic discovery by the Walker party. "In the last two days traveling," says Leonard, "we have found some trees of the Redwood species, incredibly large—some of which would measure from 16 to 18 fathoms round the trunk at the height of a man's head from the ground." No one could have invented that description, and it was published long before anyone else claimed to have seen the Big Tree of the Sierra. It stands, therefore, as the first mention of that sylvan marvel, now known as *Sequoia gigantea*. It is worthy of note that Leonard observed the similarity to the redwoods which he must have seen later in the Santa Cruz Mountains.[10]

It would be interesting to continue with Walker's party down to the plain and across the San Joaquin to San Francisco Bay, thence to the ocean, where they found an American ship, and finally to San Juan and Monterey. But, as we are concerned primarily with the Sierra Nevada, we must turn the pages of Leonard's narrative until we come again to the mountains on the return trip. Walker had no desire to repeat his experiences among the rocks and cliffs and snows, and, having learned from Spaniards that there was a way around the mountains to the south, he turned in that direction when he set out in the spring of 1834. The Spaniards presumably had in mind a route across the Tehachapi, but Walker met some Indians who told him that he could cross at the head of a river that came out of the mountains directly to the east. In this way Walker discovered the pass that has ever since been known by his name. Leonard records the event: "We continued traveling in this way for four days, when we landed safely on the opposite side of the mountain, in a temperate climate, and among tolerable pasture, which latter was equally as gratifying to our horses as the former was to the men." The party continued north along the base of the Sierra through Owens Valley. After a nearly disastrous detour they reached at length the tracks of their outward journey. Rejoicing to find themselves on familiar ground, they made rapid progress up the Humboldt. Joseph Walker and his companions by this time knew more about the Sierra Nevada than anyone else in the world. His knowledge was to prove of great value in the tide of immigration soon to follow.

NOTES AND REFERENCES

1. Alice Bay Maloney, "Peter Skene Ogden's Trapping Expedition to the Gulf of California, 1829-30," *CHSQ*, December, 1940, 19:4.

2. *Kit Carson's Own Story of His Life, as dictated to Col. and Mrs. D. C. Peters about 1856-57, and never before published*, edited by Blanche C. Grant, Taos, New Mexico, 1926; slightly different wording in De Witt C. Peters, *The Life and Adventures of Kit Carson ... from facts narrated by himself*, New York, 1859.

3. J. J. Warner's "Reminiscences of Early California from 1831 to 1846," *HSSCA*, 1907-1908, 7:2-3. Here Warner is talking about his own experiences, so his testimony should be given more weight than his comments on Jedediah Smith. (Michel La Framboise is "Mike the Raspberry.")

4. Washington Irving, *The Rocky Mountains: or, Scenes, Incidents, and Adventures in the Far West; digested from the journal of Captain B. L. E. Bonneville*, 2 vols., Philadelphia, 1837; also, in 3 vols., London, 1837. Author's revised edition, with a new title, *The Adventures of Captain Bonneville, U.S.A., in the Rocky Mountains and the Far West*, New York, 1850. There are numerous later editions.

5. William Henry Ellison, "From Pierre's Hole to Monterey," *PHR*, March, 1932, 1:1; *The Life and Adventures of George Nidever (1802-1883)*, edited by William Henry Ellison, Berkeley, 1937.

6. *Narrative of the Adventures of Zenas Leonard*, written by himself, printed and published by D. W. Moore, Clearfield, Pa., 1839 (*Farquhar* No. 1). The editors of recent editions have perpetuated an error in the name of the newspaper in which the narrative was first printed, calling it the Clearfield *Republican*. Although no copies of the newspaper containing the narrative have been reported, I have seen files for 1835 and 1836 which bear the names *Pioneer & Banner and Democratic Free Press* and *Pioneer & Banner and Democratic Republican*, and also the issue of Nov. 27, 1839, with the name *Democratic Banner*. The winds of politics seem to have blown upon the masthead. In the issue last mentioned Mr. D. W. Moore has an advertisement: "We now have the gratification to inform the public that the Journal of ZENAS LEONARD has been printed and forwarded to the binder, at Harrisburg. Unless something unexpected occurs, they will be ready to deliver to subscribers in two or three weeks. The work forms a handsome volume of near 100 large octavo pages. Price per copy, muslin binding, 75 cents." Recent quotations have reached several thousand dollars.

7. A number of well-reasoned attempts have been made to trace Walker's route from this point, with a remarkable diversity of conclusions. Those most familiar with the eastern side of the Sierra tend to take him up the Carson; but there they run into a dilemma. It is difficult to follow the description of the territory after reaching the crest. If the party had continued down the Stanislaus or Mokelumne the way would have been shorter and easier than that described by Leonard. On the other hand, if they had tried to follow along the crest all the way to the Tuolumne, they would never have arrived. A plausible argument has been made

for a crossing as far south as Lee Vining Creek, or even Rush Creek. A key point here, and one hard to account for in any other way, is Leonard's mention of a lake with water "similar to lie, admirably calculated to wash clothes without soap," and "with pummice stone floating on the surface of the water." It is possible that Leonard saw Mono Lake, but his subsequent descriptions do not fit the terrain he would have reached had he made an ascent of the Sierra from that vicinity.

F. N. Fletcher, of Reno, takes the party up the Carson, but says that "from this point to the valley of the San Joaquin is not clear" (*Early Nevada: The Period of Exploration, 1776-1848*, Reno, 1929). W. M. Maule, U.S. Forest Supervisor at Minden, Nevada, believed that the party crossed the Pine Nut Range in Nevada before crossing the Sierra near Carson Pass and continued by way of the South Calaveras Grove of Big Trees. William M. Maule, *A Contribution to the Geographic and Economic History of the Carson, Walker and Mono Basins in Nevada and California*, San Francisco: U.S. Forest Service, 1938 (large folio, maps; copy in CHS).

8. This passage is on p. 41 of the 1839 edition; p. 174 of the 1904 edition; and p. 79 of the edition of 1959.

9. Leonard describes the meteor shower: "On the night of the 12th our men were again thrown into great consternation by the singular appearance of the heavens. Soon after dark the air appeared to be completely thickened with meteors falling towards the earth, some of which would explode in the air and others would be dashed to pieces on the ground, frightening our horses so much that it required the most active vigilence of the whole company to keep them together." The next morning they reached tidewater.

10. The trees Leonard described could be either those of the Tuolumne Grove or those of the Merced Grove, possibly both. They were certainly not those of the Mariposa Grove, nor could they have been those of the Calaveras groves unless our suppositions about the route are all wrong.

VI

THE FIRST IMMIGRANTS
AND THEIR STRUGGLES

When Joseph Walker returned to Captain Bonneville's camp in the summer of 1834, with many experiences to relate, but few beaver pelts, his employer was grievously disappointed. Bonneville did not realize that the era of beaver skins and trappers was drawing to a close while that of the settler and the covered wagon was about to begin. Oregon had already become a goal for seekers of new lands, and now the call of California was becoming increasingly audible. Restless pioneers were taking heed, and in the spring of 1841 immigrants began to assemble in Missouri and Kansas.[1] Prominent in the first party were some notable names—John Bidwell, Josiah Belden, John Bartleson, Joseph B. Chiles. It could be called the "J. B." party, but it has gone down in history as the "Bartleson–Bidwell" party. In addition there were the Kelsey brothers, Andrew and Benjamin, and Benjamin's young wife Nancy and their year-old daughter Ann, destined to be the first woman and the first child to cross the Sierra. A popular young man called Talbot H. Green was also in the party. All the men were young and vigorous; none had experience in the kind of pioneering they were about to undertake.

Despite inexperience and inept leadership, the J. B. party survived the perils of the overland journey and at length, in October, came to the base of the Sierra Nevada on the West Walker River. Long before that they had abandoned their wagons and were now short of provisions. They were in an unknown country and no one had any idea how many miles lay ahead. Bidwell wrote in his journal, October 16: "This morning 4 or 5 men started to ascend several of the high peaks to ascertain if it was possible to pass the mountains."[2] Could this have been the first mountain climb ever made in the Sierra? It seems so; but what peak or peaks? Josiah Belden furnishes a few additional facts. He identifies himself as one of the climbers, and reduces the number to three. "One day two others and myself left the party, and went up to some of the higher peaks of the mountains to explore and see if we could find any place where we could get across."[3] The report was not favorable; nevertheless, a vote of the whole party was taken and by a majority of one it was decided to go ahead. "We finally reached the summit with great labor and difficulty," continues Belden, "and after getting a little beyond the summit on the other side, we struck a little stream of water that seemed to run westward, and we judged we had got over the divide. After passing the summit, and striking this stream, we worked our way along down for some distance, occasionally having to leave the track and go on to the ridges, to avoid getting into deep cañons, blocked with immense boulders. We finally succeeded in working down to the north side of the river, and finding difficulty there, got on to the south side. We went a little ways from the river, working down that side, and passed I suppose the neighborhood of where Sonora is now."

Bidwell's journal amplifies the picture: "Having ascended about half a mile, a frightful prospect opened before us: naked mountains whose summits still retained the snows perhaps of a thousand years: for it had withstood the heat of a long dry summer, and ceased to melt for the season. We wound along among the peaks in such a manner as to avoid most of the mountains which we had expected to climb—struck a small stream descending towards the west, on which we encamped, having come 15 miles. The rivulet descended with great rapidity and it was the opinion of all that we were at least a mile perpendicular below the place where we began to descend. The stream had widened into a small valley. Cedars of uncommon size, pines the most thrifty, clothed the mountains. All were pleased to think that we were crossing the mountain so fast."[4]

They were far from being out of trouble, however, and soon were floundering among the Stanislaus canyons. They encountered Indians, who endeavored to lead them into a trap and stole their horses. Bidwell scouted ahead alone for several days, but ineffectually. Many years later he wrote a memoir of the trip, and in recalling it says: "Just at dark I came to an enormous fallen tree and tried to go around the top, but the place was too brushy, so I went around the butt, which seemed to me to be about twenty or twenty-five feet above my head. This I suppose to have been one of the fallen trees in the Calaveras Grove of *Sequoia gigantea* or mammoth trees, as I have since been there and to my own satisfaction identified the lay of the land and the tree."[5] It is possible that Bidwell did reach one of the Calaveras groves, although there is no mention of it in his contemporary journal. His claim that he was the first white man to see the *Sequoia gigantea* was voided however when Leonard's journal of the Walker expedition became known.

Nancy Kelsey, more than fifty years later, described some of her experiences on the Sierra crossing.[6] She carried her baby on the horse but at times had to get off and walk. Nicholas Dawson, a young man of the party, wrote, "I looked back and saw Mrs. Kelsey a little way behind me, with her child in her arms, barefooted, and leading her horse—a sight I shall never forget."[7]

The party eventually reached the site of Knights Ferry on the lower Stanislaus and arrived at Dr. Marsh's ranch near Mount Diablo on the 4th of November, thus concluding without serious casualty the first overland migration of American settlers across the Sierra.[8]

Several members of the party became distinguished citizens. John Bidwell was the founder of the city of Chico and a leader in the development of California agriculture. Charles M. Weber was the founder of Stockton. Josiah Belden became a wealthy citizen of San Jose and was elected mayor; later he moved to New York, where he lived in opulence and respectability. A touch of melodrama is introduced in the person of "Talbot H. Green." In Monterey he rose quickly to fame and fortune.[9] He moved to San Francisco (then Yerba Buena) and took an active part in civic affairs. He married and had a son. Green Street was named for him. He was about to run for mayor when he was confronted by a Philadelphia lady who exclaimed, "Paul Geddes, I know you!" It turned out that Paul Geddes had plundered a bank and had vanished, leaving a wife and children. The popular "Talbot H. Green" hastily took ship for the East, again leaving a family behind him. "Green Street" remains.[10]

Joseph Chiles had a different career and one that brought him again into the pioneers' struggle with the Sierra Nevada. While in California he became enthusiastic about the prospects of a good life in the Napa Valley, where he visited his old Missouri friend George Yount. But before settling, he felt that he must go back to Missouri and persuade another friend, William Baldridge, an expert millwright, to come to California with mill equipment.[11] Yount saw an opportunity to bring his daughters, whom he had not seen for many years, to California, and Chiles agreed to escort them.[12] Early in 1842, Chiles started eastward with a few companions. He avoided the wintry mountains by taking a detour south of Walker Pass.

Once back in Missouri, Chiles proceeded to organize a party for permanent settlement in California. Baldridge as well as Yount's daughters, Frances and Elizabeth Ann, were ready to go, together with Frances' husband, Bartlett Vines, and their two small children. Chiles, now an experienced leader, thought that he knew what should be done. Wagons were the thing. So he filled them with provisions, goods for sale in California, and Baldridge's machinery, piled in the women and children, and set out for California in the spring of 1843. He must have planned before he started to send the wagons around the Sierra by a southern route; and when, on the way, he met Joseph Walker and was able to hire him as a guide, the plan looked even better. Now he could put the wagon party in the charge of the veteran, while he and some of the younger men, who could travel faster on horseback, would go around the northern end of the Sierra and come back over the mountains to meet them with provisions. But it didn't work out quite that way. The Sierra again proved too formidable a barrier. The northern route proved to be a long way around, and by the time Chiles and his mounted group reached Sutter's Fort the snows of winter had sealed the mountains. Meanwhile the southerly party also failed in its objective. They were forced to abandon the wagons. The mill machinery, hauled so painfully all the long way, had to be abandoned and was buried in the sand not far from Owens Lake. The women and children were placed on the faltering horses, and, with the wagons out of the way, the party uneventfully completed the journey over Walker Pass.[13]

Up to this time no one had succeeded in finding a way over the Sierra that would permit the use of wagons. But a route was about to be discovered that would eventually breach the barrier and open the way to thousands. Back in Missouri the overland parties of 1844 were assembling in larger numbers than any theretofore. Wagons were now standard equipment for Oregon and were known to be practicable as far as the Sierra Nevada. It was not known whether Chiles had succeeded in getting his wagons through, but at any rate wagons were essential for the large family groups that were now setting out, and it was felt that a way would be found somehow. Several families united to form the California-bound party, including eight women and fifteen children. There was no lack of candidates for leadership. Martin Murphy, though head of the largest family—he had eight grandchildren along—was not ambitious. The veteran mountain man, Isaac Hitchcock, was perhaps best qualified by experience, and Dr. Townsend was best educated, and certainly most vocal. But Elisha Stephens was the one chosen, and as the Stephens party it is best known.[14] Hanging on the outskirts of the group was "Old Greenwood." He claimed to be eighty years old and no doubt was, but, as his biographer says, he was just beginning the most notable episode of his career.[15] He had with him two sons by a Crow woman. Near the other end of the life scale was young Schallenberger, not yet eighteen, but destined to be the near-hero of the party.[16]

Throughout its progress the Stephens party was well-conducted and on the whole fortunate, and arrived at the Sink of the Humboldt in good condition. There a momentous decision was made which led to success and fame. Instead of turning south as Joseph Walker and the Bartleson–Bidwell Party had done, they followed the advice of an old Indian who told them, by signs and by diagrams drawn on the ground in a way that Old Greenwood seemed to understand, that if they went directly west they would come to a river that came out of the mountains. The Indian's name sounded something like "Truckee," and when, as he said they would, they came to the river they named it for him.[17] This they followed through desert canyons to a large meadowland, where the city of Reno now stands; then they continued with ever-increasing difficulty up into the mountains. At last they emerged onto a high mountain meadow where two forks joined.[18]

It was now mid-November and snow was beginning to fall. Which branch of the river should they take? The records of the Stephens party are not contemporary but consist of later recollections. They are not always fully in accord. One version of what occurred is that "as there was some difference of opinion as to the best route to follow in crossing the mountains, certain of the party who were impatient to reach the other side determined to leave the main body with the wagons, and to push forward on horseback up the main stream, and so reach some settlement on the western slope."[19] On the other hand, Moses Schallenberger, whose version throughout seems most authentic, says that the separation was a fully considered plan: the fast party was to go to the settlements and send back relief if the others did not arrive, while the wagon party "should go by way of the tributary, as that seemed to be the more promising route for vehicles."[20] The latter remark was prophetic, for the "tributary" came from the pass now used by the railroad as well as by thousands of vehicles on the highway known as U. S. 40, or Interstate 80.

First, let us follow the horseback party, for their story is short and simple. The party consisted of the brothers Daniel and John Murphy and their sister Ellen; Dr. Townsend's wife Elizabeth, who was Moses Schallenberger's sister; and two hired men, the French-Canadians Deland and Magnent. They kept to the east bank of the Truckee until they reached Lake Tahoe. There they crossed the river and kept along the west shore of the lake for some distance. It is not known exactly where they turned off from the lake, but it seems probable that it was at McKinney Creek. They crossed over the mountain to the Rubicon; thence down to the American River, and without too much difficulty reached Sutter's Fort.

The story of the wagon party was quite different. The wall above Donner Lake appeared to be impassable, but after desperate exploration a way was found. About half the party decided to leave their wagons at the lake until the following spring and try to get through by backpacking. Three young men, Joseph Foster, Allen Montgomery, and Moses Schallenberger, volunteered to stay and guard the wagons and their valuable contents. The Murphy contingent, with five other wagons, decided to try to get across. Schallenberger furnishes the following account: "The snow on the mountains was now about two feet deep. Keeping their course on the north side of the lake until they reached its head, they started up the mountain. All the wagons were unloaded and their contents carried up the hill. The teams were doubled and the empty wagons were hauled up. When about half way up the mountain they came to a vertical rock about ten feet high. It seemed now that about everything would have to be abandoned except what the men could carry on their backs. After a tedious search they found a rift in the rock, just about wide enough to allow one ox to pass at a time. Removing the yokes from the cattle, they managed to get them one by one through this chasm to the top of the rock. There the yokes were replaced, chains were fastened to the tongues of the wagons, and carried to the top of the rock, where the cattle were hitched to them. Then the men lifted at the wagons, while the cattle pulled at the chains, and by this ingenious device the vehicles were all, one by one got across the barrier."[21] The day was November 25, 1844, a notable one in the chronology of the Sierra.

Troubles were not over, however, for winter now descended upon the party. Though the most formidable barrier had been passed, the way was blocked to further travel by wagon. Somewhere on the upper Yuba River camp was made for the women and children, and there the five wagons were laid up for the winter. All but two of the men set out for Sutter's Fort, and since the snow gave less and less trouble as they descended, they were not long in completing the journey. Meanwhile there had occurred another "first" in the annals of the Sierra—a child was born to Mrs. Martin Murphy and named Elizabeth Yuba Murphy.[22] A few years later other little girls were to be given names derived from places in the same vicinity—"Alta" and "Summit." Relief ultimately arrived for the women and children, and by March all had safely reached the pleasant valley of California.

Moses Schallenberger and his two companions remain to be accounted for. Schallenberger gives us such a vivid picture of their winter that his narrative will be quoted rather fully.[23] "The morning after the separation of our party, which we felt was for only a short time, Foster, Montgomery and myself set about making a cabin, for we determined to make ourselves as comfortable as possible, even if it was for a short time. We cut saplings and yoked up our poor cows and hauled them together. These we formed into a rude house, and covered it with rawhides and pine brush. The size was about twelve by fourteen feet. We made a chimney of logs eight or ten feet high, on the outside, and used some large stones for the jambs and back. We had no windows; neither was the house chinked or daubed, as is usual in log-houses, but we notched the logs down so close that they nearly or not quite touched. A hole was cut for a door, which was never closed. We left it open in the daytime to give us light, and as we had plenty of good beds and bedding that had been left with the wagons, and were not afraid of burglars, we left it open at night also. This cabin is thus particularly described because it became historic, as being the residence of a portion of the ill-fated Donner party in 1846."

Snow began to fall, and then more snow. The cows were starving without feed and had to be killed. The frozen meat lasted for a while, but it was obvious that it would not suffice for three all winter. The snow was ten feet deep and too soft to bear any weight. They made some crude and clumsy snowshoes, and, faced with starvation, made up light packs and set out for the pass. Inexperience, and soon exhaustion, conspired against them. Schallenberger, younger than the other two and lacking endurance, finally gave up, and with a "Good-bye, Mose" from his companions returned to the cabin. He was now alone, to lead the life of a Robinson Crusoe, as Erwin Gudde has remarked, but with this difference: there was very little to be found in this wintry isolation for sustaining life.[24] Fox and coyote tracks abounded, but in the deep snow the animals themselves were unattainable. Mose bethought himself of some traps that Stephens had left, and hope revived. The first catch was a coyote. "I soon had his hide off and his flesh roasted in a Dutch oven. I ate the meat, but it was horrible. I next tried boiling him, but it did not improve the flavor. I cooked him in every possible manner my imagination, spurred by hunger, could suggest, but could not get him into a condition where he could be eaten without revolting my stomach. But for three days this was all I had to eat. On the third night I caught two foxes. I roasted one of them, and the meat, though entirely devoid of fat, was delicious." Thereafter he caught more foxes and an occasional coyote which he placed in cold storage for a reserve against the last stages of starvation. He acquired a great affection for foxes. He had enough coffee for just one cup, "and that I saved for Christmas."

Christmas came and went. "My life was more miserable than I can describe. The daily struggle for life and the uncertainty under which I labored were very wearing. I was always worried and anxious, not about myself alone, but in regard to the fate of those who had gone forward. Fortunately, I had plenty of books, Dr. Townsend having brought out quite a library. I used often to read aloud, for I longed for some sound to break the oppressive stillness. I thought the snow would never leave the ground, and the few months I had been living here seemed years." At last the break came. "One evening, a little before sunset, about the last of February, as I was standing a short distance from my cabin, I thought I could distinguish the form of a man moving towards me. I first thought it was an Indian, but very soon I recognized the familiar face of Dennis Martin." When the relief had been sent up from Sutter's Fort, Dennis was particularly anxious to go, for his elderly father had been one of the two men left at the snowy camp on the Yuba. Mrs. Townsend had pleaded with Dennis to keep on over the pass and find out if her brother was still alive. The Martins were Canadians, and Dennis was adept at snowshoes. When he arrived at the cabin he lost no time in making a pair for Mose, and the next morning the two, spurred by the threat of another storm, crossed the pass and reached the Yuba camp and safety. The following July, some of the men returned and found their possessions quite thoroughly looted. The wagons themselves were retrieved and brought over the pass and on to Sutter's Fort. The first wagon trail across the Sierra was completed.

Before entering into an account of Frémont's adventures in the Sierra in the years 1843-1844 and 1845-1846, it seems convenient to continue with the immigrants for a while. As far as the Sierra Nevada is concerned, the so-called "Pathfinder" had no influence on their movements. Other influences were at work, however. Old Greenwood, who had come with the Stephens party, had added to his general knowledge of the West an intensive experience with the Sierra crossing and despite his age, stood ready to guide all comers. Then and there a campaign was begun that was to continue for a century, the campaign to bring settlers to California.

Greenwood and his two sons returned to Fort Hall, near the junction with the Oregon trail, and endeavored to divert as many as possible from their original Oregon destination and set them instead on the road to California. Whether seduced by Greenwood or not, a substantial number did change their minds and headed for California. For several reasons the 1845 parties encountered fewer difficulties than had their predecessors. In the first place, it was known that a practical route existed and that wagons had actually passed the barrier of the Sierra. Old Greenwood, who had just been there, was with them to show the way. Moreover, he had scouted a route by which some of the difficulties of the canyon of the Truckee could be bypassed. Most important of all, however, was the fact that this year the immigrants reached the mountains before the winter storms set in.

Difficulties enough remained, nevertheless, as is shown by sundry diaries and reminiscences. Take, for instance, the account of William Ide's experiences.[25] Greenwood had insisted that the wagons would have to be taken to pieces and hauled up by ropes. "Our Yankee adventurer thought he would find a better way. He took a survey of the premises, on foot, climbing up the rugged cliffs of rock till he reached the plain above, and finally concluded there *was* a better way. Accordingly, he went to work, with as many of the men as he could induce to assist him, removing rocks and trees and grading a patch six or seven feet wide up the several steep pitches and levels to the summit." Hitching and hauling, backing and hitching and hauling again, they got their wagons to the top. Ide's daughter says: "It took us a long time to get about two miles over our rough, new-made road up the mountain, over the rough rocks in some places, and so smooth in others that the oxen would slip and fall on their knees. It was a trying time—the men swearing at their teams and beating them most cruelly."

A diarist of another party writes under the date of September 21, 1845, that they passed a log cabin built by the emigrants of the preceding year (Schallenberger's, at Donner Lake). He continues: "At this lake we commenced ascending the rugged side of the mountain. It is composed of masses of granite. In many places large detached pieces are thrown in the way, rendering it impossible for horses to get a foothold, and in many others it is so smooth that it is as bad for the animals as the more rugged parts. We were obliged to lead our horses until we arrived at the summit."[26]

Once over the summit the several parties found their way down the Yuba and Bear and arrived safely at Sutter's Fort. One other party came over the mountains before the end of the year. Captain Sutter recorded in his diary: "December 25th.—Arrived Capt. Hastings direct from the U. States crossing the mountains with 11 men. Among them was Dr. Semple. If they had arrived one day later they would have been cut off by the immense quantity of snow."[27] In modern terms: "U. S. Highway 40 Closed."

The year 1846 was truly a "Year of Decision," with profound changes throughout the land.[28] It was the year of the Mexican war, and it was the year in which California became *de facto* United States territory. And it was the year in which took place the most celebrated attempt to cross the Sierra. The story of the Donner Party has been told at such length and so often that its dreary, gruesome details need not be repeated here.[29] And yet some of its features cannot be overlooked. Why did so many of its members fail to get over the pass where others had been successful? What really happened in that long winter camp by the lake, where today thousands pause for a few moments to gaze at the scene of starvation and cannibalism? There is a heroic side, too—men voluntarily braving storm and deep snow in efforts to rescue the weak and the starving.

The answer to the first question involves that same Hastings who arrived at Sutter's Fort on Christmas Day, 1845, barely in advance of the winter's snow. He had written an "Emigrants' Guide" and was advocating a variation of the route east of Salt Lake, by which the journey to California could be shortened.[30] When it became necessary to make a choice between the established route and Hastings' tempting propaganda, several groups, to be known later as the Donner party, decided upon the latter course. For some it was a fatal decision, for the "Cut-off," while decreasing the distance, greatly increased the time. How much blame for the results should be attached to the untested assurances of Hastings and how much to the incapacities of the party is still a subject of debate. At all events, when the Donner party arrived at last at the foot of the pass of the Sierra it was too late in the season. Snow had come earlier than usual, and the pass was closed. Three or four men did manage to get through to Sutter's Fort and bring news of the beleaguered families, but relief had to wait until spring. One man, Stanton, gallantly returned from safety, only to be among those who perished. Another, Reed, desperately tried to take provisions back to his family, but the snow halted him only a few miles from his goal. Late in December fifteen of those who had remained at Donner Lake succeeded in getting over the pass on crude snowshoes. Of these, eight men perished, while two men and five women reached safety, but not without frightful agony and a last resort to cannibalism.

Those who remained at the Lake—Donner Lake, though the Donners had little to do with it—crowded into Schallenberger's old cabin and into two others that they built for themselves. Snow soon covered everything. Provisions gone, cattle gone, nothing left but the flesh of the dead: all winter long starvation and horror prevailed. Meanwhile, the Californians were aroused and relief parties were organized. For a long time deep snow repelled all assistance, but the emaciated survivors were finally brought out, the last not until the 21st of April. The final tally of those who had reached Donner Lake: 47 survivors, 35 dead.[31]

Three men emerge as outstanding: Stanton and Reed, for their gallant efforts at relief, and Eddy, whose courage and persistence brought half the snowshoe party through alive. Of the Donners, little need be said, save of Tamsen, pathetic mother, who sacrificed herself for husband and children. We might add little Eliza Donner, to represent the bewildered children. She survived to attain a dignified and gracious maturity.

Nothing like the Donner tragedy ever happened again, though many a man has suffered and died in the High Sierra, even in summer, through failure to realize that the forces of nature can be far more destructive than might be expected from their benign appearance at other times.

NOTES AND REFERENCES

1. There is a vast literature about this migration. The best background for present purposes is George R. Stewart, *The California Trail: An Epic with Many Heroes*, New York: McGraw-Hill, 1962.

2. The unique copy of John Bidwell's *A Journey to California* in the Bancroft Library was reprinted in 1937 (San Francisco: John Henry Nash) with an introduction by Herbert Ingram Priestley, and again in 1964 (Berkeley: Friends of the Bancroft Library) with an introduction by Francis P. Farquhar. Bidwell's *Echoes of the Past*, Chico, Calif., 1914, reprinted in 1928 (Chicago: Lakeside Press), contains the account in modified form.

3. *Josiah Belden, 1841 California Overland Pioneer: His Memoirs and Early Letters*, edited and with an introduction by Doyce B. Nunis, Jr., Georgetown, Calif.: Talisman Press, 1962.

4. William G. Paden, "Bidwell's Route of the Sierras, a Field Study," unpublished M.A. thesis, University of California, Berkeley, 1940 (copy in BL), follows the route in detail, with the conclusion that the crossing of the Sierra crest was several miles north of the present Sonora Pass.

5. John Bidwell, "The First Emigrant Trail to California," *Century Magazine*, November, 1890; reprinted in *In California Before the Gold Rush*, Los Angeles: Ward Ritchie Press, 1948, with a foreword by Lindley Bynum. From an eastern point of view these pioneers were "emigrants," but viewed from the west they were "immigrants."

6. *San Francisco Examiner*, February 5, 1893; reprinted in *The Grizzly Bear*, February, 1915, and again February, 1937. The Kelseys lived for a while in Lake County; Kelseyville was named for the family. Nancy died in 1895.

7. *Narrative of Nicholas "Cheyenne" Dawson*, introduction by Charles L. Camp, San Francisco: Grabhorn Press, 1933.

8. Bancroft, *California*, IV; George D. Lyman, *John Marsh, Pioneer*, New York: Scribner's, 1930. In the Bancroft Library there is a manuscript dictated by Chiles in 1878, in which it is stated that Dr. Marsh lived near *San* Diablo. Thus was the devil made a saint—a splendid example of antisyzygy.

9. Rev. Walter Colton, U.S.N., *Three Years in California*, New York, 1850.

10. *Dawson*; Stewart, *California Trail*; John Adam Hussey, "New Light upon Talbot H. Green," *CHSQ*, March, 1939, 18:1.

11. Biographical sketch of William Baldridge in *History of Napa and Lake Counties*, San Francisco, 1881.

12. "The Chronicles of George C. Yount," *CHSQ*, April, 1923, 2:1.

13. *Napa and Lake Counties*; "Chronicles of George C. Yount," *op. cit.*; Bancroft, *California*, IV.

14. Experts differ in the spelling of his name. In Kern County, where he spent his last years, the name is recorded as "Stephens," and that is the preference of Charles L. Camp and Dale L. Morgan. On the other hand, Bancroft uses "Stevens" and George R. Stewart prefers it that way. The two former have persuaded me to use "Stephens."

15. Charles Kelly, *Old Greenwood*, Salt Lake City, 1936.

16. George R. Stewart, *The Opening of the California Trail*, Berkeley, 1953 (not the same book as *The California Trail*, 1962, cited in n. 1), gathers scattered accounts of the 1844-1845 crossing of the Sierra, including Moses Schallenberger's narrative, "Overland in 1844." Also, see Erwin G. Gudde, "Robinson Crusoe in the Sierra Nevada," *SCB*, May, 1951, 36:5; and Bancroft, *California*, IV.

17. "Trip of the Murphy Party," edited by Horace S. Foote, *San Jose Pioneer and Historical Review*, April 15, 1893. On T. H. Jefferson's map of the Emigrant Road, 1849 (*Wheat* 624), it is spelled "Truckey."

18. Near the present city of Truckee.

19. Bancroft, *Chronicles*, III.

20. Stewart, *Opening*.

21. Stewart, *Opening;* also Bancroft, *Chronicles*, III. Kelly, in *Old Greenwood*, is inclined to exaggerate Greenwood's part in the crossing; on the other hand, most historians have perhaps unduly ignored him.

22. The middle name was doubtless added later, for Mrs. Murphy could hardly have known the name of the river at the time.

23. "Overland in 1844," which is the "text" in Stewart's *Opening*.

24. Gudde, *op. cit.*

25. Simeon Ide, *A Biographical Sketch of the Life of William B. Ide*, Claremont, N. H., 1880. Portions are reprinted in Fred B. Rogers, *William Brown Ide, Bear Flagger*, San Francisco: John Howell Books, 1962. See also Bancroft, *California*, IV.

26. "The Diary of Jacob R. Snyder," *Quarterly of the California Society of Pioneers*, December, 1931, 8:4.

27. *The Diary of Johann August Sutter*, San Francisco: Grabhorn Press, 1932.

28. Bernard DeVoto, *The Year of Decision: 1846*, Boston: Little, Brown, 1943.

29. The literature of the Donner party is voluminous. The best account is George R. Stewart, *Ordeal by Hunger: The Story of the Donner Party*, Boston: Houghton-Mifflin, 1960. (Originally published in 1936, the later edition contains much supplementary material.) Before Stewart, the standard work was C. F. McGlashan, *History of the Donner Party: A Tragedy of the Sierra*, Truckee, 1879, and subsequent editions. There are other accounts, including a blank verse poem by Julia Cooley Altrocchi, *Snow Covered Wagons: A Pioneer Epic*, New York: Macmillan, 1936.

30. Lansford W. Hastings, *The Emigrants' Guide to Oregon and California*, Cincinnati, 1845, reproduced in facsimile by Princeton University Press, 1932.

31. John Muir's comment: "They were not good mountaineers. The whole winter could have been spent delightfully in so beautiful a spot." Linnie Marsh Wolfe, *Son of the Wilderness*, New York: Knopf, 1945.

VII

FRÉMONT'S WANDERINGS

John Charles Frémont, 2nd Lieutenant in the U. S. Topographical Engineers, was thirty years old and quite sure of himself when he set out in the spring of 1843 on his Second Exploring Expedition. He had already made a creditable expedition to the Rocky Mountains, and now, under the patronage of his influential father-in-law, Senator Thomas Hart Benton of Missouri, he was on the way to greater things.[1] His instructions were to connect his previous reconnaissance with the surveys of Commander Wilkes on the California–Oregon coast. This he did by carrying a line of astronomical observations through to the Columbia River and the Pacific. After that he proceeded pretty much according to his own ideas, or perhaps those of his sponsors in Washington who wanted to know more about California. At any rate, he turned south from Oregon and professed to be on the homeward journey, in the course of which he would explore "the Great Basin between the Rocky mountains and the *Sierra Nevada.*"[2] One of the objects, he declared, was to ascertain the character and existence of "the reputed *Buenaventura* river, which has had a place in so many maps, and countenanced the belief of a great river flowing from the Rocky mountains to the Bay of San Francisco." If Frémont really believed there was such a river he was woefully lacking in geographic sense and carelessly oblivious of his predecessors in the field; the alternative is that he deliberately introduced the Buenaventura into his report as an excuse for his actions.[3]

For a month he wandered through the bleak region of northwestern Nevada until he reached Pyramid Lake, which he named, and the mouth of the Truckee, which he called "Salmon Trout River." Here he met some Indians who "made on the ground a drawing of the river, which they represented as issuing from another lake in the mountains three or four days distant, in a direction a little west of south; beyond which they drew a mountain and further still, two rivers; on one of which they told us that people like ourselves traveled." Here was a description of Lake Tahoe, or perhaps Donner Lake, and the American and Yuba rivers. If Frémont had followed this lead he would have saved himself much trouble and would have anticipated the Stephens party by nearly a year. Instead, he kept on south until he came to another river, the Carson. Here he took account of stock and found that the feet of the animals were "so much cut up by the rocks, and so many of them lame, that it was evidently impossible that they could cross the country to the Rocky mountains." He therefore determined to abandon the eastern course and instead "to cross the Sierra Nevada into the valley of the Sacramento, wherever a practical route could be found." The Pine Nut Mountains were nearby, and he climbed one of the summits and had a view of the Carson Valley and the Sierra beyond. "I sometimes regret," he says, "that I did not make the trial to cross here; but while we had fair weather below, the mountains were darkened with falling snow, and, feeling unwilling to encounter them, we turned away again to the southward." He was in an excellent position to carry out his plans if he had patiently waited for better weather while his able scouts, Kit Carson and Thomas Fitzpatrick, looked for a pass. But instead he spent the next ten days in futile wanderings that brought him as far south as Bridgeport Valley before he turned back. At the West Walker River some Indians gave a confusing account of white men who had crossed the mountains in that vicinity several years before. "I believe," says Frémont, "that this was a party led by Mr. Chiles, one of the only two men I knew to have passed through the California mountains from the interior of the Basin—Walker being the other."

It was the last day of January when Frémont again camped by the waters of the Carson, supposing himself back on his "Salmon Trout" river. By this time the Pathfinder was definitely lost. It was beginning to snow again and the men were getting restive. He had to do something. He made a speech, reminding his men "of the beautiful valley of the Sacramento, with which they were familiar from the descriptions of Carson," and assuring them that with one effort they would "place themselves in the midst of plenty."

Frémont was now at his best. No longer hesitant, he boldly led on into the wintry Sierra in frontal attack. Up the East Carson, past the site of Markleeville, the party began to encounter deep snow. An old Indian warned: "Rock upon rock—rock upon rock—snow upon snow—snow upon snow. Even if you get over the snow you will not be able to get down from the mountain." An Indian who had been engaged as a guide deserted. But Frémont no longer wanted a guide; he would spy out the land himself. On February 6 he set out with a few others on snowshoes to reconnoiter. "Crossing the open basin, in a march of about ten miles we reached the top of one of the peaks, to the left of the pass indicated by our guide. Far below us, dimmed by the distance, was a large snowless valley, bounded on the western side, at the distance of about a hundred miles by a low range of mountains, which Carson recognized with delight as the mountains bordering on the coast. 'There,' said he, 'is the little mountain—it is 15 years ago since I saw it; but I am just as sure as if I had seen it yesterday.' [4] Between us, then, and this low coast range, was the valley of the Sacramento; and no one who had accompanied us through the incidents of our life for the past few months, could realize the delight with which at last we looked down upon it."

Frémont crossing the Sierra in February, 1844, from a drawing in Frémont's report.

The following night the thermometer fell to three degrees below zero, but although extremely cold it was perfectly clear. "Scenery and weather combined," writes Frémont, "must render these mountains beautiful in summer; the purity and deep-blue color of the sky are singularly beautiful; the days are sunny and bright, and even warm in the noon hours; and if we could be free from the many anxieties that oppress us, even now we would be delighted here; but our provisions are getting fearfully scant." Thus for a moment the spell of the High Sierra was upon him. And mark it up to Frémont's credit that, even though provisions were scant and there were many anxieties, his sensitive nature perceived the beauty that surrounded him. Almost immediately, however, the perils of the situation were brought back to his attention. The weather changed, the wind rose to a gale, and it began to snow again. Yet even in the midst of these difficulties he was able to note the character of the trees and the rocks. For several days the struggle continued through wind and snowfall, followed by bright sun and thaw. Snow blindness, fatigue, and hunger were countered by resolution and resourcefulness.

To one member of the party, however, the stark necessities of survival were more important than scenery. Charles Preuss, the German topographer, was not so inured to hardship as were others of the party. His diary furnishes some realistic commentaries.[5] Writing on February 3, he says, "We are getting deeper and deeper into the mountains and snow. We can make only a few miles each day." A little later: "Today the 'field marshal' marched out with a party on snowshoes to open up a way to the summit, about ten miles distant, it appears. Tomorrow we shall probably know whether it is possible to get through. No longer any salt in the camp. This is awful." "We are now completely snowed in," he continues. "The snowstorm is on top of us. The wind obliterates all tracks which, with indescribable effort, we make for our horses. At the moment no one can tell what will really happen. It is certain that we shall have to eat horse meat. I should not mind if we only had salt." Soon afterward Preuss's mule was killed, then their little dog. Frémont writes, "We had tonight an extraordinary dinner—pea soup, mule, and dog."

The following day, February 14, Frémont mentions almost casually, and Preuss not at all, what to us now seems an event to be celebrated. "With Mr. Preuss, I ascended today the highest peak to the right: from which we had a beautiful view of a mountain lake at our feet, about fifteen miles in length, and so entirely surrounded by mountains that we could not discover an outlet." Here is the first recorded mention of one of the great scenic features of the Sierra, Lake Tahoe. It is also the first account of an *identifiable* mountain ascent in the Sierra. They were on Red Lake Peak.[6] Frémont with the spirit of a true mountaineer not only climbed to observe the lay of the land but remained on top to enjoy the view. "From the immediate foot of the peak," he says, "we were two hours in reaching the summit, and one hour and a quarter in descending. The day had been very bright, still, and clear, and spring seems to be advancing rapidly. While the sun is in the sky, the snow melts rapidly, and gushing springs cover the mountain in all exposed places; but their surface freezes instantly with the disappearance of the sun."

But though the illusion of spring was in the air, it was nevertheless mid-winter and the party was in a serious predicament. They had gained the Sierra crest at a point a little south of the present Carson Pass and now considered themselves victorious over the mountain. They soon found out, however, that many difficulties intervened between them and the promised land. The second day after they crossed the pass they "were forced off the ridges by the quantity of snow among the timber, and obliged to take to the mountainsides, where, occasionally, rocks and a southern exposure afforded us a chance to scramble along. But these were steep, and slippery with snow and ice; and the tough evergreens of the mountain impeded our way, tore our skins, and exhausted our patience." That afternoon they reached the South Fork of the American River a short distance above Strawberry Valley. Carson, who was in advance, leaped across at a narrow spot between two rocks, but when Frémont attempted it his smooth moccasin slipped and he fell into the water; whereupon Kit jumped in and rescued him; they dried off before a large fire—a scene to be recalled when driving along U. S. 50 on a winter's day.

The barrier had been surmounted, and, although hunger and hardship were still with them, from that time on they were definitely on the way to warmth and safety. The Lieutenant went on ahead with Carson, Preuss, and a few others, while Fitzpatrick rounded up the lagging animals with such baggage as they had been able to carry. On the 6th of March the advance party was greeted by Captain Sutter at New Helvetia, and two days later the others, emaciated and exhausted, at last found haven. Of the large band who started across the mountain not one had failed to arrive, although one man did come in somewhat deranged in his mind. Of the sixty-seven horses and mules, thirty-three reached Sutter's Fort. Had the winter been as severe as some of those immediately before and after, the story would have been quite different and Lieutenant Frémont's career would have ended abruptly.

After recuperating for two weeks Frémont was ready to resume his journey, with newly acquired livestock and provisions. It was clearly his duty to get back to the United States as soon as possible. "Our direct course home," he writes, "was east; but the Sierra would force us south, about five hundred miles of traveling, to a pass at the head of the San Joaquin river. This pass, reported to be good, was discovered by Mr. Joseph Walker, of whom I have already spoken, and whose name it might, therefore, appropriately bear. To reach it, our course lay along the valley of the San Joaquin—the river on the right, and the lofty wall of the impassable Sierra on the left." During the next two weeks the party followed substantially the route of the modern Highway

99. There were frequent rains, and Frémont remarks: "On our left, the Sierra maintains its snowy height, and masses of snow appear to descend very low towards the plains; probably the late rains in the valley were snow on the mountains." On the 6th of April he says: "Here we found the San Joaquin coming down from the Sierra with a westerly course, and checking our way, as all its tributaries had previously done." On the 8th they came to Kings River, which Frémont calls "the River of the Lake." Continuing south and crossing the delta of the Kaweah, they "approached considerably nearer to the eastern Sierra, which shows very plainly, still covered with masses of snow." They were looking directly up at the Great Western Divide and the Kaweah Peaks. Presently they came to Kern River, "the swiftest stream we have crossed since leaving the bay."

A pass was now in sight toward the southeast, which Frémont supposed was the one by which Walker had left the valley ten years before. Walker, however, on the advice of some helpful Indians, had turned here to the east, while Frémont unknowingly missed the turn and headed for the Tehachapi. On the 14th of April, 1844, from the summit of that pass he took a parting view of the California Valley and of the Sierra Nevada. And here, in his Report, with a grand gesture, he dismissed the Buenaventura. His journey, he says, had "cleared up some points in geography on which error had long prevailed. It had been constantly represented, as I have stated that the bay of San Francisco opened far into the interior, by some river coming down from the base of the Rocky mountains, and upon which supposed stream the name Rio Buenaventura had been bestowed. Our observations of the Sierra Nevada show that this neither is nor can be the case. No river from the interior does, or can cross the Sierra Nevada. There is no opening from the bay of San Francisco into the interior of the continent." Thus did Frémont unmask a bogey of his own creation and announce what had been common knowledge throughout the West for at least ten years and in California for half a century.

When Frémont returned to Washington he at once set to work upon his report, ably assisted by his wife, while Preuss prepared the maps and illustrations. The work was finished barely in time for the newly breveted Captain to head another expedition. That the main object of the "Third Expedition" was closely connected with Senator Benton's plans for acquiring California there is little doubt. The expressed object was "to extend the survey west and southwest of the great range of the Cascade Mountains and the Sierra Nevada, so as to ascertain the lines of communication through the mountains to the ocean." Frémont adds that "in arranging the expedition, the eventualities of war were taken into consideration."[7]

The journey across the continent was made rapidly, with little time for lateral exploration. Before reaching Walker Lake the Captain with a select group of fifteen men left the main party and sought the fastest way to California. He found the river which on his previous journey he had called the Salmon Trout (the Truckee) and made rapid progress up it, endeavoring to reach the pass before a heavy fall of snow should come. In this he succeeded, and arrived at Sutter's Fort on the 9th of December, where he received "the same friendly hospitality which had been so delightful to us the year before." Here they camped for a few days while Frémont negotiated for fresh horses and a small drove of cattle, and on the 14th set out to look for the other section of the expedition.

Meanwhile, the larger group, in charge of Theodore Talbot and guided by the veteran Joseph Walker, proceeded south from Walker Lake to Walker Pass. It was planned that the parties would unite at a river called the "Lake Fork of the Tulare Lake." This to Frémont was Kings River and familiar ground. From Sutter's Fort he moved south through the valley and up to "a beautiful country of undulating upland, openly wooded with oaks, principally evergreen, and watered with small streams which together make the *Mariposas River*."[8] Here he encountered a band of the Horse-thief Indians and conflict arose. With such phenomenal marksmen and skilled Indian fighters as Carson, Owens, Godey, and Maxwell in his train, not to mention the Delaware Indians whom he had brought from the East, Frémont was much better equipped than were most small parties; the losses were all on the side of the Indians. Returning to the valley, he reached the "Lake Fork," confident that he would find the Talbot–Walker party somewhere along the river. But they were not there.

We now come to one of the most extraordinary episodes in High Sierra history—Frémont with sixteen men on horseback herding a number of cattle, venturing into an utterly unknown country up to eleven thousand feet, in midwinter. Frémont's narrative gives very few landmarks, but there are enough, together with the maps, to indicate fairly well the route he took. Apparently he started on the north bank of Kings River and followed bottomlands for a while until the narrowing canyon forced him to climb out. He found the general character of the country similar to that farther north, but the timber more open and "some trees extremely large." These can hardly be other than the Big Trees (sequoias) of the North Fork of Kings River. He kept on into the upper basin to its extremities, Burnt Corral Meadow, or perhaps Blackcap Basin. In the *Memoirs* is a description of the region that should be in any anthology of the literature of the High Sierra:

"I found the mountain extremely rocky in the upper parts, the streams breaking through the canyons, but wooded up to the granite ridges which comprise its rocky eminences. We forced our way up among the head springs of the river and finally stood upon the flat ridge of naked granite which made the division of the waters and was 11,000 feet above the sea. The day was sunny and the air warm enough to be not only very agreeable, but with exercise exhilarating, even at that height. Lying immediately below, perhaps 1,000 feet, at the foot of a precipitous descent was a small lake, which I judged to be one of the sources of the San Joaquin. I had grown, by occasional privation, to look upon water as a jewel beyond price, and this was rendered even more beautiful by its rough setting."[9]

We shall probably never know the precise point at which Frémont stood looking down upon this sparkling lake. There are a dozen different places corresponding to the description and the circumstances. That night camp was made immediately below the ridge where some pine furnished welcome shelter from a threatened change in the weather. "The sky clouded over and by nightfall was a uniform dull gray, and early in the night the roar of the wind through the pines had at times the sound of a torrent." It was a gloomy camp, for they were "disappointed and perplexed, wondering what had become of our people." They themselves were in real danger, for had they not moved promptly the next morning, they would have been trapped. They chose a different way down, but it was not much better. "The old year went out and the new year came in, rough as the country." Snow began to fall, and soon they had to abandon their cattle, for it was impossible to drive them over the treacherous ground. They had difficulty enough themselves getting out from the snow and had misgivings as they "rode through the forest, silent now without a sound except where we came within hearing of water roaring among rocks or muffled under snow." But they were presently out of trouble, among the oaks, "where spring weather, rain and sunshine, were found again." Descending to the valley, they traveled "among multitudinous herds of elk, antelope, and wild horses." They searched a little farther up the San Joaquin Valley, without avail, then turned back to Sutter's Fort, confident that the others, doubtless delayed, would soon come to this region of abundant game.

While all this was going on, what had become of Talbot, Walker, Kern, and the main body of the expedition? After the Captain left them at Walker Lake, they remained for ten days to recruit their animals. Then, skirting the margin of the lake past the site of the present town of Hawthorne, Nevada, they took a general southwest direction until they came to Owens River.[10] For several days they followed the course of the river and on the night of December 19 camped near the lake at its mouth. Here at Owens Lake they were looking directly up at Lone Pine Peak, with Mount Whitney, not then known, just beyond. Continuing south they came to Little Lake. On the way they found the cache left by the Chiles–Walker party, where the contents of the wagons and the set of mill irons lay buried. They saw what appeared to be a pass over the mountains, but it was so steep that it was not attempted and they kept on toward Walker Pass. "Our Christmas," writes Kern, "was spent in a most unchristmaslike manner. Our camp was made on the slope of the mountain, at some Indian wells of good water." Fuel was furnished by an abundance of yucca trees.[11] "The camp-fires blazed and cracked joyously, the only merry things about us, and all that had any resemblance to that merry time at home." Christmas dinner was, "by way of a change, on one of our tired, worn mules, instead of a horse."

Next day they crossed the pass to the headwaters of a river, which they followed down to its forks. They were on Kern River. This they supposed to be the rendezvous, and there they remained for nearly three weeks, living on acorns and a meager supply of very poor venison. The situation was becoming intolerable, and as Frémont failed to appear, they raised camp and struck north across the Greenhorn Mountains and down to the valley, where young grass and a few flowers were beginning to put forth. They pressed on to Kings River, but too late to meet Frémont on his return from the High Sierra. Of this excursion of course they had no knowledge; nor did they recognize the misunderstanding that had caused Walker to suppose the rendezvous to be on the Kern, while Frémont supposed it to be on the Kings. Each was familiar with his own river and knew nothing of the other. For a day or two the Talbot–Walker party floundered in the tulare sloughs, but eventually extricated themselves and pushed on toward Sutter's Fort. On the way they met a mountain man who told them that their Captain had gone to the Pueblo of San José, and a few days later the entire party of some sixty men was united. The Exploring Expedition was ended and a new era was about to begin.

The events that followed are no part of the history of the Sierra Nevada except as they brought about for Frémont one more crossing of the range—this time not as a daring leader, but as a humiliated subordinate. His brief tenure as Military Governor of California had ended with the departure of Commodore Stockton. General Stephen Watts Kearny took command, but Frémont refused to acknowledge his authority and was placed under arrest.[12] When Kearny was ready to return to Washington, with California now securely part of the United States, the recalcitrant Frémont was ordered to follow in his wake. In June, 1847, they set out over the Sierra by the now well-established Donner Route, accompanied by certain members of the Mormon Battalion returning east to Salt Lake. Crossing Donner Pass they came upon the ruined cabin and grisly remains of the "Cannibal Camp" of the preceding winter. Sergeant Daniel Tyler, of the Mormon party, reports in his diary: "The General ordered a halt and detailed five men to bury the dead that were lying on the ground," after which, "they set fire to the cabin and left the horrible place."[13] Frémont is mentioned as passing by at this time. Such was his grim farewell to the High Sierra.

NOTES AND REFERENCES

1. The best present-day biographies are Allan Nevins, *Frémont, Pathmarker of the West*, New York, 1939 (superseding the same author's earlier work, *Frémont, The West's Greatest Adventurer*, New York, 1928), and Cardinal Goodwin, *Frémont, An Explanation of His Career*, Stanford, 1930. Frederick S. Dellenbaugh, *Frémont and '49*, New York, 1914, is useful for the geographical background. Best of the earlier biographies is John Bigelow, *Memoir of the Life and Public Services of John Charles Frémont*, New York, 1856 (*Wagner-Camp* 271A). For a more critical examination of Frémont's conduct in California, see Josiah Royce, *California*, Boston, 1886; new edition, 1948. Frémont's own story is set forth in *Memoirs of My Life*, Chicago, 1887, of which only the first volume was published.

2. The report of the 1843-1844 Expedition was printed in 1845 both by the Senate and by the House of Representatives in large editions (*Wagner-Camp* 115), accompanied by a large map (*Wheat* 497). The report has been reprinted and paraphrased many times. Quotations here are from the House edition, and from the *Memoirs*, which repeat verbatim many passages from the *Report*.

3. Frémont may not have had far to go to obtain his ideas about the Buenaventura River. There was probably visible at the time in more than one Washington office a large wall map by Dr. John Hamilton Robinson, 1819 (*Wheat* 374), which showed, among other apocryphal features, a river flowing from far in the interior to the Pacific, on a course, as Wheat says, "untrammeled by geography or topography" (*Wheat*, II). If Frémont took his ideas from this map it is small wonder that he strayed from the path. There were genuine maps available before 1843, which, if he had consulted them, would have set him straight: by Gallatin, 1836 (*Wheat* 417); by Bonneville, 1837 (*Wheat* 424); and especially by Burr, 1839 (*Wheat* 441). The origin and propagation of the Buenaventura myth are discussed by Dale L. Morgan in *The Humboldt, Highroad of the West*, New York, 1941, and in his *The Great Salt Lake*, Indianapolis, 1947; and by C. Gregory Crampton in *PHR*, May, 1956.

4. The "little mountain" was presumably Mount Diablo.

5. Charles Preuss, *Exploring with Frémont*, translated and edited by Edwin G. and Elisabeth K. Gudde, Norman, Okla.: University of Oklahoma Press, 1958.

6. I formerly thought that this was Stevens Peak (Farquhar, "Frémont in the Sierra Nevada," *SCB* February, 1930, 15:1), but Vincent P. Gianella in a well-reasoned article, "Where Frémont Crossed the Sierra Nevada in 1844," *SCB*, October, 1959, 44:7, has convinced me that it was Red Lake Peak. Gianella's other identifications are equally convincing.—F. P. F.

7. It is clear that in Frémont's mind the "eventualities of war" quite overshadowed all other considerations. Upon his arrival in California he even found it difficult to wait for eventualities and soon became involved in a train of circumstances that violently changed the whole course of his life. One consequence was that he had neither the time nor the inclination to prepare an official report of this expedition comparable to that of the previous one. The *Memoirs*, published long afterwards, furnish most of the information.

A map, however, was an urgent necessity. This work he placed in the hands of Charles Preuss, who, although he had not accompanied the Third Expedition, was sufficiently acquainted with the West to enable him to produce one of the finest maps of the period, with an especially good portrayal of the Sierra Nevada (*Wheat* 559). The tributaries of the Sacramento and the San Joaquin are shown in their correct positions and in most instances under their present names. Several names appear for the first time: Carson River, Walker River, Kern River, and Owens Lake, which Frémont named for his companions; why Fitzpatrick, Godey, and especially Preuss himself, are left out is not explained.

Frémont put together a brief *Geographical Memoir upon Upper California, in Illustration of His Map of Oregon and California*, which was published by the Senate in 1848 and a year later by the House (*Wagner-Camp* 150). A new edition was published by the Book Club of California in 1964.

8. The Captain could have had no intimation that he was on the margin of a tract that in a little more than a year would be his own property. When the Mariposa Grant was acquired by him, more or less by accident, it was suitable merely for a poor cattle range. Then gold was discovered on the property and Frémont overnight became a millionaire. (See chap. IX.)

9. Frémont, *Memoirs*.

10. The journal of Edward M. Kern is included in Captain J. H. Simpson's *Report of Explorations Across the Great Basin of the Territory of Utah . . . in 1859*, Washington, D. C., 1879, Appendix Q. For biographical data and commentaries, see William Joseph Heffernan, *Edward M. Kern: The Travels of an Artist–Explorer*, Bakersfield, Calif., 1953, and Robert V. Hine, *Edward Kern and American Expansion*, New Haven, Conn., 1962.

11. The Tree Yucca (*Yucca brevifolia*) is described by Jepson (*Silva of California*, Berkeley: University of California Press, 1910) as "commonly 20 to 30 feet high with an open crown of arm-like branches, the columnar trunk 8 to 15 feet high and 1 to 3 feet in diameter." It is distributed from the western arm of the Mojave Desert to Walker Pass. According to Jepson, the name "Joshua Tree" was given to it by Mormons of southern Utah; Kern says it was nicknamed "Jeremiah" by the men of his party; Joshua has prevailed over Jeremiah.

12. The dispute between Kearny and Frémont, the arrest of Frémont, and his courtmartial and conviction for insubordination are treated at length in innumerable writings about Frémont, and more recently in Dwight L. Clarke, *Stephen Watts Kearny, Soldier of the West*, Norman, Okla., 1961.

13. Sergeant Daniel Tyler, *A Concise History of the Mormon Battalion in the Mexican War, 1846-1847*, Salt Lake City, 1881; the incident is also discussed in Clarke, *op. cit.*

VIII

GOLD AND THE WAY TO THE MINES

▸▸

Discovery of gold on the American River in January, 1848, brought changes far out of proportion to the value of the metal itself. Pastoral California disappeared forever; an expansive American life sprang into being. The foothills of the Sierra became alive with frenzied searchers for the fabulous wealth one and all expected to pick up on every river bank and gravel bar. Tent camps blossomed, presently to be replaced by shacks and cabins, which in an incredibly short time became towns. "Never before in history," writes Carl Wheat, "had men so rapidly overrun so vast an unoccupied territory."[1] All this had an immediate effect upon the Sierra, causing intensive exploration of the central region and the conclusive breaching of the mountain barrier by sheer force of numbers. The Gold Rush was on. From 2,000 Americans in California at the beginning of 1848, the number grew to over 53,000 by the close of 1849.[2] Although most of the travelers came by sea to the port of San Francisco, thousands of others came overland. Most of those who journeyed overland in 1848 followed the established Truckee route, but some tried experiments. One contingent followed Peter Lassen through the region north of the Sierra to which his name thereafter became attached. A few, hearing of the newly opened Carson Pass, brought their wagons that way.

The new Carson Pass route was discovered and made passable, not by Kit Carson, but by a remnant of the disbanded Mormon Battalion which had stayed behind at Sutter's Fort in 1847.[3] After the gold discovery they lingered for a while to try their luck in the "diggings" before they set out to rejoin their brethren at Great Salt Lake. Early in May, when they were ready to go, an advance party was sent to see if there might be a practicable way for wagons directly east. "Three days' travel brought this company to Iron Hill, where they found the snow so deep they could travel no farther. A donkey belonging to one of the men was completely buried in the snow, except his ears. On this occasion, these appendages were not to be despised, ugly and unique as they usually appear, for one or two of the men got hold of them and dragged Mr. Donkey on to terra firma and saved his life."[4] Here there is note of another mountain ascent, peak not specified. "Brothers Willis, Sly and Evans ascended to the summit of a mountain. Seeing nothing but snow-capped mountains in advance of them, it was decided not to abandon but to postpone the enterprise until a later period. So far as they could judge, a wagon road would at least be possible and perhaps a success."

Later, toward the end of June, three others, Browett, Allen and Cox, essayed a second exploring tour, against the advice of their companions who were fearful of Indians. The three did not return. In the middle of July the whole company, about thirty-seven, with sixteen wagons, started for the mountains. "They had no guide, nor as far as known, had the foot of white man ever trod upon the ground over which they were then constructing, what subsequently proved to be a great national highway for overland travel."[5] In time they came to a spring, where someone about to quench his thirst picked up a bloodstained arrow. The worst fears of the company were soon confirmed; the bodies of their missing friends were found in a shallow grave, terribly mutilated. The bodies were reburied and a memorial monument erected. They named the place "Tragedy Springs," a name it still bears.[6] Continuing, the party passed near Silver Lake and across the meadow now occupied by Twin Lakes. "This day," writes Bigler, "I gathered flowers with one hand and snow with the other." They crossed the pass and "camped at the head of what we called Hope Valley, as we began to have hope."[7]

Among the westward-moving immigrants diverted to the new pass by the success of the Mormon party was Pierre Barlow Cornwall. "One night, after a day of more than the usual difficulties, they came to camp upon a high, level ground with a peak rising to the southeast. At sunrise the two Cornwalls [Pierre and his younger brother Arthur] went on ahead to view the prospect from this eminence. As they reached the summit a most glorious panorama lay outstretched before them. At their feet lay the rolling declivities of the Sierras, finally stretching out into the vast fertile valley of the Sacramento. The sun glinted upon the river as it wound its course down to the sea. Verily the children of Israel could not have looked upon the Promised Land with greater gladness. It was one of the most joyful moments of a lifetime, and the scene inspired awe and thanksgiving in the hearts of the beholders."[8]

Carson Pass is vividly described in the diary of one of those who crossed that way a year later: "The principal obstructions that interposed themselves to our march were the large piles of granite that had broken off the walls of the mountains which stood on either side thousands of feet above us—and overhanging us as it were—and rolled down into the gorge, forming piles from 1 to 300 feet high. We were compelled to force our wagons over, around, and through, many of these places by manual labor, the turns being too short to be made with the team hitched on." And, next day: "Large trees have been felled to the ground and a kind of road made above it by throwing brush and dirt on it to gain the upper side of some large stone, which forms a kind of road again until another turn can be effected. We have to lift our wagons around frequently and make a square tack to the right or left." At the summit: "Nothing in nature I am sure can present scenery more wild, more rugged, more bold, more grand, more romantic, and picturesquely beautiful than this mountain scenery."[9]

There are many accounts of the troubles and trials of the forty-niners as they struggled across the last great barrier to the land of gold. One more may suffice to round out the picture. For this, Wakeman Bryarly's diary will serve.[10] On August 21, 1849, camp was made below Donner Lake. Next day: "Early everything was in motion. In one mile we crossed a little stream to the left, which runs from the Lake. Here we stopped, and cut sufficent grass for a feed. After rolling one mile farther we struck the foot of the mountain. The road was very rough and in many places steep both going up and coming down. Every now and then there was a little table upon which there was a little grass. We rolled thus two miles when we nooned (or rather rested, not taking our mules out) upon one of these tables. We stopped two hours, when we ascended a very steep and very rocky road with many short turns around the large rocks and trees. One mile brought us to the foot of the 'Elephant' itself. Here we 'faced the music' and no mistake. We immediately doubled teams, and after considerable screaming and whipping, thus arrived safely at the top. We were but four hours ascending, and we were much disappointed, but agreeably so, in not finding it much worse. Certainly this must be a great improvement upon the old road, where the wagons had to be taken to pieces and packed across."

It was, therefore, a blow when they found that they were still far from their goal. They descended a steep hill, only to climb up again. There were pretty valleys and many lakes, but the road was rougher than ever. They crossed a divide and came to Bear River. "Everyone is liable to mistakes," writes Bryarly, "and everyone has a right to call a road *very bad* until he sees a worse. My mistake was that I had said I had seen 'The Elephant' when getting over the first mountain. I had only seen the tail. This evening I think I saw him in toto."[11] There was further letting down of wagons by ropes; "down a hill and immediately up another so steep and rough that some of our teams had to double." They came to Bear Valley, where there was a fine stream and plenty of grass. Then another "Elephant," and at last down to a stream where men were digging. Hundreds must have had similar experiences, and yet, like Bryarly and his companions, they came through.

It was not so bad when there were no wagons. The diarist of one Forty-nine party records a journey of only three days from "Truckie's" (Donner) Lake to the first diggings on Bear River, but even he conceded that the road was rough. "Our road soon struck off for Bear River," he writes, "over a high rough mountainous region. We got off from our road this morning and went several miles out of our way. The road this afternoon has been most horribly bad, and I more than once congratulated myself that I have got away from the ox teams —wagons would have to be let down with ropes in many places, and if they make five miles a day they will do well." He traveled thirty miles that day.[12]

The rapid increase in the population of the mining camps and their uncontrolled activities began to create problems hitherto not considered. It was quite natural for the Indians to attack and commit depredations upon the swarms of strangers invading their territory; and it was quite natural for the whites to retaliate. Something had to be done to prevent open warfare. The military command at Monterey recognized this and in the summer of 1849 sent Brigadier General Bennet Riley to look over the situation. Temporary camps were set up at several points, but the most important was near Johnson's Ranch on Bear River, the present Wheatland, where the immigrants were pouring over the mountains.[13] Lieutenant George H. Derby of the Topographical Engineers was instructed to lay off a square mile for an army post, which was established as "Camp Far West." Derby summarizes its significance: "The Truckee emigrant route, over which was passing an average of one hundred wagons and two hundred emigrants per diem, the wagon road to the Yuba mines, that to the Feather River 'dry diggins,' and the paths to the Bear Creek diggings, all intersect at this point." Derby prepared a map to show the situation. On a similar map of a reconnaissance a little earlier in the summer, the diggings south of the American River are shown, and on this map are several significant names— Angel's, Jamestown, Sonoran Camp—the beginning of permanent settlements in the mining region and the bases for future exploration.[14]

Marysville was already a small city, when, suddenly at the opening of the mining season of 1850, it became temporarily almost deserted. There are several versions of the "Gold Lake stampede" that brought this about, but the one generally accepted stems from a man named Stoddard.[15] According to his story he was crossing the mountains in 1849 and, while hunting with a companion, lost the way. They came upon a small lake the shores of which were covered with gold, some in large chunks, with gold slabs at the bottom shining in the clear water. They were attacked by Indians and the companion was killed, but Stoddard escaped and reached the mining camps. It was too late in the season to return to the lake, but in the spring Stoddard offered to lead a party in search of the spot. Meanwhile the story became augmented by all kinds of imaginative embellishments, some obviously (to us) out-and-out hoaxes, but in their time and circumstances wishfully plausible. A Sacramento newspaper reported that Marysville was thrown into great excitement by "a report that mines, exceeding in their richness the wildest dreams of the visionary, have been discovered a considerable distance to the northeast," between the Feather and the Yuba, where a lake had been found to which the name "Gold Lake" was given.[16] Another report said that a vein of quartz was found "where the pure ore was observed in threads and spangles, beautiful to look upon." The stories grew, and a few days later, "We are informed by a gentleman from Marysville that it is currently reported there that the Indians upon this lake use gold for the commonest purposes—that they have a rude way of knocking out square blocks, which they use for seats and couches." Then, "Another man reported that he had found a lake somewhere at the head of the rivers on whose shore clean gold could be scraped by the pound." One old man at Marysville told of packing mules with three hundred pounds of gold each, but having to lighten the loads by sorting over the big chunks and throwing out all those "weighted with quartz stickin' to 'em."[17] How could such tales be believed? It seems incredible. But there were those who believed at least part of them, for hundreds scrambled up into the mountains in search of Gold Lake, which, however fantastic, might exist after all.

As day after day went by and no gleaming chunks of gold were seen at the bottoms of the numerous lakes visited, and no golden pebbles on their shores, the glittering visions began to dissolve and the disillusioned miners took counsel. The first impulse was to hang Stoddard, but on second thought it began to be evident that Stoddard was just a bewildered old man, probably crazy, and that the fault lay with themselves. Although that was the end of the Gold Lake dream, all was not lost. A very thorough exploration of the upper Yuba and Feather rivers had been made and not a little gold was discovered. In sentimental remembrance, one of the many lakes of the region still bears the name Gold Lake.

NOTES AND REFERENCES

A portion of this chapter appeared in *Westways*, June, 1964.

1. Carl I. Wheat, *The Maps of the California Gold Region, 1848-1857*, San Francisco, 1942.

2. Charles Howard Shinn, *Mining Camps, A Study in American Frontier Government*, New York, 1885; new edition, 1948.

3. There are two contemporary accounts: (1) Sergeant Daniel Tyler, *A Concise History of the Mormon Battalion in the Mexican War*, Salt Lake City, 1881; and (2) *Bigler's Chronicle of the West*, edited by Erwin G. Gudde, Berkeley and Los Angeles, 1962. Also see Allen Fifield, "Wagons East Across the Sierras," *HSSCA*, 1961.

4. Tyler, *op. cit.*

5. *Ibid.* The Carson Pass Road, now known as Route 88.

6. *Ibid.*; also Gudde, *op. cit.* Fifield, *op. cit.*, argues that the men were killed not by Indians but by bandits, for their gold.

7. Gudde, *op. cit.*

8. Bruce Cornwall, *Life Sketch of Pierre Barlow Cornwall*, San Francisco, 1906.

9. Dale L. Morgan, editor, *The Overland Diary of James A. Pritchard from Kentucky to California in 1849*, Denver, 1959.

10. *Trail to California: The Overland Journal of Vincent Geiger and Wakeman Bryerly*, New Haven, 1945.

11. George P. Hammond, *Who Saw the Elephant? An Inquiry by a Scholar Well Acquainted with the Beast*, CHS, 1964. (An explanation of the phrase.)

12. *Diary of Henry R. Mann, 1849.* (Photocopy in BL.)

13. Stewart, *California Trail,* New York, 1962, estimates that in 1849, 7,000 came by the Truckee route, 8,000 by the Lassen route, and 6,000 by the Carson.

14. Farquhar, "The Topographical Reports of Lieutenant George H. Derby," *CHSQ,* June, 1932, 11:2; reprinted separately, 1933. *Senate Ex. Doc. 47 and H. R. Ex Doc. 17,* 31st Cong., 1st Sess., 1850. Wheat, *Maps of the California Gold Region,* items 79 and 149.

15. Farris & Smith, *Illustrated History of Plumas, Lassen & Sierra Counties,* San Francisco, 1882. Also see George and Bliss Hinkle, *Sierra-Nevada Lakes,* 1949.

16. *Sacramento Transcript,* June 14, 1850.

17. J. C. Tucker, *To the Golden Goal and Other Sketches,* San Francisco, 1875.

IX

MARIPOSA AND YOSEMITE

The second season of gold mining, the summer of 1849, found thousands of prospectors seeking new fields, from the Yuba and the Feather in the north to the Stanislaus and the Tuolumne in the south. A few hardy explorers penetrated to the canyon of the Merced and on up to the Mariposa country.[1] Frémont's barren cattle ranch now began to take on a new aspect; with the magic of gold it might be worth something after all. Frémont sent one of his trusted aides, Alexis Godey, with a few Mexican miners, to look things over. Gold was there all right, and they were soon panning it out of Agua Fria Creek. But the Mexicans knew more about gold than the American newcomers and began looking for the *veta madre*, the "mother vein," or "mother lode," which they reasoned must be nearby. They found the quartz vein they were looking for and before long had a crusher in operation. Frémont became a millionaire. But questions arose. Did Frémont's title to the land give him rights to the gold? Further, and more important, did he actually have a valid title at all? Years of litigation followed, which, together with huge debts and wasteful mining practices, resulted in bankruptcy. He was a millionaire no longer.[2]

Meanwhile, avid prospectors swarmed over the property and over the surrounding country, building for themselves trouble that at first they scorned, then resented. The Indians, tired of working for small pay in goods and food, began to raid the stores that enterprising traders had set up. From the white man's point of view the Indians were savages, to be subdued or annihilated. The Indians had similar views of the white men and proceeded to wipe them out. Then the horrors of war began.

Protagonist of the Mariposa Indian War was James D. Savage.[3] He occupied a unique position, since he was both closely associated with the red raiders and a victim of their raids. One of the earliest prospectors on the Merced, he had established a camp at the junction of the South Fork with the main river. He had had long experience with Indians and was quick to learn their ways and speak their language. He married into the "best families" and had access to their councils. Some say he had five, some say over twenty, Indian wives, who, in addition to their marital duties, aided in panning for gold. As the population of gold-seekers increased, Savage saw a way to make profits faster than by tedious efforts on the gravel bars. In the spring of 1850 he abandoned his Merced River enterprise and set up a trading post at Agua Fria, near Mariposa, followed soon after by one on the Fresno River, near Coarsegold. During the year mining activities and Indian troubles increased until they culminated in an Indian raid on Savage's Fresno River store and the murder of the men in charge. A posse was formed at Agua Fria and a small battle fought. To prevent reprisals, an appeal was made to the Governor of the newly formed State, who authorized the organization of a volunteer militia. Savage was appointed Major of this "Mariposa Battalion," with three companies under elected captains.[4] Before action could be taken, however, three United States Commissioners arrived and ordered a halt in proceedings while they attempted to persuade the Indians to sign treaties and settle on reservations.

Although most of the Indians accepted the treaties, some of the wilder ones failed to come in, retreating to remote hiding places in the mountains. Major Savage received orders to seek them and bring them in. Captain John J. Kuykendall, with Company C, was detailed to the Fresno and the San Joaquin and ordered to pursue recalcitrants up the Kings and the Kaweah. Companies A and B, under Captains John Bowling (or Boling) and William Dill, respectively,[5] with Major Savage in charge, set out to find a mysterious valley said to be the stronghold of a hostile group known as the "Yosemites."[6] Deep wet snow on Chowchilla Mountain delayed Savage's men before they arrived, by a long night march, at a suitable camping spot on the South Fork of the Merced, near the present Wawona. Here they were met by a chief of the Yosemites, called Teneiya,[7] who agreed to lead Savage to his *rancheria* in the valley. As it was deemed unnecessary to send the entire party, footraces were held to determine the most fit. In the morning some fifty or sixty men set out, following a route that later became the stage road from Wawona to Yosemite. On the way they met some of Teneiya's people, coming in to surrender, so Teneiya turned back with them, leaving a younger Indian to guide the party to the rancheria. Fortunately for the history of this event there was in Captain Bowling's company a young man of twenty-seven, Lafayette Bunnell, who had the ability to observe, and later to record, what went on.[8] At Old Inspiration Point, which Bunnell calls "Mount Beatitude," they suddenly came into full view of Yosemite Valley. "The grandeur of the scene," writes Bunnell, "was softened by the haze that hung over the valley—light as gossamer—and by the clouds which partially dimmed the higher cliffs and mountains. This obscurity of vision but increased the awe with which I beheld it, and as I looked, a peculiar exalted sensation seemed to fill my whole being, and I found my eyes in tears with emotion." The others of the party appeared indifferent to the scene and were more interested in getting into camp. Hastening down, they arrived at a meadow in full view of Bridalveil Fall—the first known camp of white men in Yosemite Valley. The date was March 27, 1851.[9] That evening around the campfire it was proposed to give a name to the valley. Bunnell suggested "Yosemity," the name of Teneiya's tribe as he understood it.[10] The following

Early photograph of Yosemite from Inspiration Point.

C. E. Watkins

day the men explored the valley from end to end. There was abundant evidence that Indians had occupied their huts as recently as the night before, but all had disappeared. Bunnell, with a few others, went a long way up Tenaya Canyon and found tracks which ultimately eluded them. He returned greatly impressed by the views of Mirror Lake, Half Dome, and the waterfall of the South Canyon.[11] A small squad explored above Vernal and Nevada falls as far as Little Yosemite, undoubtedly the first to see them. Next day all left the valley and rejoined their comrades at the camp near Wawona. "During these three days of absence from headquarters," writes Bunnell, "we had discovered, named and partially explored one of the most remarkable of the geographical wonders of the world."

Were the members of the Mariposa Battalion actually the first to enter Yosemite Valley? It has long been presumed that they were, assuming that the Walker party merely looked upon it from above. Yet there was always the chance that some adventurous explorer had found his way there. Savage claimed that he had gone a long way up the Merced Canyon, perhaps to Cascade Valley, and there were rumors that others had gone even farther, but nothing definite was known until, in 1947, there came to light the diary of William Penn Abrams, unquestionably genuine and contemporary.[12] It contains the following entry under date of October 18, 1849: "Returned to S.F. after visit to Savages property on Merced River, prospects none too good for a mill. Savage is a blasphemous fellow who has five squaws for wives for which he takes authority from the Scriptures. While at Savage's Reamer and I saw grizzly bear tracks and went out to hunt him down, getting lost in the mountains and not returning until the following evening, found our way to camp over an Indian trail that led past a valley enclosed by stupendous cliffs rising perhaps 3,000 feet from their base and which gave us cause for wonder. Not far off a waterfall dropped from a cliff below three jagged peaks into the valley, while farther beyond a rounded mountain stood, the valley side of which looked as though it had been sliced with a knife as one would slice a loaf of bread and which Reamer and I called the Rock of Ages."

It is not easy to determine just where Abrams and Reamer went on this two-day trip. They certainly saw Bridalveil Fall and Half Dome. Did they go all the way up the Merced through the canyon, or did they climb out to the south and east from near El Portal? The latter route, which corresponds to the old Hennessy Trail, would have brought them to the vicinity of Old Inspiration Point, which would have provided the view recorded. They may have then returned by the bed of the canyon. This would have been a natural route and about all they could do in two days. The fact remains that they reached Yosemite Valley, and as the record now stands they were the first to do so.

This does not in the least detract from the credit due Bunnell and his companions of the Mariposa Battalion. It was they who first explored Yosemite and made it known to the world. Moreover, they followed their first exploration with a more extended one a few weeks later. The first efforts to round up the Indians and take them to reservations were not entirely successful. Not only did a considerable number remain at large, but many of those who had been brought in, including the Yosemites, strayed away, and one night a whole group of them vanished. A more vigorous campaign was ordered. The principal effort was directed toward the Chowchilla tribe, a Yokuts people, who had taken refuge in the upper San Joaquin. In the subsequent pursuit, members of the Battalion covered a considerable portion of the territory north and northeast of the present Bass Lake (at that time called Crane Flat), in which Beasore Meadow and Kaiser Creek are recognizable with the aid of the diary of Robert Eccleston, a member of Company C.[13] Under date of April 19 Eccleston records: "We saw a noble Red wood tree on the mountain which would measure all of 60 ft close to the ground & 4 ft from the ground about 50 ft. It tapered slowly til over half way up & it was of majestic height." The context indicates that this was in the Fresno Grove, at the head of Nelder Creek, a region that was so heavily logged in later years that there is little chance that Eccleston's majestic tree can be identified, even if it remains. The Chowchillas proved elusive, but were eventually brought to terms by the destruction of their food supply, as the white men burned their caches of acorns wherever found. A treaty was concluded at the end of April that ended hostilities.

Major Savage was now free to attend to the recalcitrant Yosemites. He ordered Captain Bowling to take thirty-five men from Company B and endeavor to surprise the Indians in the stronghold previously visited, while he himself would outflank them by going up the San Joaquin and crossing over to the Merced. Little did the Major realize what he was getting into. Reporting on this expedition, Sergeant Major Russell writes to his adjutant: "I am aware that you have been high up and deep in the mountains and snow yourself, but I believe this trip ranks all others. The Major himself has seen cañons and snow peaks this trip which he never saw before. It is astonishing what this man can endure. Traveling on day and night, through the snow and over the mountains, without food is not considered fatigue with him, and you are well aware the boys will follow him as long as he leaves a sign."[14] Dr. Crampton has traced the route as well as can be conjectured from Eccleston's diary. From Beasore Meadows, which the Battalion had visited on the Chowchilla campaign, the party traveled by night, across Chiquito Creek, probably to Jackass Meadow. Eccleston writes, "We had some ugly streams to cross, & in one place one of the pack mules came near drowning. We had to wade these streams up to our knees which made our traveling very uncomfortable as it was a cold night & wet feet were far from pleasant." Sergeant Major Russell amplifies the story: "Among others the animal of Orderly Sergeant Bishop was washed down into the deep water, where it remained for some time, apparently feeling for the bottom, letting him into the water up to his waist, where he remained for some time on account of the strength of the current, which prevented the mule from swimming as it was disposed to do. The animal, however, finally succeeded in getting foothold, and brought its frozen rider safely to shore. The stream was immediately christened Bishop's River, which our orderly does not admit as being sufficient compensation for such an untimely bath."[15]

Snatches of Eccleston's diary reveal the extent to which they had penetrated the High Sierra. "We had some dangerous places to climb," he says, "along the rocks to which we were obliged to go bare footed." And again, "The scenery here is magnificently wild. Whole mountains of solid rock are not infrequent & many beautiful pictures of tremendous waterfalls on stone by the Oldest Master enliven the stream. The snowy peaks, the summit of the Sierra Nevada, show out nobly." They were in full view of the Ritter Range and the Minarets. The route of the next few days is not as clearly identifiable as one would like, but Crampton's interpretation is plausible that they crossed the San Joaquin–Merced divide at Isberg Pass and recrossed a few days later by Fernandez Pass, thence back to the Fresno River camp. "In terms of discovery," Crampton concludes, "this campaign into the Sierra was an important achievement but this was not the objective of the volunteers." Their hard work went for nothing at the time, as the Yosemites were far away on another escape route and no Indians were captured.

Meanwhile, the other division of the Battalion was more successful. Captain Bowling tells the story in a letter to the Major, written from Yosemite Valley on May 15, and Bunnell at considerably greater length in his book.[16] Briefly, what happened was this: Bowling and his men reached the Valley with the expectation of surprising the Yosemites, but evidently they had been forewarned and had fled. Next day five young Indians were seen scrambling along the talus on the north side of the Valley and were captured. They were held as hostages while an effort was made to reach the Chief and persuade him to come in with his band. Meanwhile one of the hostages was wantonly shot, and two others escaped. It was found that the main group of the Yosemites had retreated up Indian Canyon, but Teneiya was captured after a skirmish and was brought into camp, only to recognize the body of the murdered Indian as his son. The Chief was carefully guarded while further efforts were made to discover and capture the fugitives. A thorough exploration of the escape route up Indian Canyon was made, and during the search Captain Bowling reached the top of Yosemite Falls. On another trip Teneiya was taken along as guide, and Bunnell says they went as far as the open rocks at the foot of Mount Hoffmann. Returning from that trip Teneiya brought them to the Valley by a "short cut" along a ledge near Royal Arches, down the sloping side of an immense detached rock, and finally through the top of an oak tree to the base of the cliff. After a detachment came back from Fresno River with a replenishment of supplies, Captain Bowling made a final determined attempt to end matters and took the Chief along to exhort his people to return. Horses were left behind and all went on foot up Tenaya Canyon and Snow Creek until they reached "an elevation almost entirely covered with snow." There was evidence that spies were watching them, and on chase being given there came into view a dim circle of blue smoke under the lee of a large granite knob. "As I lowered my line of vision to the base of the cliff to trace the source of the smoke," writes Bunnell, "there appeared an Indian village, resting in fancied security, upon the border of a most beautiful little lake." To this lake Bunnell gave the name of the captured Chief—Lake Tenaya. Bunnell continues his account of a vigorous and successful day: "After collecting together all the Indians found in this encampment, the total number was found to be but thirty-five, nearly all of whom were in some way a part of the family of the old patriarch, Teneiya. These were escorted to our camp, the men placed under guard, but the women and children were left free. This was accomplished before sundown, and being relieved of duty, a few of us ran across the outlet of the lake, and climbing the divide on the south side of the lake, beheld a sunset view that will long be remembered. It was dark when we reached camp, and after a scanty repast, we spread our blankets, and soon were wrapped in slumber sweet." It was about the 5th of June. In the morning Bunnell found ice on the shore of the lake strong enough to walk on.

Climbing up from Tenaya Lake on the bare granite, the group was overtaken by the rising sun. "Although not sufficiently elevated to command a general outlook, the higher ridges framing some of the scenery to the north and eastward of us, the westerly view was boundless. The transparency of the atmosphere was here extreme, and as the sun illumined the snow-clad and ice-burnished peaks, the scene aroused the enthusiasm of the command to a shout of glad surprise." Without further incident Bowling's party reached the Yosemite Valley camp and a few days later delivered their captives at headquarters on the Fresno. The campaign of 1851 was over, and the Mariposa Battalion was mustered out.

Yosemite was not to be a peaceful place just yet, however. At Fresno River there was a general air of relaxation. In order to be rid of his constant pleadings and complaints, Teneiya was granted permission, on pledge of good behavior, to return to his mountain valley and take with him his immediate family. Later a few of the Yosemites slipped away from the reservation and joined him. The winter of 1851-1852 was quiet, but in the spring a fresh outbreak occurred. In late April or early May a party of eight miners left Coarsegold on the Fresno and passed through the Mariposa Grove of Big Trees, on the way to Yosemite Valley. The story of their adventure is told most convincingly by Stephen F. Grover, somewhat different in detail from the long-accepted versions of Bunnell and Hutchings.[17] On reaching the Valley the miners camped by the river.

Grover and two others remained in camp next day while the five others went up the valley prospecting and looking for game. Suddenly there was heard screaming and firing. Two of the men came rushing into camp, wounded by arrows. One of the party, Rose, a Frenchman, was seen to fall and, as he did so, screamed, " 'Tis no use to try to save ourselves, we have all got to die." According to Grover, two others, Sherburn and Tudor, were killed. (Other versions say that Rose was killed and that Tudor was badly wounded, but they make no further mention of the latter.) After a desperate retreat, the five survivors reached Coarsegold in five days. A company of twenty-five went to the valley and buried the bodies of the two victims. Shortly afterwards Rose turned up near Coarsegold and reported that the whole party had been killed except himself. When he heard that some of the party had returned he disappeared. Grover states that Rose had been a partner of Sherburn and Tudor in a gold mine, and that on his return he took possession of it and sold it, and then disappeared. He intimates that Rose purposely lured his partners into the hands of the Indians, whom he incited to kill them. But whether it be Sherburn and Rose or Sherburn and Tudor, two men lie buried in the meadow below Bridalveil Fall.

The final episode in the Yosemite Valley hostilities came shortly afterwards. A station of the Regular Army had been established on the San Joaquin, called Fort Miller, from which Lieutenant Tredwell Moore, U.S.A., was dispatched with a small company to finish off the Yosemite Indians once and for all. Augustus A. Gray, who had been with Bowling's company the previous year, served as guide. They entered the Valley at night and surprised and captured five Indians. Clothing belonging to the murdered men was found in their possession, and with this evidence Lieutenant Moore ordered the captives executed by a volley of musketry. Teneiya, who was still in the Valley with a few of his people, on hearing of this, fled at once, and without stopping at Tenaya Lake took refuge with the Monos beyond the Sierra. Moore pursued in vain, but in doing so, opened a new route for white men, via Tuolumne Meadows and Mono Pass. Bunnell says: "He made some fair discoveries of gold and gold-bearing quartz, obsidian and other minerals, while exploring the region north and south of Bloody Cañon and of Mono Lake." His return to Fort Miller is said to have been east and south of Yosemite, presumably by the route later known as the Sunrise Trail and above Nevada Fall.[18]

It remains to record the sad demise of Chief Teneiya. After a year of refuge with the Monos he made one more attempt to occupy his old home in Yosemite Valley, accompanied by a few of his retainers. This time it was not the whites who caused his downfall, but his own people and his former friends the Monos. The latter had stolen horses from some white men in the south and had brought them to their camp near Mono Lake. Teneiya's young bucks, in a night raid, captured some of these horses for themselves and drove them all the way to Yosemite. While they were feasting on the twice-stolen delicacies the Monos caught up with the banqueters and slaughtered them. They found the old Chief and stoned him to death.[19] Warfare ceased in Yosemite.

NOTES AND REFERENCES

1. A contemporary guidebook says: "Supposing our miner to have arrived at Stockton and he proposes to go to the Mokelamy, he would have to cross the Calaveras at the distance of about 15 miles, and strike the Mokelamy diggings 70 miles distant from the above mentioned town. If he should like to go south, he would find diggings on the Stanislaus, about 40 miles distant from Stockton; then he might pass on to those of the Tuolomy, 20 miles distant from the latter, and farther on he would meet at the distance of 30 miles with those of the stream *La Merced*, then at the distance of about 20 miles he would come to the stream *Mariposa*." F. P. Wierzbicki, *California As It Is & As It May Be, or a Guide to the Gold Regions*, San Francisco, 1849; reprinted by the Grabhorn Press, San Francisco, 1933.

2. Charles Gregory Crampton has made a thorough study of these questions in "The Opening of the Mariposa Mining Region, 1849-1859, with particular reference to the Mexican Land Grant of John Charles Frémont," unpublished Ph.D. dissertation, University of California, Berkeley, 1941 (copy in BL).

3. The history and character of James D. Savage have been exhaustively treated by a number of writers: Carl P. Russell, *100 Years in Yosemite*, Stanford University, 1931, and later editions; Lafayette H. Bunnell, *Discovery of the Yosemite, and the Indian War of 1851 Which Led to That Event*, Chicago, 1880, and later editions (*Farquhar* 15); Newell D. Chamberlain, *The Call of Gold*, Mariposa, Calif., 1936; Raymund F. Wood, *California's Agua Fria*, Fresno, Calif., 1954; Jill L. Crossley-Batt, *The Last of the California Rangers*, New York, 1928; James O'Meara, "A White Medicine Man," *The Californian*, February, 1882, reprinted in *YNN*, November and December, 1951, 30:11 and 12; Annie R. Mitchell, "Major James D. Savage and the Tulareños," *CHSQ*, December, 1949, 28:4, and *Jim Savage and the Tulareño Indians*, Los Angeles, 1957.

4. The principal source of information regarding the Mariposa Battalion are Bunnell, *op. cit.*, and *History of Fresno County*, Wallace W. Elliott & Co., San Francisco, 1881.

5. The *History* contains a "muster roll" of the three companies, where Captain Bowling's name is spelled in that fashion, as it is in the *Daily Alta California*, June 12 and 14, 1851. Bunnell and Russell use the form "Boling."

6. The true name of these people was "Ahwahneechee" or "Awanis," signifying "dwellers in the village of Ahwahnee, or Awani." Galen Clark, *Indians of the Yosemite*, Yosemite Valley, 1904. "Awani, the name applied by the natives of the valley, was the principal village, which by extension was given to the whole valley and its inhabitants." F. W. Hodge, *Handbook of American Indians North of Mexico*, Washington, D. C., 1906; see also James E. Cole, *YNN*, July, 1936, 15:7.

7. The earlier accounts use the spelling Teneiya, but today the established form is Tenaya. Here the former spelling is used for the old Chief, the latter for the lake and canyon.

8. Lafayette Houghton Bunnell was born in Rochester, N. Y., 1824; spent his boyhood in Michigan and Wisconsin, where he became familiar with Indians and their ways; served in the Mexican War; came to California in 1849, and was in the Mariposa country when the Battalion was organized. His Yosemite experiences are fully recounted in his book. After these events he remained in California for several years, then returned to Wisconsin. He enlisted in the Union Army at the outbreak of the Civil War, serving as a hospital steward. He advanced to Surgeon by the end of the War. With this as experience, he was given the honorary degree of M.D. from La Crosse Medical College, Wisconsin. His later life was spent in Minnesota, where he died in 1903. Howard A. Kelly, "Lafayette Houghton Bunnell, M.D., Discoverer of the Yosemite," *Annals of Medical History*, 1921, 3:2.

9. The date of the entry of the Mariposa Battalion into Yosemite Valley is given by Bunnell as "about the 21st of March, 1851" (*op. cit.*, 1911 ed., p. 78). Discovery of the diary of Robert Eccleston, however, fixes the precise date, March 27. Eccleston's entry for that day begins, "Today about noon Major Savage started for the Yosemita Camp with 57 men & an Indian Guide." *The Mariposa Indian War, 1850-1851, Diaries of Robert Eccleston: The California Gold Rush, Yosemite, and the High Sierra*, edited by C. Gregory Crampton, Salt Lake City, 1957.

10. The change in spelling is explained by Bunnell: "Lieutenant Moore, of the U.S.A., in his report of an expedition to the Valley in 1852, substituted *e* as the terminal letter, in place of *y*, in use by us; no doubt thinking the use of *e* more scholarly, or perhaps supposing Yosemite to be of Spanish derivation." Bunnell, 1911, ed., *op. cit.* The present spelling was not established, however, without further argument. When J. M. Hutchings visited the Valley in 1855 he was told by his Indian guides, "No, *Yo-Semite; Yo-Hamite*." Hutchings published a lithograph from a drawing by Thomas A. Ayres with the title "Yo-Hamite," but after correspondence with Bunnell reluctantly dropped his *h*. He asserted his individualism, nevertheless, by using the form *Yo-Semite*, or *Yo Semite*, long after the current *Yosemite* was generally accepted. J. M. Hutchings, *Scenes of Wonder and Curiosity in California*, San Francisco, 1860, and *In the Heart of the Sierras*, with places of publication given as Yo Semite Valley and Oakland, 1886, (*Farquhar* Nos. 4 and 18.).

11. The names of specific features in Yosemite Valley have undergone numerous changes. Bunnell writes: "The names 'North Dome,' 'South Dome' and 'Half Dome' were given by us during our long stay in the valley from their localities and peculiar configuration. Some changes have been made since they were adopted. The peak called by us the 'South Dome' has since been given the name of 'Sentinel Dome,' and the 'Half Dome,' Tis-sa-ack, represented as meaning the 'Cleft Rock,' is now called by many the 'South Dome.' The name for the 'North Dome' is To-ko-ya, its literal signification 'The Basket.' The name of 'The Royal Arch' was given to it by a comrade who was a member of the Masonic Fraternity, and has since been called 'The Royal Arches.'" Names given by Bunnell and the Mariposa Battalion at the time of their visits and remaining unchanged are Mirror Lake, Clouds Rest, Little Yosemite, Yosemite Falls, Vernal Fall, Nevada Fall, Three Brothers, El Capitan, and Tenaya Lake (except for the spelling). The

"waterfall of the South Canyon" refers to what is now called Illilouette Fall, a name apparently originating with the Whitney Survey in the 1860's, and a preposterous corruption of what Bunnell gives as "Too-lool-we-ack." Bunnell goes on to say, "The strict literal interpretation of this name would be inadmissable, but it is well enough to say, that to the unconscious innocence of their primitive state, the word simply represented an effort of nature in the difficult passage of the water down through the rocky gorge." Bunnell, *op. cit.*, 1911 ed.

12. The Abrams diary was first brought to the attention of Yosemite historians in 1947 by William C. Barry of Glendale, and the passage quoted here was first published in *SCB*, May, 1947, with an explanatory note by Weldon F. Heald, who gave a more extended account of the diary and its contents in *Westways*, March, 1954. It has been only briefly mentioned in a few other publications. As Heald says, it is worthy of wider fame. William Penn Abrams was born in Sanbornton, N. H., in 1820, and died in Portland, Ore., in 1873. With his friend U. N. Reamer he arrived in San Francisco from New Orleans, via Panama, August, 1849, and promptly set out for the diggings. Abrams was a carpenter and millwright and received a commission to search for a millsite on the Merced to furnish lumber for the mines; hence the visit to Savage's camp and the adventure that led to Yosemite.

13. *Eccleston Diary*.

14. Letter from H. E. Russell, Serg't Major California Battalion, to M. B. Lewis, Adjutant, published in the *Daily Alta California*, June 12, 1851.

15. Samuel Addison Bishop (1825-1893), a native of Virginia; California pioneer of 1849; an early settler in Owens Valley; town of Bishop and Bishop Pass named for him; constructed the first streetcar line in San Jose, 1868.

16. Captain Bowling's letter was published in the *Daily Alta California*, San Francisco, June 12. It is undoubtedly the first letter written from Yosemite. It is printed, practically in full, in Carl Russell's *100 Years in Yosemite*. Bunnell's account runs through chaps. 9 to 14 of his *Dicovery of the Yosemite*.

17. Stephen Frealon Grover (1830-1907), a native of Maine; in later years engaged in lumber operations in the Santa Cruz mountains. Grover's reminiscences were obtained from him by Mrs. A. E. Chandler, of Santa Cruz, who sent the manuscript to Galen Clark in Yosemite. On Clark's death it came into possession of the photographer George Fiske, and upon his death it went to the Yosemite Museum.

18. Information about Lieutenant Moore and his punitive expedition is very meager. The present account is taken almost entirely from Bunnell, who says he got his information from an old-timer named Gus Gray. It is unfortunate that we do not have more about Moore, for he seems to have pioneered a good deal of interesting territory. He comes into the Sierra story again in connection with the Ebbetts Pass exploration of 1853. This we know of him: Tredwell Moore (1825-1876), a native of Ohio, was graduated from West Point in 1847. Following the two episodes in the Sierra he was in San Diego. The *San Diego Herald*, May 27, 1854, gives a hint of his personality: "Lieut. Moore, U.S.A., a member of Gen. Wool's staff, arrived here on Wednesday. We hope the handsome Lieutenant will not show himself too much among our susceptible young ladies, while he is in this region, for there is already sufficient jealousy and heart-burning among the daughters of Saint James." He saw service in the Civil War and was brevetted Brigadier General in 1865 for "faithful and meritorious services."

19. There are other versions, but the fact remains—Teneiya was killed.

X

BIG TREES

****

The Big Tree is nature's forest masterpiece, and so far as I know, the greatest of living things. It belongs to an ancient stock, as its remains in old rocks show, and has a strange air of other days about it, a thoroughbred look inherited from the long ago—the auld lang syne of trees.

JOHN MUIR

In the summer of 1848 three prospectors worked their way up the Stanislaus, trying their luck, with notable success. One, George Angel, founded Angels Camp, a name that should ring a bell with readers of Bret Harte. Another, James Carson, pioneered the rich discoveries at Melones and Carson Hill. The third, John Murphy, one of the immigrants of 1844, set up camp at the flat soon to be known as Murphys Camp. There he struck it rich, and as the news spread throngs of miners hastened to the feast. Water was needed in greater quantity than the local streams afforded and it became necessary to import water from the Stanislaus River fifteen miles away. Ditches were not enough; flumes and trestles had to be built. That required lumber, and lumber required sawmills. Soon there was a lot of activity in the woods above Murphys. To feed the construction workers as well as the miners, hunters were employed to get fresh meat. Presently they were going farther and farther away in search of it.[1]

One day in the spring of 1852, one of the hunters, A. T. Dowd by name, had an extraordinary experience. Following a wounded bear, he suddenly found himself in the presence of a tree, a tree larger than he had ever seen before. As he looked he observed others equally large. He could hardly believe his eyes. On his return to camp he related what he had seen, but in spite of his repeated affirmations he was ridiculed. Seeing that he could not convince his companions with words, he resorted to a ruse. The next Sunday, when the men were loafing, he hurried into camp pretending that he had "killed the largest grizzly bear that I ever saw in my life." He persuaded the whole camp to follow him and bring in the bear. Dowd led the party over ridges and through brush until at last they came to his tree. "Pointing to the immense trunk and lofty top, he cried out, 'Boys, do you now believe my big tree story? This is the large grizzly bear I wanted you to see. Do you still think it's a yarn?' "[2]

The immensity of the tree was recognized at once and the news quickly spread that a modern wonder of the world had been discovered. In the words of J. M. Hutchings a little later, "But a short time was allowed to elapse after the discovery of this remarkable grove, before the trumpet-tongued press proclaimed the wonder to all sections of the State, and to all parts of the world, and the lovers of the marvelous began first to doubt, then to believe, and afterwards to flock to see with their own eyes the objects of which they had heard so much."

For a while it was supposed that Dowd had been the first man to see the Big Trees. At that time Zenas Leonard's account of Walker's expedition of 1833 was unknown and Bidwell had not yet advanced his claim. Presently, however, an inscription was discovered, carved on one of the trees, "J. M. Wooster, June 1850." When this was made known it was proposed to give credit to Wooster. But when he heard of it Wooster wrote to a local newspaper: "Happy as I should be to be able to claim the honor of the first discovery, justice to others and the truth would prevent my doing so." He followed with an account of a certain Whitehead, who had come across these trees about twelve days before he did.[3] It matters little, however, who was the first; the important thing is that it was Dowd's discovery that brought the Big Trees of California to the attention of the world.

The immediate result was exploitation. Men saw a chance to make money. Promptly a preemption claim was filed by William W. Lapham. He built a cabin and for several years entertained visitors to the Big Trees until he sold out to James W. Sperry and moved to Lake Tahoe, where he became a celebrated hotel owner and boat operator. At about the same time it was proposed to cut down one of the largest trees, remove the bark and send it to the eastern cities for exhibition. Captain H. W. Hanford, head of the Union Water Company, who had built the flume to Murphys, undertook the enterprise. But to cut down one of these huge trees proved to be no ordinary task. Axes and saws would not suffice. Resort was made to drilling by pump augurs through to the center from opposite sides. It is said that it took five men twenty-two days to accomplish this. It required wedges to complete the work until finally the great tree fell with a crash that was heard for miles around. The bark was stripped off the fallen log for a length of fifty feet, and carefully marked in sections so that it could be placed as it originally stood.[4] The bark was then hauled to Stockton and shipped by boat to San Francisco, where it was exhibited before being sent around the Horn to New York. There Hanford's venture ran into trouble. It arrived just in time to be a rival to Barnum's Crystal Palace, and Barnum would have none of it. For a while the exhibit was set up at the Racket Court on Broadway,[5] but the show failed and not long afterward the bark was destroyed by fire.[6]

Meanwhile a new enterprise was under way. In the summer of 1854 another entrepreneur, George L. Trask, erected a scaffolding around a large tree known as "The Mother of the Forest," and had the bark removed to a height of 116 feet. Trask's exhibit took the same course as Hanford's, but reached New York at a more propitious time. The Crystal Palace venture was on the brink of failure, and this time the Big Tree came to the rescue. Early in 1855 the New York papers advertised "The Tree Mastodon: a mountain of wood—a single tree taller by a hundred feet than the Bunker Hill monument. Great attraction at Crystal Palace." Another advertisement declared, "The big-tree exhibited in this city several months ago was almost a pigmy compared with this mastodon."[7] As an exhibitor and despoiler, Trask outclassed Hanford. Trask's victim, "though naked and miserable," remained alive for years. In 1878 the far-traveled Scottish lady, Constance Frederica Gordon Cumming, wrote: "I can see her from where I now sit—a ghastly object—her sides still transfixed with wooden instruments of torture—the St. Sebastian of the forest."[8] The exhibit continued triumphantly on its way. In 1857 it went to London and was housed at full height in London's Crystal Palace, admired by gaping thongs until a fire put an end to it in 1866.[9]

While Hanford and Trask were bringing the Big Trees to the world, the world was beginning to come to the Big Trees. As if the trees themselves were not sufficient, added attractions were devised to supplement them. The stump

Hutchings' Magazine

Dancing on the Big Tree stump.

of the tree that had been felled was smoothed off, and on it thirty-two persons were able to dance a cotillion. With modern dancing styles the number could doubtless have been doubled. Soon a pavilion was erected over the stump; theatricals were performed; and for a short time in 1858 a newspaper was printed there.[10] Nearby, on the flattened surface of the trunk, a bowling alley was constructed, "for a distance of eighty-one feet, affording ample space for two alley-beds, side by side." A hotel, providing room for sixty people, was built by Sperry in 1856. It continued to accommodate visitors from all parts of the country and from abroad until 1943, when it was destroyed by fire. A popular pastime for visitors seems to have been to give names to the individual trees. At one time a name could be purchased, complete with carved marble slab to be attached to the tree. Some of the names were fanciful—*The Three Graces, Pride of the Forest, Fallen Hercules.* Others were patriotic, political, or literary—*Washington, Webster, Clay, Longfellow, Bryant.* There was a

Section of Big Tree felled in 1853.   Interior of pavilion on the Big Stump.

spate of state names—*Old Dominion, Bay State, Kentucky*.[11] Many were personal, trivial, soon forgotten. Among these, perhaps not to be forgotten after all, were *Ada* and *Mary*, "named for the first two ladies who ever came here in a buggy. The former is fifty-one, the latter sixty-one feet in circumference, straight, solid, handsome."[12] *The Horseback Ride* came to a sad end in 1863. Professor Brewer wrote in his journal: "One prostrate tree was hollow; it had been burned out and the cavity was large enough for a man to ride through eighty feet on horseback. Only three days before I arrived it split in pieces and caved in. No one will ride through it again."[13]

Hotel at Calaveras Grove.   "The Horseback Ride."

Far more important than the names of the individual trees is the name of the tree itself. Hardly had the news of the discovery reached the world than botanists began to argue about its classification. Albert Kellogg and Herman Behr, of the California Academy of Natural Sciences, considered that it belonged to one of the many species of Cypress or Juniper and gave it the name *Taxodium giganteum*.[14] When the discovery was first announced in Europe, in July, 1853, the tree was called simply a giant cedar. Later that year some specimens of branches and cones reached England, sent by William Lobb, a collector for a London nursery.[15] They came into the hands of Professor John Lindley, regarded as the foremost botanist in Britain. He announced a new genus and bestowed upon it a name in the following magniloquent terms: "We think that no one will differ from us in feeling that the most appropriate name to be proposed for the most gigantic tree which has been revealed to us by modern discovery is that of the greatest of modern heroes. Wellington stands as high above his contemporaries as the California tree above all the surrounding foresters. Let it then bear henceforward the name of WELLINGTONIA GIGANTEA."[16] Hear! Hear!

Several months later the French reopened the case, and though polite enough not to say so, they doubtless took some satisfaction in pushing the Duke off his arboreal pedestal. At a meeting of the Société Botanique de France, in June, 1854, Joseph Decaisne presented specimens of the Big Tree received from the French consul in California. Decaisne pointed out certain similarities to the Coast Redwood (*Sequoia sempervirens*), disputed Lindley's claim of a separate genus, and gave the name *Sequoia gigantea*.[17] The fight was on. The British stood firm for *Wellingtonia*; Americans tried to substitute *Washingtonia*. Variations were proposed. Thus, besides *Sequoia gigantea* and *Wellingtonia gigantea*, we find in manuals of good repute: *Sequoia wellingtonia* and *Sequoia washingtoniana*. Professional botanists have their own rules, but sometimes seem to have difficulties in applying them. To set matters straight, J. T. Bucholz in 1939 declared they were all wrong, and that it should be *Sequoiadendron giganteum*.[18] In a questionnaire sent to California botanists in 1943, out of 29 replies, 24 stated that they would continue to use *Sequoia gigantea*, while only three were inclined to adopt *Sequoiadendron*.[19] There may have been converts, or apostates, since then. Complications arose when, in 1945, *Metasequoia glyptostroboides*, sometimes called "Dawn Redwood," was discovered in China. We won't go into that, but let the phytologists fight it out.[20]

There is another aspect. What are we to call the tree in common parlance? For a time Big Tree, Mammoth Tree, Mastodon, and Vegetable Monster appear to have sufficed.[21] But when it became known that the Big Trees of the Sierra were related to the Redwoods of the Coast, there was trouble. The latter were also known as Big Trees, the former were also known as Redwoods. Professor Emanuel Fritz of Berkeley, an eminent authority, prefers to distinguish them as Sierra Redwoods and Coast Redwoods. Time alone will tell. For the present the unlearned will probably continue to use the names prevalent in their own localities; in the Sierra these are Big Tree, Giant Sequoia, or just plain Sequoia.

Although the Calaveras Grove, whence came the type-specimens, was for a long time the most famous grove of Big Trees, it soon became known that there were other groves, from the Middle Fork of the American River on the north to the Tule River on the south.[22] None, however, were ever found elsewhere than in the Sierra Nevada. After a while the Mariposa Grove, on the southern approach to Yosemite, came to rival the Calaveras Grove as a tourist attraction, especially when someone conceived the idea of cutting a tunnel through a living tree, large enough for a stagecoach to be driven through. The tunnel is still there, and self-conscious tourists pose for their pictures, now in automobiles. Finest grove of all is the one that John Muir named the Giant Forest, in Sequoia National Park. It is heartening to know that after many years of effort practically all of the Big Trees of the Sierra are in public ownership, preserved for as long a time as the trees may stand, which is likely to be a very long time indeed.

Someone may ask, "Haven't I seen Sequoias growing elsewhere than in California?" You certainly have; they are growing all over the world. But they are all from California seeds or seedlings. No sooner had the new genus or species been announced in Great Britain than its phenomenal character aroused the interest of the proprietors of lordly estates. Nurseries were besieged with inquiries and traffic grew apace. Hundreds of little Sequoias (pardon me, Wellingtonias) were soon sprouting in all parts of the country. At Stratfield Saye itself, residence of the Great Duke, a tree was ceremoniously planted in 1857 by the second Duchess. Today it is magnificently massive and tall. Nearby there is an avenue lined with 35 Sequoias on each side, and, not far away, at Finchampstead, there is an avenue with 110 of these trees on each side. In Dorset, especially, there are many fine specimens. In fact, they are growing everywhere in the British Isles.

The fad spread to the Continent. At first the Sequoia was merely another ornamental companion to other exotic trees such as the Cedar of Lebanon. Today, a century after their introduction, they have grown to overtop all other trees, and one is suddenly aware of new points on the European horizon. As one drives along the shore of Lac Leman from Geneva to Montreux he can count more than a hundred Sequoias, easily distinguished by their height and pointed tops. In front of the Bar-au-lac Hotel in Zurich there is a handsome Sequoia. A placque dates it from 1842, which is clearly an error—ten years too early at least. There are two notable Sequoias in the French hill-town of Vézelay and many others scattered throughout France. Germany has hundreds of them. In Spain there is one by the Genil River, visible from the Alhambra, and two beauties in the garden of El Palacio at Granja. And there is one in Zagreb, Yugoslavia. Not only in Europe, but far away in New Zealand the Sequoia has become a stately fixture in the landscape.

The Sierra Nevada of California has shared its beauty with the world.

Sequoia at Bar-au-Lac Hotel, Zurich, Switzerland, 1957.

NOTES AND REFERENCES

This chapter in substantially the same form was published in *American West*, August, 1965.

1. The literature of the period is extensive, notably, Bancroft, *California*. For Murphy's Camp a good sketch is Richard Coke Wood, *Murphys: Queen of the Sierra*, Angels Camp, 1948; also Joseph Henry Jackson, *Anybody's Gold*, New York: Appleton, 1941. Most writers give the name *George* Angel as the founder of Angels Camp, but recent investigations indicate that it may have been *Henry* Angel.

2. *Hutchings' California Magazine*, March, 1859; J. M. Hutchings, *Scenes of Wonder and Curiosity in California*, 1860 (*Farquhar* No. 47); Hutchings, *In the Heart of the Sierras*, 1886 (*Farquhar* No. 18).

3. *The San Andreas Independent*, October 3, 1857, as reprinted in the *Calaveras Californian*, Angels Camp, May 20, 1937. Hutchings, in the 2d edition of *Scenes of Wonder*, states that Wooster acknowledged the priority of Whitehead. Rodney Sykes Ellsworth, "Discovery of the Big Trees of California," unpublished M.A. thesis, University of California, Berkeley, 1933 (MS in BL), goes very thoroughly into the parts played by Wooster and Whitehead. It appears that "Whitehead" was not a real name, but was given because of his white hair. He was reputed to have discovered a fabulously rich gold mine, but no one could track him to it. "No one knew whence he came, no one knew whither he went" (*San Francisco Chronicle*, December 28, 1902).

4. *Gleason's Pictorial Drawing-Room Companion*, October 1, 1853; reprinted in *Description of the Great Tree* (see n. 5 below).

5. *Description of the Great Tree, Recently Felled upon the Sierra Nevada, California, now placed for Public Exhibition in the spacious Racket Court of the Union Club, No. 596, Broadway, adjoining the Metropolitan Hotel, New York* (*Farquhar* No. 2). This rare pamphlet was reprinted for private distribution, San Francisco, 1960 (copy in BL).

6. Norman Taylor, *The Ageless Relicts*, New York, 1962. The exhibits are discussed at length.

7. New York papers of July, 1856, as quoted by Taylor, *op. cit.*

8. C. F. Gordon Cumming, *Granite Crags*, 1884 (*Farquhar* No. 17).

9. *Description of the Mammoth Tree from California, now erected at the Crystal Palace, Sydenham*, London, 1857 (*Farquhar* No. 3).

10. *Big Tree Bulletin, and Murphys Advertiser*, "Published every Tuesday and Friday by John Heckendorn. Office on the stump of the Big Tree." Only a few copies are known to have survived (one in BL).

11. Names given to the trees are listed in a number of publications, notably Whitney, *Yosemite Guide-Book*, 1869 (*Farquhar* No. 7); Williams, *Mammoth Trees*, 1871 (*Farquhar* No. 9); *Report on the Big Trees of California*, U. S. Department of Agriculture, Division of Forestry, 1900.

12. *Transactions of the California State Agricultural Society During the Year 1859.* (For this bit of serendipity I am indebted to Robert H. Becker, Bancroft Library.)

13. *Brewer Journal.*

14. *Proceedings of the California Academy of Natural Sciences*, meeting of February 12, 1855.

15. William Lobb, born in Cornwall, 1809; died in San Francisco, 1863. *Illustrated London News*, February 11, 1854.

16. John Lindley (1799-1865), in *The Gardeners' Chronicle and Agricultural Gazette*, December 24, 1853.

17. *Bulletin de la Société Botanique de France*, 1854.

18. J. T. Bucholz, *American Journal of Botany*, July, 1939.

19. William A. Drayton, "The Names of the Giant Sequoia," *Leaflets of Western Botany*, San Francisco, April, 1943, bibliography. See also Willis Linn Jepson, "Scientific and Vernacular Names for the Species of Sequoia," *SCB*, February, 1933, 18:1.

20. Erwin G. Gudde, "The Two Sequoias," *Names* (journal of the American Name Society), June, 1953.

21. There was also a local Indian name. Stephen Powers, *Tribes of California*, 1877, says that the Paiutes called it *"woh-woh-nah,* a word formed in imitation of the hoot of the owl, which is the guardian spirit and deity of this great monarch of the forest. It is productive of bad luck to fell this tree, or to mock or shoot the owl."

22. *Report on the Big Trees of California*, prepared in the Division of Forestry, U.S. Department of Agriculture, Washington, 1900.

Calaveras Big Trees, with camels entering the grove, 1862.

Edward Vischer

XI

OPENING THE PASSES

The Constitution of the State of California defines the state's eastern boundary as "commencing at the point of intersection of the 42nd degree of north latitude with the 120th degree of longitude west from Greenwich, running south on the line of the said 120th degree of west longitude until it intersects the 39th degree of north latitude; thence running in a straight line, in a southeasterly direction, to the River Colorado, at a point where it intersects the 35th degree of north latitude." Sounds very simple. But just where are those intersections? It took more than forty years to find an acceptable answer.[1]

The importance of determining the boundary was recognized immediately. Residents of the Carson Valley, in particular, made urgent inquiries. Did they live in California or in the then Territory of Utah? And who was to pay for roads? It was the duty of the Surveyor General of California to find out. William M. Eddy, the incumbent in 1852, went to Placerville, took astronomical observations for latitude, and made inquiries of knowledgable residents about the distance to Carson Valley. He was "reluctantly forced to the conclusion that the valley was from twelve to fifteen miles out of the State," and he did not "feel warranted in going over there at the expense of the State, as it was useless to pursue the matter any farther."[2] A comfortable way to make a survey! He was several miles off his latitude, to be sure, but he guessed right about the Carson Valley, so no harm was done.

The intersection of the 120th degree of longitude with the 39th degree of latitude was presently found to be somewhere in the middle of Lake Tahoe (Bigler, as it was then called). But precisely where? A very slight error in observation or computation would have a far-reaching effect. And so it turned out. For more than a decade the mining town of Aurora was the county seat of Mono County, California, but there were those who doubted, and in the spring of 1863 the residents of that town elected one of their number to the legislature of the Territory of Nevada (which by that time had been carved out of the Territory of Utah) and at the same time they elected another to the California legislature.[3] In September of that year Aurora was found to be in Nevada, three miles east of the California boundary, and the Mono county seat was moved to Bridgeport. Although further revisions of the line have been made, Aurora stays in Nevada. Nevertheless, a lingering doubt remains about the exact point of intersection at Lake Tahoe. Is it possible that gambling, legal in Nevada, may be going on illegally in California because of the slip of a slide rule?

The same Eddy who guessed right about the Carson Valley also made a map, in which his guesswork was not as successful. His "Official Map of the State of California" was characterized by one of his successors as a "broad burlesque on the topography of California, and no mortal foot has ever trodden over the roads delineated upon it."[4]

Roads, real roads that could be traversed by wagons, were an immediate necessity. The roads of the 1840's were merely improvised ways through, hardly sufficient to encourage settlers with families. California needed population, especially farm people, and there were thousands ready to come across the plains if only decent wagon roads could be provided over the mountains. As the need became apparent, it also became apparent that there was a wide difference of opinion about where the roads should be. Each town on the west side of the mountains wished to be the terminal for overland traffic. The Immigrant Route over Donner Pass presented too many difficulties for wagons, but a way was found to bypass these difficulties by leaving the Truckee River at the site of the present Verdi, then by Dog Valley and the Little Truckee over a comparatively easy pass to the headwaters of the North Fork of the Yuba and on to Downieville. This route, said to have been discovered by a man named Henness, for a while took a considerable part of the overland immigration.

At about the same time Jim Beckwourth (or Beckwith) discovered a pass a little farther north.[5] His autobiography records the discovery. "It was the latter end of April [1851] when we entered upon an extensive valley, already robed in freshest verdure, contrasting most delightfully with the huge snow-clad masses of rock we had just left. Flowers of every variety and hue spread their variegated charms before us. Nowhere visible were any traces of the white man's approach, and it is possible that our steps were the first that ever marked the spot. We struck across this beautiful valley to the waters of the Yuba, from thence to the Truchy, which latter flowed in an easterly direction. This, I at once saw, would afford the best wagon road into the American Valley." He made known his discovery at Bidwell's Bar and at Marysville, with enthusiastic response. He expected a substantial recognition, but received practically nothing for work and money expended. "There is one thing certain," he declared, "when I go out hunting in the mountains for a road for everybody to pass through, and expend my time and capital upon an object from which I shall derive no benefit, it will be because I have nothing better to do."[6] Alas for ingratitude! It was a useful pass and was used by thousands who came to the northern mines, but it was too long a detour ever to become the primary east-west route. In recent years it has come into its own as the scenic and low-level freight route of the Western Pacific Railroad.

The direct route from Carson Valley over Carson Pass to Placerville had proved passable for wagons, but the difficulties in Carson Canyon and at the summit were discouraging. An alternative was very much needed. This was found in 1852, or perhaps even earlier, by John Calhoun Johnson, known by courtesy as "Colonel" but more familiarly as "Cock Eye" Johnson.[7] Starting from Carson Valley, he went straight up the mountainside to what is now known as Spooner Summit. Instead of descending directly to Lake Tahoe, he kept high up along the ridge around the southeastern side of the lake, eventually reaching the site of Meyers, and thence up a very steep grade to Echo Summit. Crossing to the South Fork of the American River, he completed "Johnson's Cut-off."

While wagon roads were being demanded locally, a far greater project was being debated in Washington—a transcontinental railroad. Congress in the spring of 1853 authorized a survey of possible routes, with the Secretary of War in charge. He placed the work in the hands of the Corps of Topographical Engineers, who proceeded that summer on a series of "Explorations and Surveys to Ascertain the Most Practicable and Economic Route for a Railroad from the Mississippi River to the Pacific Ocean." It became clear at once that for political reasons a survey of a possible central route was not to be included in the program. A route in the south over Walker Pass and one outflanking the mountains on the north were to be considered. The northerly route was fruitless as far as a railroad was concerned, although it produced useful information for making wagon roads. In the south, Lieutenant Robert S. Williamson made a thorough examination of Walker Pass and concluded that the approaches were not suitable for a railroad. He moved on to "Tah-ee-chay-pah" (Tehachapi), which he recommended as the only practicable route.[8] That ended any attempt by the Federal Government to look for a railroad route across the Sierra. It remained for private enterprise to continue the effort.

Late in the summer of 1853 a group of citizens held a meeting in San Francisco to organize the Atlantic and Pacific Company for the purpose of constructing a railroad that would connect San Francisco with Las Vegas de Santa Clara, believed to be one of the most likely points to be reached if the Federal Survey resulted in selection of a southern route.[9] Money was raised for a survey and Major John Ebbetts[10] was placed in charge of an exploring expedition. The same Lieutenant Tredwell Moore who had chased the Yosemite Indians across the Sierra to Mono Lake was assigned as Engineer, and a young English surveyor named George H. Goddard became Assistant Engineer.[11] It was a strong party, but its objectives were utterly hopeless. They were to proceed to the headwaters of the Stanislaus, cross the main divide of the Sierra, and, after exploring 200 miles eastward, return by the Tuolumne. There were alternative courses, but they were not attempted, nor was the return made by the Tuolumne.[12] After organizing at Stockton, the Ebbetts party proceeded to Sonora, which they left on October 11, rather late in the season for such an enterprise. They followed in general the line of the present Sonora Pass road along the ridge between the South Fork of the Stanislaus and the North Fork of the Tuolumne, past Pinecrest. Keeping south of the present highway, they came to Relief Valley and Emigrant Meadow, from which a comparatively easy grade led them over the Sierra crest to the headwaters of West Walker River. So far the way had not been too bad, although there were signs that immigrants coming from the opposite direction were having a hard time. Bodies of animals and fragments of wagons were strewn about.[13] The crossing was made about eight miles south of the spot we now know as Sonora Pass. The descent to Leavitt Meadow was steep and rough, so instead of continuing down West Walker River through Pickel Meadow, they turned north to Lost Cannon Creek. There Ebbetts and Moore recognized the region as one they had visited together in April, 1850.[14] They now decided to examine it more closely. Ebbetts records that he and Goddard now "ascended a very steep mountain with great fatigue." "It affords us a very fine view of the whole surrounding country," he says, and "there is no difficulty in reaching this pass by an easy grade from the valley in the east." They made no further exploration of the pass, and it was not until later that the name of Ebbetts Pass was given to it.

The Ebbetts party continued eastward for another month, far into Nevada, before exhaustion of their animals and lack of provisions forced them to return. It was late in November when they reached Mormon Station in Carson Valley. Thence, leaving Goddard to dispose of all but a few of the mules, Ebbetts and Moore rode up a steep trail that brought them over the ridge to Johnson's Cut-off, where a sign read "60 miles to Placerville." After recuperating at Smith's Ranch,[15] they climbed up to Echo Summit and camped for the night. "We have passed the two summits of the Sierra," writes Ebbetts, "stopped nearly two hours, and from the distance we have made, 22 miles, it will be seen there are no great difficulties to be met with." Next day, after encountering considerable snow, they descended into the bottom of the canyon of the South Fork of the American River and a day and a half later reached Placerville. Ebbetts concludes his report by stating that the nature of the country at the headwaters of the Stanislaus "will never admit of a railroad being constructed. It has been passed by wagons of every grade, but they met with great losses, and I would advise none to undertake it hereafter." Ebbetts Pass was suggested for further exploration and Johnson's Cut-off was praised; but no recommendation was forthcoming for a railroad route.

Seneca Hunt Marlette,[16] a man of energy and ability, became Surveyor General of California in 1854. He at once sought competent help and found it in Sherman Day,[17] who became his chief field assistant, and George H. Goddard, who had been with the Ebbetts–Moore party. Both were well-qualified civil engineers. Day shortly afterwards became a member of the State Senate, where he urged the vital importance of a reliable map as well as adequate communications across the Sierra. On April 28, 1855, a bill was passed providing for survey and construction of a wagon road. The appropriation, however, was declared unconstitutional.[18] Nevertheless, in the hope that money would eventually be forthcoming, Marlette proceeded with a reconnaissance by soliciting funds from the communities interested, even advancing expenses out of his own salary. Camptonville in Yuba County, Fiddletown in Amador County, Murphys in Calaveras County, and other communities professed interest, but did not provide the capital needed for the survey. A little help was reluctantly furnished by El Dorado County, and Georgetown raised enough money to send Sherman Day to look over a wagon route by the headwaters of the North Fork of the American River to Lake Bigler (Tahoe). He reported that "although this route might ultimately be an available one for the people of Yankee Jim's, Auburn, and Nevada City, to connect with a road through Carson Canyon, yet it would seem to be a very circuitous one for the people of Georgetown to take to get around the south shore of Lake Bigler."[19]

The rest of the summer of 1855 was spent by Day and Goddard, part of the time accompanied by Marlette, in going over the Carson Pass Immigrant route (with variations proposed by local residents) and in traversing Johnson's Cutoff. Day commented that, although Carson Pass had the disadvantage of snow remaining on the pass until late in the spring, Hope Valley presented a good natural road, with an easy grade. Carson Canyon, "formerly the terror of all travelers on account of the enormous granite boulders with which the road was obstructed," had recently been improved by clearing out the roadway and erecting two bridges. In the latter part of August Goddard came to a point "which commanded a very extensive view of the mountains to the southeast. Two lofty double-headed peaks lay to the east, the southern of which I recognized as that pointed out to me from near Walker's River in October, 1853, by my esteemed friend the late lamented Major Ebbetts, whose untimely end has delayed the exploration of the pass discovered and named after him." Late that afternoon they came to the summit of the "Great Carson Spur, which being the highest point on the wagon road, is generally called Carson Pass, although in reality it is not on the divide of the Sierra." Goddard and Day ascended a peak east of the pass for observation. They recognized Mount Diablo on the western horizon. That night and for several nights thereafter they camped at what they called Clear Lake, now Twin Lakes Reservoir. Goddard went down Carson Canyon to Mormon Station for a fresh supply of provisions and on the way back turned off at Hope Valley to explore Luther Pass[20] before rejoining Day at the Clear Lake camp. Day then returned to Placerville, while Goddard went back over Luther Pass to Lake Tahoe. The entire Carson Pass area had been thoroughly examined and many observation points occupied for mapmaking.

On the shores of Lake Tahoe Goddard continued his surveys in a further attempt to fix the angle of the eastern boundary of California. But the weather was not favorable, and on September 22 he broke camp and returned to Carson Valley. At the end of the month he set out on his return to Placerville, continuing the reconnaissance of the Johnson route that had now been traversed several times by the Marlette Survey. The combined reports of Day and Goddard provide a comprehensive view of the proposed wagon route, soon to be the principal way across the Sierra until replaced a decade later by the railroad over Donner Pass. Starting from Mormon Station three routes converged upon Lake Valley: the first, up Carson Canyon and over Luther Pass; the second, Johnson's route, rising steeply to the rim of the Tahoe basin (Spooner Summit) and then skirting the Lake high up to avoid the difficulties of the shore; the third, a horse trail over Daggett Pass.[21]

Sherman Day's report provides a description of the remainder of the proposed road to Placerville. "The most difficult portion," he says, "is encountered in the ascent from Bigler Lake Valley to the western summit, about 1,000 feet above the valley. It attains the summit by a length of only three-fourths of a mile, which gives a grade of over 14½ degrees.[22] Continuing westward from the summit, the road descends by a fair grade through a valley of pines to a rocky canyon above Slippery Ford. From this point, where Johnson's Cut-off turns to ascend the high ridge, a new road is proposed, not following the narrow bottom of the creek, but maintaining a proper grade along the spurs 100 to 300 feet above. At Sugar Loaf Rock, about 11½ miles below Slippery Ford, the road descends to the bottom, and after about two miles again winds around among the benches of the spurs. At 22 miles below Slippery Ford it is proposed to cross to the south side of the South Fork by a bridge and ascend by an easy grade to the ridge leading to Placerville."

Slippery Ford has long since disappeared from the traveler's ken, but in its day it was a famous spot. Goddard describes it as he saw it in 1855: "The Slippery Ford Creek is the most northern branch of the South Fork and drains the mountains from Pyramid Peak to the main summit, which form a grand amphitheater around its headwaters. There is no spot on the road more strikingly wild. It is a naked basin of white granite rocks. On the south side of the river is a lofty cliff of dark granite, which contrasts finely in color and abruptness of form with the neighboring mountains." Slippery Ford was later displaced as a crossing by Twin Bridges; today a modern highway (part of U. S. 50) carved out of the granite slope on a long slant continues to offer a spectacular view toward Pyramid Peak.

While the Day and Goddard surveys had recommended the Johnson Immigrant route for the state wagon road, the fact that there was no state money available left the way open to proponents of other routes if they could raise the funds. The counties took the matter in hand, and several private companies were formed for making toll roads. O. B. Powers, of Calaveras County, surveyed and advocated a road from Calaveras Big Trees that followed the ridges of the Mokelumne until it crossed over and joined the Carson Canyon road. But in the end the Johnson route prevailed, and by the summer of 1858 Jared B. Crandall, of the Pioneer Stage Company, was operating a stage over a partially completed road from Placerville to Carson Valley. But it was tough going, and heavy snows put an end to it for the winter season. Nevertheless, a beginning had been made and soon mail was being carried with more or less regularity across the mountains. Further county financing, together with contracts for toll roads, brought improvements, but the problem of winter snows was not solved for wheeled vehicles. The mail did go through, however, by pack mule and horse, except in the worst weather, and presently in a more spectacular manner. In January, 1856, "Snow-shoe" Thompson began a remarkable series of trips across the Sierra on skis, which he continued for twenty years.[23] He

Thayer's Marvels of the New West, *1887*

Snow-shoe Thompson in action.

made his skis from recollections of his boyhood in Norway. They were ten feet long and very heavy. At first he used the Placerville–Johnson–Luther Pass route, but later the Big Tree route to Hope Valley, where both routes continued down Carson Canyon to Genoa. With fifty to eighty pounds on his back he would make the eastward journey in three days and the return often in two. He carried no blankets, nor did he even wear a heavy overcoat, relying on his exertions to keep him warm while traveling, and on campfires at night. There are many tales of his wintry experiences, saving lives and rescuing lost travelers. He himself was never lost, nor did he ever suffer a mishap, even in the most violent blizzards. He rarely received any compensation for his serv-

Cedric Wright

Snow-shoe's grave, Genoa, Nevada.

ices—many promises, but little cash. "He took pride in the work," writes his biographer. "It challenged the spirit of adventure within him. It was like going forth to battle, and each successive trip was a victory. His equal in his peculiar line will probably never again be seen. The times and conditions are gone that called for men possessing the special qualifications that made him famous. It would be hard to find another man combining his courage, physique, and powers of endurance—a man of such thews and sinews, controlled by such a will."

Of quite different character was another picturesque episode in trans-Sierra travel that flourished briefly in 1860—the Pony Express.[24] Designed for the speedy transport of the overland mail, its backers proposed to accomplish this between St. Joseph, Missouri, and Sacramento in ten days—and they did, at least a few times. The first eastbound trip left Sacramento on April 3, 1860, and arrived at St. Joe on the 13th, in spite of a severe blizzard in the Sierra. Starting at the same time in the opposite direction, the riders from St. Joe delivered the mail at Sacramento on the 14th. This schedule was kept by the most adept and daring riders and an elaborate system of relays and remounts. The route across the Sierra was at first substantially that of the Johnson Immigrant road, from Placerville to Lake Valley, and by Luther Pass to Woodfords, but almost immediately it was changed to take advantage of the nearly completed Kingsbury Grade between Genoa and Daggett Pass.[25] It was a bold and spectacular gesture, but it lasted hardly more than a year and was ended by a synchronization of three events—completion of the Overland Telegraph, the financial collapse of the promoters, and the Civil War.

Meanwhile, an event of major importance in Nevada brought new pressure upon the passes. Bonanza in Washoe! Blue mud, which had hampered the working of gold placers, turned out to be silver—almost solid silver.[26] News of fabulous values sped across the Sierra to the towns of the foothills and on to Sacramento and San Francisco. The rush to Washoe was on. From the northern mines over Henness Pass, and from farther south over the Johnson and Carson routes, poured the avid seekers for fortunes. The whole character of Sierra travel changed, flowing in reverse from the accustomed pattern. Roads were worked over, stages and wagons rumbled through, feeding stations for man and beast sprang into being and became crowded and overcrowded with travelers—Berry's Station (Strawberry), Swan's Toll House at Slippery Ford, Yank's in Lake Valley, Friday's Station on the western approach to Daggett Pass. Stage passengers, drivers of mule-team freighters, weary Washoe-bound hopefuls on foot, all manner of men and beasts of burden, clamored for food and a lodging for the night. No time for the amenities of life, only the urge to find fortune on the Comstock, where Virginia City, out of nothing, was becoming a great western metropolis.

A similar though smaller tide was flowing over the Big Tree route through Hermit Valley. One day in the fall of 1862 an astonishing sight met the unbelieving eyes of the traveler—a group of camels. One-humped camels had been known in the Southwest for several years, brought from Mediterranean lands. But what were these two-humped fellows doing here? They were Bactrian camels, imported from Siberia, destined to carry burdens in Nevada.[27] The camel experiment did not prove much of a success, either in the Southwest or in Nevada. It was objected that the strange beasts scared the honest, hardworking mules and horses, and eventually most of them were turned loose. For a while there was a law in Nevada prohibiting loose camels on the highways.[28]

The big bonanza in Washoe stimulated search for silver in every direction. In an obscure valley at the head of East Carson River some Norwegians made a strike. They called their camp "Kongsberg" for their hometown, soon corrupted to "Konigsberg"; but when others swarmed in the name was changed to the more alluring "Silver Mountain." Whitney and Brewer, of the State Geological Survey, visited it in 1863.[29] "Silver Mountain," writes Brewer, "is a good illustration of a new mining town. We arrived by trail, for the wagon road is left many miles back. As we descend the canyon from the summit, suddenly a bright new town bursts into view. There are perhaps forty houses, all new and as bright as new, fresh lumber, which but a month or two ago was in the trees, can make them. There are town lots and streets, although as yet no wagons. It is probably all a 'bubble'—but little silver ore has been found at all—people are digging, hoping to strike it. One or two mines may pay, the remaining three hundred will only lose." Before leaving, Brewer and Whitney climbed the peak of Silver Mountain. "It is over eleven thousand feet high, the highest in the region, and commands a very extensive view. In the north we look into the Carson Valley and even see the mountains of Washoe; in the west is the summit of the Sierra Nevada, the volcanic crests here worn into fantastic outlines; on the southeast are the mountains near Mono Lake and about Aurora; and in the east chain after chain, extending far beyond the state line into the territories." By the end of that summer a rough wagon road was completed from Hermit Valley and Ebbetts Pass was open.[30]

The people of Sonora and adjacent communities were not content to see traffic diverted to the northerly passes without making an effort to have a road of their own. The legislature was persuaded to provide for a direct road over the mountains from Sonora to the mining regions of Mono and Aurora. First an attempt was made by way of the Clark Fork of the Stanislaus, but that proved unsatisfactory. On March 31, 1863, an act was passed authorizing a commission from the four counties concerned to select another route. Bonds were to be issued for each county's share, to be reimbursed from tolls. A new route, up Deadman Creek and over the crest at approximately the present site, was surveyed and work was begun that summer. A passable road was constructed, but it was many years before the Sonora Pass road attained the standards of those farther north.

By the middle of the 1860's freight, passengers, and mail were moving by one means or another, and in all kinds of weather, over all the Sierra passes from Sonora Pass to Beckwourth Pass. All except one, and that the most obvious and the most neglected—Donner Pass. That was reserved for the first great engineering feat in the High Sierra, construction of the Central Pacific Railroad.

Notes and References

For further discussion of some of the events of this chapter, see *California Highways and Public Works*, Centennial Edition, September 9, 1950, especially chap. xi, Stewart Mitchell, "Crossing the Sierra."

1. A detailed account of the various surveys is given in *Oblique Boundary Line Between California and Nevada*, Appendix No. 3, Report for 1900, U.S. Coast and Geodetic Survey, Washington, 1901.

2. William M. Eddy, *Annual Report of the Surveyor General of California for 1852*.

3. Thompson and West, *History of the State of Nevada*, 1881.

4. John A. Brewster, *Annual Report of the Surveyor General of California for 1856*. (The Eddy map referred to is described in Carl I. Wheat, *The Maps of the California Gold Region*, San Francisco: Grabhorn Press, 1942.)

5. "The name of this remarkable prevaricator was not Beckwourth until his biography came to be written. In the days when he was a roustabout on Mississippi River steamboats, or a wild savage among his adopted tribe, he was plain Jim Beckwith, and is so carried on the rolls of the American Fur Company" (H. M. Chittenden, *Fur Trade of the Far West*, New York: Press of the Pioneers, 1935, vol. II). The name has sometimes been confused with that of Lieut. E. G. Beckwith, U.S.A., who was on the Pacific Railroad Survey a little farther north. The U.S. Geographic Board, *Sixth Report*, 1933, says "Beckwith Pass," as does Erwin G. Gudde, *California Place Names*, Berkeley and Los Angeles: University of California Press, 1960. On the other hand, Drury, *California: An Intimate Guide*, New York: Harper, 1947, and Rensch and Hoover, *Historic Spots in California*, Stanford, Calif.: Stanford University Press, 1933, use "Beckwourth."

6. T. D. Bonner, *The Life and Adventures of James P. Beckwourth*, New York, 1856, and later editions. Although purported to be from Jim's dictation, the passages quoted indicate substantial ghost writing.

7. *Historical Souvenir of El Dorado County*, Paolo Sioli, publisher, Oakland, 1883. John Calhoun Johnson was born in Ohio, 1822; came overland to California, 1849; had a ranch six miles north of Placerville; was a member of the California legislature, 1856; and was killed by Apache Indians in Arizona, 1876 (Pioneer Records, CSL).

8. *Report of Explorations in California for Railroad Routes*, by Lieut. R. S. Williamson, 1853 (*Pacific Railroad Reports*, V, 1856).

9. Access to Las Vegas is sought today for other purposes.

10. Very little biographical information about Major Ebbetts has come to light other than his explorations in the Sierra and his death when the steamboat *Secretary* burst her boiler on the way from San Francisco to Petaluma, April 15, 1854, killing about thirty persons and injuring many more (*Alta California*, April 16, 1854). He had relatives in San Francisco, but his name does not appear in the early directories.

11. George Henry Goddard, born in Bristol, England, 1817; came to California by Cape Horn, 1850; lived in Sacramento until 1862, when he moved to San Francisco; died in Berkeley, December, 1906, brokenhearted over the loss in the San Francisco fire of his vast lifetime collection of maps and sketches.

12. An account of the expedition was recorded at length in the *San Francisco Herald*. Major Ebbetts' journal was printed in full in the issues of December 19 and 20, 1853. Portions of the report are included in Stewart Mitchell, "A Forgotten Experiment," *CHSQ*, September, 1955, 34:3.

13. Very little is recorded about the immigrants who came by this route, and there are conflicting dates. There is a brief account in *Tuolumne County, California*, issued by the *Union Democrat*, Sonora, 1909, but the sources are vague.

14. There are several references to this earlier trip, but no details. Some say 1850, some say 1851.

15. Martin Smith built a cabin here in 1851 and operated a trading post and way station for several years. He was followed by Ephraim Clement, known as "Yank," because no one could pronounce "Ephraim" correctly; so it was "Yank's Station" for a while. In 1873 it was purchased by George Henry Dudley Meyers, and the site has since then been "Meyers" (Edward B. Scott, *The Saga of Lake Tahoe* Crystal Bay, Nevada: Sierra-Tahoe Publishing Co., 1957).

16. Seneca Hunt Marlette (1824-1911), a native of New York State; graduated from Rensselaer Institute as civil engineer; to California via Cape Horn, 1849; surveying in San Francisco; mercantile business in Mokelumne Hill; Surveyor General of California, 1854-1855; moved to Washoe, 1860, and became the first Surveyor General of Nevada; acquired lumber and water interests near Lake Tahoe. A lake created by a dam to store water for local mills, later for flume and pipeline, was named Marlette Lake. He disposed of his Tahoe interests in the 1880's and moved to southern California (J. M. Guinn, *A History of California*, Los Angeles, 1907).

17. Sherman Day (1806-1884), born in New Haven, Conn.; graduated, 1826, from Yale, of which his father was president; to California in 1849; engaged in civil and mining engineering; State Senator, 1855-1856; U.S. Surveyor General for California, 1868-1871. An original trustee of the University of California and for a time Professor of Mine Construction and Surveying there.

18. People *v.* Johnson, 6 Cal, 493, Oct. 1856. The court was alarmed because the legislature had authorized indebtedness for road construction exceeding the limit stated in the Constitution of California (Article VIII), which forbade a debt of more than $300,000 unless voted by the people. We repeat here the admonition of the Court in the hope that it will discourage further extravagance: "If we were at liberty to decide this case on grounds of public policy, we could not hesitate one moment between bankruptcy and ruin, or credit and prosperity. It is time that the axe should be laid at the root of this political evil; that this system of extravagance, which has been the curse of the State for the last five years, exhausting the substance of the people, destroying our credit abroad, and corrupting and demoralizing our citizens at home, should be stopped,

and that honesty, prudence and economy should preside over the legislature of the State, and the administration of her affairs."

19. Accounts of the surveys of 1855, including detailed reports by Day and Goddard, are in S. H. Marlette, *Annual Report of the Surveyor General of California for 1855*.

20. Ira Manley Luther (1821-1890), born in New York State; came to California, 1850; had a ranch near Genoa, 1856; member Nevada Territorial Legislature, 1861-1862; returned to New York State, 1865. He discovered a pass from Hope Valley to Lake Valley in 1852 and took the first wagons across in 1854 (Pioneer Records, *CSL*; Scott, *Saga of Lake Tahoe*).

21. The approach to the pass began at the home of Dr. Charles Daggett, about three miles south of Genoa.

22. It actually was steeper than that. Shortly afterwards Asa Hawley built a road to Echo Summit by a better grade.

23. The chief source of information about Snow-shoe Thompson's career is an article in *Overland Monthly*, October, 1886, by "Dan De Quille" (William Wright), editor of the *Territorial Enterprise* of Virginia City, and first published in that paper after an interview with Thompson in 1876, just before he died. It has frequently been copied, in whole or in part: *Daily Alta California*, February 20, 1876; *Hutchings' California Magazine*, February, 1857, and *SCB*, February, 1935, 20:1. Thompson was born in Norway, 1827, and came to the U.S. when ten years old, and to California at twenty-four. He died at his ranch in the Carson Valley, May 15, 1876. His tombstone in the little cemetery at Genoa is remarkable for a pair of crossed skis carved above his name, which is there given as "John A. Thomson." This is the correct Norwegian spelling, but by "Snow-shoe Thompson" he is known to history, and it would be as difficult to eradicate the "p" from his name as it would be to change the spelling of "Arkansas."

24. The Pony Express has been the occasion for celebrations, the theme of postage stamps, and the inspiration of fiction to such an extent that it may be presumed that everyone knows all about it. Should a refresher be desired, consult Roy S. Bloss, *Pony Express—the Great Gamble*, Berkeley, Calif.: Howell–North, 1959; and sundry encyclopedias.

25. David Demmen Kingsbury and John McDonald constructed the Kingsbury Grade up Haines Canyon, 1858-1860. It has since been partly relocated.

26. The story of the Great Bonanza is available in many histories. One of the liveliest is George D. Lyman, *The Saga of the Comstock Lode*, Scribner's, 1934; add Charles Howard Shinn, *The Story of the Mine*, D. Appleton, 1896, and you have a sufficient account of the events that caused a mighty arch to span the Sierra from San Francisco to the Nevada mines.

27. The camel episode, both the importation from the Mediterranean and that from the Amoor River in Siberia, is summarized and documented in articles in *CHSQ*, December, 1930, 9:4: by A. A. Gray ("Camels in California"), F. P. Farquhar ("Camels in the Sketches of Edward Vischer"), and W. A. Lewis ("A Contribution Towards a Bibliography of the Camel"). The scene at Hermit Valley is depicted in *Vischer's Pictorial of California*, 1870, No. 19; there are several other camel scenes in the *Pictorial*. There is also Vischer's *Mammoth Tree Grove Album* of lithographed plates, 1862, in which plate IX shows camels passing through the Calaveras Grove on the way to Nevada.

28. *Statutes of the State of Nevada*, 1875, pp. 53-54, Secs. 4799 and 4800, "An Act to prohibit camels and dromedaries from running at large on or about the

public highways of the State of Nevada," approved February 9, 1875. Although the Act was probably invalidated by revision of the Statutes later on, nevertheless one can never be sure about such things and you are hereby warned that the penalty for letting your camels run loose on the highways of Nevada may be "a fine not less than twenty-five (25) or more than one hundred (100) dollars, or imprisonment not less than ten or more than thirty days, or by both."

29. *Brewer Journal.*
30. R. Coke Wood, "Ebbetts Pass" (pamphlet, n.d.).

XII

THE CENTRAL PACIFIC RAILROAD

The man who opened the gate for a railroad across the Sierra was a young engineer named Theodore Dehone Judah. He had come to California in 1854 to be chief engineer of the Sacramento Valley Railroad, a new project designed to connect Sacramento with the mining regions through Folsom and Placerville and through Marysville and the Yuba River towns. Judah came with a fine reputation in the East and soon showed that it was deserved.[1] From the beginning, however, his thoughts were on a more ambitious plan than local railroads. He was convinced that a transcontinental railroad could be built, that it would be built, and that he was the man who would build it. So when the Sacramento Valley Railroad failed to come up to expectations financially, he resigned and was presently absorbed in an effort to arouse interest in his project. He went to Washington and diligently pressed his plan upon Congress. He wrote and distributed a pamphlet in which he said, "Let the Pacific Railroad be properly constructed, with a double track, and a trip from St. Louis to San Francisco and back can be made in one week, with perfect ease and safety."[2] Judah's proposals may have sounded rhapsodical, but he never lost sight of sound engineering. He knew that facts rather than dreams were required for raising money. Facts he had and facts he would continue to produce. But as Congress was not yet convinced, Judah went back to California for more facts and for a demonstration that private capital would be available if Congress did its part.

In October, 1859, a convention met in San Francisco to pursue the matter. Judah was appointed its agent to urge Congress to provide for a survey of a central route across the Sierra and to give aid by granting rights of way on public lands and by guaranteeing interest on railroad bonds. Judah was by now well acquainted in Congress, and his straightforward presentations created a favorable opinion that produced the Pacific Railroad Act, approved by President Lincoln July 1, 1862.[3] Under the terms of this act, two railroad companies, the Union Pacific in the East, and the Central Pacific in the West, were to be allotted bonds in proportion to miles of road constructed, except that the amount of bonds was to be tripled for construction over the mountains. In addition to the right of way the act provided for timber and quarrying rights and for ten sections of land for each mile of rail. It was now up to the surveyors and the financiers.

In the intervals between trips to Washington, Judah had been busy looking over the lay of the land with an eye for details that would determine the actual route across the Sierra. The old wagon routes were examined, including the Georgetown route, the Henness Pass, and finally the almost forgotten route over Donner Pass. The last he approached by way of Dutch Flat, where he became acquainted with Daniel W. Strong, the local druggist. Dr. Strong's familiarity with the region was of great help, but it was Theodore Judah's knowledge of railroad grades that settled the matter. Ignoring the temptation to start up the river canyons, he held as nearly as possible to the long ridge north of the American River and found that he could reach the summit, a rise of seven thousand feet, in seventy miles, with a maximum grade of 105 feet per mile. Describing the route in his report, Judah emphasized a characteristic that is apparent to the traveler today, a hundred years later, as he looks out of his Pullman car window: "The line of top or crest of ridge being far from uniform, of course the lowest points or gaps in ridge become commanding points, and it was found necessary to carry the line from gap to gap, passing around the intervening hills, upon their side slopes."[4] Thus we have Clipper Gap and Emigrant Gap, with their spectacular views down into the adjacent canyons. From Emigrant Gap Judah carried the line along the side of the ridge above the Yuba to Summit Meadow, now occupied by Lake Van Norden.

All this could not be accomplished without trestles and fills and a number of tunnels. The final crossing of the Sierra crest, or rather under it, was to be made by a very long tunnel, which turned out later to be even more difficult than Judah had foreseen. Once over the summit the way would be considerably easier, although there would still be problems. The first of these was how to get down to the level of Donner Lake. The old wagon routes were far too steep for a railroad. No feasible way was found on the north, but Judah's practiced eye discovered a solution. "Pursuing its course from the summit easterly," he reported, "the line commences its descent with maximum grade, and, passing to the right, is carried for next two miles over a steep, rocky side-hill, on which will be found quite heavy rock cutting: thence turning abruptly to the right, it enters upon side-hill of Strong's Ravine, and, running up the same, about one mile, crosses over, and is carried down over a smooth side-hill, to a point 600 feet higher than the south-west corner of Donner Lake, thence pursuing its course along the side-hill for about three miles, it encounters Coldstream Ravine, and runs up the same a little over a mile. Crossing Coldstream, the line follows along down its south side-hill to within about a quarter of a mile of the Main Truckee, where turning to left, it crosses the valley of Donner Creek, accomplishing the descent in about 11 ½ miles of downward maximum grade."[5]

Before actual construction could begin two very important matters had to be settled. First, what was to be the gauge of the tracks? The Act of 1862 left the matter for the President to determine. At that time there were several different gauges in effect among the eastern railroads, and each group wanted the new railroad to conform to its own gauge. Lincoln listened to the arguments and decided upon a 5-foot gauge. But pressure groups were active then as now, and the strongest prevailed upon Congress to override the President's decision and make the gauge 4 feet 8½ inches, the width that has since become standard for all major American railroads. Another matter left for determination by the President was the location of the western base of the Sierra Nevada. This was vital for the financiers, for at that point the increased allotment of bonds would begin. Lincoln asked for professional opinions from California.[6] First to respond was Professor J. D. Whitney, State Geologist. He cited Professor James D. Dana's decision about the Rocky Mountains as a precedent and declared that "with regard to the Sierra Nevada, it would seem that a strictly accurate determination of the position of its western base would place it where the upward rise of the surface commences." He concludes that "the point where the line of the Central Pacific Railroad crosses Arcade Creek may with propriety be taken as the base of the Sierra, as from there commences a regular and continuous ascent." Edward F. Beale, U. S. Surveyor General for California, had a different idea. After a philosophical discussion in which he intimated that the base was really at sea level, he swung over to the popular concept that the base means "the point where the ascent becomes plainly perceptible, not to be geometrically ascertained, but merely by observation—where the mountains presented the first considerable obstruction." He concluded that "a point should be taken about midway between Sacramento and Folsom." This seemed to make sense, but as the railroad didn't run in that direction, Beale's opinion had little value. In a third opinion, J. F. Houghton, State Surveyor General, concurred with the conclusion of Professor Whitney, although on different grounds. Referring to the provision that the bonus was for the 150 miles of most difficult construction, he thought that "the two extremities of the 150 miles should rest upon corresponding grades, the one to the west, the other to the east of the mountains." From Judah's survey profiles Houghton found that "seven miles from the city of Sacramento, at a point marked Arcade Creek, a grade of 21 feet per mile occurs, and at a distance of 150 miles from this point the route reaches the Big Truckee Meadow," where the same grade prevails. With these rather specious opinions before him, President Lincoln gave his decision: "The point where the line of the Central Pacific Railroad crosses Arcade Creek in the Sacramento Valley is hereby fixed as the western base of the Sierra Nevada Mountains." The railroad promoters were delighted; the decision was final, and the bonds were subsequently issued for these miles of "most difficult construction."[7]

Without waiting for these details to be settled, the railroad had already started on its way east from Front Street, Sacramento, on January 8, 1863, with prayers and speeches and shovels. Three of the men who would presently be known as the "Big Four" were on hand: Leland Stanford, Governor of California, who delivered an oration; Charles Crocker, merchant and contractor, who stimulated the applause; Mark Hopkins, hardware dealer, who modestly kept in the background. The fourth member, Collis P. Huntington, was in New York, pulling strings in financial and legislative circles. Theodore Judah was also present, impatiently waiting for the fuss to subside and the real work to begin. Alas for poor Judah, his impatience was to carry him far from the scene of his high endeavor. Frustrated by delays and the divergent views of his associates, he soon departed by sea for the East to seek help from others. In Panama he caught yellow fever and barely reached New York before he died. He was not quite thirty-eight years old.

The story of the Big Four and their financial and political dealings has been told often and at length.[8] With such matters the Sierra Nevada is only indirectly concerned, but with the actual construction it is very much concerned.[9] The nature of the range, with its extremes of weather unprecedented in the building of railroads, demanded extraordinary procedures. Cuts and fills, bridges and trestles, and especially tunnels required labor and the logistics of supplies on a huge scale. A separate company, the Dutch Flat and Donner Lake Wagon Road Company was organized on the side by some of the promoters, partly as an adjunct to financing, partly for hauling supplies. The operation was highly successful. Not only were the materials, including rails and even engines, moved "over the hill" ahead of construction, but practically all freight was diverted from the Johnson and Carson routes with substantial profit to the new company.

There were no trucks and tractors, no giant earthmovers in those days, only mules and dumpcarts, shovels and manpower, and more manpower. Labor was scarce. Irishmen predominated at first, but competition from the mines was too great, and in their place came Chinese, all who could be found in California, and then importations from China by the shipload. At one time there were more than 10,000 Chinese laborers on the job, and very effective they proved. The Superintendent of Construction, James H. Strobridge, at first opposed to them, came to have a high opinion of the Chinese. John R. Gillis, an assistant engineer, had a good word for them: "They were as steady, hard-working a set of men as could be found. They were paid from $30 to $35, in gold, a month, finding themselves, while the white men were paid about the same, but with their board thrown in."[10]

Driving tunnels through Sierra granite proved to be a very arduous task. Tunnel No. 6, more than 1600 feet in length, was the longest of the fifteen on the Sierra crossing, nearly all of which were on the summit. Before the snow began to fall in 1866, work was pushed on the headings of the tunnel. Then, when the storms came and drifts piled up, snow-tunnels were driven through them so that work could be continued through the winter. Speed was of the essence, and to increase the speed a shaft was sunk to the central point of the tunnel and work was pushed from within toward the headings. The experience of recent years in the mines had developed techniques of excavation and timbering, as well as of lighting and air supply, which were now

Railroad construction scenes.

put to good use. One of the earliest uses of the newly invented nitroglycerin was in blasting for the tunnels. It was highly effective in expediting the work, but terrible accidents elsewhere demonstrated its dangers and caused it to be discontinued.[11]

Under the rigorous conditions that prevailed that stormy winter there were remarkably few accidents. Snowslides were the greatest danger. To quote Engineer Gillis again: "Snowslides or avalanches were frequent. The storm winds, being always from the southwest, form drifts or snow-wreaths on the southeast crests of hills. When these become too heavy, which is generally towards the close of the storms, they break off, and falling start the loose snow below. This slides on the old crust. I never saw a slide from the ground. Near the close of one storm, a log-house with board roof, containing some fifteen or sixteen men, was crushed and buried at day-break. The storm ended at noon. Towards evening a man coming up the road missed the house and alarmed the camp, so that by six o'clock the men were dug out. The bulk of the slide had passed over and piled itself up beyond the house, so that it was only covered fifteen feet deep. Only three were killed; the bunks were close to the log walls and kept the rest from being crushed. The snow packed around the men so closely that only two could move about; they had almost dug their way out; over the heads of the rest little holes had been melted in the snow by their breath. Most of them were conscious, and, strange to say, the time had passed rapidly with them, although about fourteen hours under the snow. At Tunnel 10 some fifteen or twenty Chinamen were killed by a slide about this time."[12] There were twenty-four storms that winter of 1866-1867, varying, according to Gillis, from a short snow squall to a two-weeks gale. "The latter, the heaviest storm of the winter, began February 18th, at 2 P.M., and snowed steadily until 10 P.M. of the 22d, during which time six feet fell. The barometer kept low and the wind heavy from the southwest for five days more, by which time a fresh supply of damp air came up from the Pacific. It snowed steadily from March 2d, making ten feet of snow and thirteen days storm." Gillis also had something to say about snowshoes. "We started with Canadian snowshoes, but soon abandoned them for the Norwegian, each a strip of light wood ten to twelve feet long, four inches wide, and an inch and a quarter thick in the centre; they taper in thickness toward the end, are turned up in front, and grooved on the bottom. There is a broad strap in the middle to put the foot under, and a balancing-pole to steady, push, and brake with. The latter will be seen all-important, as a speed of twenty-five to thirty miles an hour is often attained on a steep hill-side."

The snowstorms and snowdrifts that created such difficulties in the construction of the railroad might be expected to interfere even more with its operation. Much thought was given to the problem. One device was to build

Thayer's Marvels of the New West, *1887*

Snowshed construction.

barriers on the upper side of the cuts and leave the rest to snowplows. But the barriers were broken down with the first storms, and the plows, no matter how powerful the engines behind them, proved utterly ineffective. There seemed to be no alternative except to put a roof over the track, and thus were born the snowsheds. The cost was appalling: hundreds of carpenters, millions of board feet of lumber were required. Yet, the order was to go ahead, and in 1867 work was begun under the direction of Arthur Brown, who had been in charge of bridges, trestles, and other structures for the past two years.[13] Nearly forty miles of track were put under cover during the next three years, causing one trainman to remark that "in all his wide experience this was the first time he ever railroaded in a barn." As time went on improvements were made in design, but from the first the snowsheds were effective, with two qualifications—they were very expensive to maintain, and they shut out the view of the most beautiful and spectacular scenery on the transcontinental route. In recent years these drawbacks have been largely overcome: the rotary snow plow has made it possible to clear the track, with the result that many miles of snowsheds have been removed and the view brought to light.

The prodigious efforts of the Big Four and their associates were crowned by achievement, and sooner than anyone had believed possible, in April, 1868, a train from the west crossed the Sierra and went on eastward.

Notes and References

1. Theodore Dehone Judah (1826-1863), born at Bridgeport, Conn., son of an Episcopal clergyman; graduated from Rensselaer Polytechnical Institute and engaged in railroad construction in New York and New England until he was called to California in 1854. (Carl I. Wheat, "Sketch of the Life of Theodore D. Judah," *CHSQ*, September, 1925, 4:1; John D. Galloway, "Theodore Dehone Judah—Railroad Pioneer," *Civil Engineering*, October and November, 1941, 11:10-12.) "In him perished a genius—one of the greatest in his important line—without whom the way over the Sierra would not have been found perhaps for many years" (Theodore H. Hittell, *History of California*, 4 vols., San Francisco, 1898, vol. IV).

2. Judah, *A Practical Plan for Building the Pacific Railroad*, Washington, 1857.

3. *An Act to Aid in the Construction of a Railway and Telegraph Line from the Missouri River to the Pacific Ocean*. Summarized in Lewis Henry Haney, "A Congressional History of Railways in the United States," *Bulletin of the University of Wisconsin*, 1910, no. 211, vol. 2.

4. *Report of the Chief Engineer on the Preliminary Survey, Cost of Construction, and Estimated Revenue, of the Central Pacific Railroad of California*, Sacramento, 1862 (in BL).

5. *Ibid.*

6. These were furnished him by Governor Leland Stanford. The respective letters and the decision of the President are in the testimony of Edward H. Miller, Jr., secretary of the railroad company, August, 1887, before the U.S. Pacific Railway Commission, *50th Cong., 1st Sess., Senate Ex. Doc. 51*, vol. VI.

7. The decision differed very much from the popular notion that mountains begin where they can be seen; but, as humorist John Phoenix remarked upon a former occasion, "there can, of course, be no disputing the elucidations of science, or facts demonstrated by mathematical process, however incredible they may appear *per se*" (George H. Derby, *Phoenixiana*, New York, 1856; reprinted San Francisco: Grabhorn Press, 1937).

8. Bancroft, *California;* Bancroft, *Chronicles;* Hittell, *History of California;* and, more particularly, Oscar Lewis, *The Big Four,* New York: Knopf, 1938.

9. Full and well-documented coverage is given in Wesley S. Griswold, *A Work of Giants,* New York: McGraw-Hill, 1962, and John Deboe Galloway, *The First Transcontinental Railroad,* New York: Simmons-Boardman, 1950; also Neill C. Wilson and Frank J. Taylor, *Southern Pacific,* New York, McGraw-Hill, 1952, and Edwin L. Sabin, *Building the Pacific Railroad,* Philadelphia: Lippincott, 1919.

10. The part played by the Chinese is covered in Gunther Barth, *Bitter Strength: A History of the Chinese in the United States, 1850-1870,* Cambridge: Harvard University Press, 1964.

11. Nitroglycerin (first known as "nitro glycerine") had recently been invented by the Swedish chemist Alfred Bernhard Nobel, founder of the Nobel Prize.

12. John R. Gillis, "Tunnels of the Pacific Railroad," *Transactions of the American Society of Civil Engineers,* 1872, vol. I.

13. Arthur Brown (1830-1917), native of Scotland, came to California by way of Canada. In addition to railway structures he designed mansions for some of the Big Four. His son, Arthur Brown, Jr., was one of the architects of the present San Francisco City Hall and a number of other buildings in the Bay area.

Lithograph from Thomas A. Ayers' drawing, 1855.

XIII

A SCENE OF WONDER AND CURIOSITY

The transition of Yosemite from a mysterious Indian stronghold to a world-famous scenic wonder was incredibly rapid. Hardly had the murderous conflicts of 1851 and 1852 subsided when rumors began to spread from Mariposa of spectacular waterfalls and immense cliffs. They caught the attention of a young Englishman, James M. Hutchings, whose experiences in the mining regions had led him to believe that an illustrated magazine, supplying the public with what he termed "solid information," would be well received.[1] If the facts about Yosemite were anything like the rumors, they were worth looking into and would be lively subjects for his magazine. Accordingly he engaged an artist, Thomas A. Ayers, who had been making a name for himself with well-executed portrayals of the California scene, and set out for Yosemite.[2] At Mariposa he had difficulty in finding anyone who knew how to get to the Valley, but at length two reliable Indians were secured as guides and late in June, 1855, Hutchings and Ayers, with two companions, Walter Millard and Alexander Stair, took the obscure trail. The first tourists to Yosemite were on their way. They spent five days in the Valley, exploring, sketching, and calculating the heights of falls and cliffs. The beauty of the scene and the magnitude of its features far exceeded expectations. Upon returning to Mariposa, Hutchings wrote for the *Mariposa Gazette* an account that marked the beginning of a century of descriptions that practically exhausted the thesaurus of adjectives.[3]

Inspired by the reports of the Hutchings party, two other groups set out for the Valley at about the same time in August: one, of seventeen, from Mariposa; the other, ten miners from nearby Sherlock Creek. Little is recorded of the former, except that it included Galen Clark, who was to be closely identified with Yosemite for the rest of his long life. The Sherlock party, on the other hand, had an able chronicler in James H. Lawrence, who wrote an entertaining account of it, albeit some years afterwards.[4] A briefer account, published earlier and quoted by Lawrence, gives additional details;[5] the group was composed of "ten as fearless spirits and noble hearted fellows as ever shouldered a rifle or gathered around a campfire." They were led by Edward W. Houghton,[6] a veteran of the Mariposa Battalion, and accompanied by "the best dog on the Pacific Coast," who answered to the name of "Ship." It was an exuberant, at times a hilarious, group, forerunner of many a jolly Yosemite camping trip. But the Sherlock boys were also energetic and daring in exploration. Before they were through they had found a way to the top of Vernal Fall, had "rediscovered" Nevada Fall, had reached Little Yosemite, and at least one of them had climbed to the top of Cap of Liberty. The Mann brothers, Milton and Houston, members of the party, were so enthusiastic and so confident of a booming tourist travel that they promptly began, and the following year completed, fifty miles of toll trail, ultimately to become the Wawona Road.

A fourth expedition in this inaugural year of Yosemite tourism was organized by the Reverend W. A. Scott, of San Francisco, after hearing of the wonders from Hutchings in person. Included in the party of eleven as it left Mariposa the middle of October were a painter, a doctor, a preacher, a colonel, and an editor. The editor was L. A. Holmes of the *Mariposa Gazette*, who wanted to see for himself the wonders he had been hearing so much about. They had two pack mules; some rode on horses, some on mules, and some on their "mother's colts."[7] "After a very satisfactory and soul-satisfying jaunt," writes Hutchings, "Dr. Scott, upon his return to San Francisco, gave several eloquent discourses, and published some tersely written articles upon it. His magnetic enthusiasm largely contributed to the development of an interest in the minds of the public to witness such sublime scenes as those he had so graphically portrayed."[8]

At the close of 1855 the total tourist travel to Yosemite had reached forty-two. Fifty years later the annual number reached 10,000; a century later 1,000,000; and in the year 1962 a million and a half visitors came to Yosemite.

The attractions of Yosemite were not left for long as a monopoly of Mariposa. When Ayers returned in June, 1856, for a second visit it was by way of "a good though very steep trail constructed by the enterprising citizens of Coulterville."[9] Ayers this time was accompanied only by "Mr. Coulter's son, a lad of thirteen." In the Valley, however, he joined a party already there at "the camp of Judge Walworth."[10] Lafayette Bunnell, late of the Mariposa Battalion, was one of the group. They had located claims to land and were engaged in building a frame house to be "opened for the accommodation of visitors early next season." This appears to be the first structure erected in Yosemite Valley, later to be rebuilt as the "Lower Hotel," and to be followed a year later by a crude shack a little farther up the Valley, which became the "Upper Hotel," later the "Hutchings House."[11]

Ayers was one of the first to explore Yosemite with an eye trained to perceive its beauties and proportions, which he presented ably both in his sketches and in a letter he wrote for the press. Of Vernal Fall, for instance, he says, "For picturesque beauty, together with the surrounding combinations of rocks and trees, this waterfall excels; yet it is the least in height, being not more than two hundred feet perpendicular. It comes over the cliff in a broad sheet, retaining its form until lost in the pool below." He and his companions crawled up through the mist "to the magnificent arch, its recesses adorned with exquisite ferns and mosses." Next day they returned and went on to Nevada Fall, where "the water descending about half way

Ansel Adams

Nevada Fall.

perpendicularly, then shooting over the shelving part of the cliff, at an angle of seventy degrees, reaches the rocky pool below in clouds of silvery spray; a small portion of the same stream comes down the rocky canyon to the left;[12] all the waters then shoot over an inclined bed of granite, reaching the deep reservoir below; collecting again, they plunge over the lower [Vernal] fall, and reach the depths of Yohemity valley by a succession of picturesque rapids some two miles below." On another occasion he visited the falls of the South Fork (Illilouette), where "the water comes over the cliff to the left like a gust of living light from heaven, foaming into feathery spray." He visited Mirror Lake, "a gem set amid the surrounding mountains, whose aerial heights with the trees upon its borders are reflected in its silvery bosom." Ayers concludes his letter: "The time passed like a dream, and it was with regret that we left the beautiful valley of the Yohemity, bound on an exploring trip to the headwaters, far among the snow-clad peaks of the Sierra Nevada, of which more anon." A tantalizing conclusion, for the "more anon" has not come to light even with the most diligent search.

There was considerable activity in the Valley in the summer of 1856. Lafayette Bunnell, with an engineer named George K. Peterson, was engaged in making a survey of the practicability of conveying waters of the Merced to the Mariposa mines. "Not long after we had gone into camp and commenced our survey," says Bunnell, "visitors began to come into the valley." In addition to the Walworth party, mentioned by Ayers, there was a group from Mariposa distinguished by inclusion of "the first white woman who visited the valley," Madame Gautier, housekeeper at one of the Mariposa hotels.[13] They were followed shortly afterwards by Mr. and Mrs. John H. Neal, who presently became the first hotelkeepers in Yosemite.

In 1857 primitive "hotel" accommodations became available. An unusual tourist party arrived, led by James Denman, a San Francisco school superintendent. Besides several men, he was accompanied by two of his schoolteachers, Miss Anna C. Park and Miss Harriet J. Kirtland.[14] Also in the party were Editor Holmes of the *Mariposa Gazette*, this time with Mrs. Holmes. On the way they were entertained by Galen Clark, who had recently established a camp near the site of the present Wawona Hotel. He had come for the recruitment of his health. It was sufficiently recruited to enable him to live there and in Yosemite Valley for the next half-century. He died in 1910 at the age of ninety-six.[15]

The year 1858 appears to have been comparatively uneventful in Yosemite, but in 1859 things began to pick up. In June of that year the Reverend Ferdinand C. Ewer, of San Francisco, came with his wife after a tour of the Calaveras Big Trees and the mining districts. "On the 19th he held the first Episcopal service ever held in the Valley, Mr. Holbrook, a minister of

C. L. Weed

"The Upper Hotel," believed to be the first photograph taken in Yosemite.

the Congregational Church, having held there the first religious service the Sunday previous."[16] Another "first" that year was the first photograph taken in Yosemite, by C. L. Weed, whom Hutchings brought in for publicity purposes. Engravings from his photographs appeared the following year in *Hutchings' Magazine*. Another artist, a German named Camerer, spent some time in Yosemite in 1859, with results almost forgotten, although a few lithographs were made from his work.[17]

James C. Lamon, a native of Virginia, came to Yosemite at this time and found himself so much at home that he built a cabin and planted a garden and an orchard. He located a preemption claim and settled down to remain there, summer and winter, for the rest of his life. He died in 1875 and is buried in the local cemetery.[18]

Other claims besides that of Lamon had been made from time to time, but, as no official survey of the land had been made, they could not be perfected. Nevertheless, in 1860, a preposterous attempt was made to gather these miscellaneous claims and pool them in a lottery scheme, which, if it had been successful, would have led to disaster. But not enough tickets were sold and the plan was abandoned, not without some scandal. This scheme, as well as the bona fide claim of Lamon and a claim asserted a little later by Hutchings, indicate the probable destiny of Yosemite Valley had not a momentous event occurred. For this event, however, some preparation was needed—the public had to be brought to a realization that the treasures of Yosemite should be public property, not to be lavished upon a few for personal gain. Two concurrent events in 1860 greatly stimulated this realization: first, the establishment of the California State Geological Survey under Josiah Dwight Whitney; second, the visit to the Valley of the Reverend Thomas Starr King. The latter had recently come from Boston to be pastor of the First Unitarian Church in San Francisco. In Boston, in addition to his ministry, he had become famous as a lecturer and for the letters he had written to the *Boston Transcript* about his excursions in the White Mountains of New Hampshire. He now wrote a similar series of letters to the *Transcript* about his excursion to the Calaveras Big Trees and Yosemite Valley.[19] Such was his fame and influence that these letters had a wide audience in the East with a substantial effect upon Yosemite's destiny. The effect of the State Geological Survey, while not so immediate, was, nevertheless, to provide a sound scientific basis for future proceedings. The Whitney Survey was of such importance in the history of the Sierra Nevada that its activities and the careers of its personnel are reserved for a separate chapter.

The "momentous event" referred to was, of course, the grant to the state of California by the federal government of the Yosemite Valley and the Mariposa Grove of Big Trees. A most important condition was attached to the grant, namely, that "the premises shall be held for public use, resort, and recreation" and that they "shall be inalienable for all time." This was an entirely new concept and one of far-reaching significance, for it marked the beginning of our system of National Parks and Recreational Areas.[20] The immediate effect was to put a stop to the acquisition of land in Yosemite by private persons and to prevent unregulated uses. Whence came this idea? And how did it come so suddenly to a realization? It came primarily from two individuals, Frederick Law Olmsted and Israel Ward Raymond, although others to a lesser extent participated. Olmsted had come to California in 1863 to manage the Mariposa Estate, which had long since ceased to be the property of Frémont. Olmsted was not a mining engineer, but the new owners had confidence in his administrative ability and in the integrity of his character. With Calvert Vaux he had been largely responsible for the creation of Central Park in New York City and had been its Superintendent. He was already well on his way to becoming the foremost landscape architect of the country. It was natural, then, that as soon as he saw Yosemite he should recognize its great scenic value and begin to think of some way to preserve it.[21] Just how and when Olmsted and Raymond got together is not known, but the conjunction was a fortunate one. Raymond was a highly respected citizen of San Francisco, a manager and agent of steamship lines, with a wide acquaintance in the business world. He had been to Yosemite and was inspired by its beauty. He was alarmed by what he saw of the tendencies to private exploitation and the threatened destruction of its trees.[22] It is probable that he had had some preliminary discussion with Olmsted before, on February 20, 1864, he addressed a letter to the junior senator from California, John Conness, urging a grant by Congress to the State of California "to prevent occupation and especially to preserve the trees." He furnished descriptions and clauses for the purpose of a bill, including the phrase, "for public use, resort and recreation." Senator Conness promptly complied and introduced a bill in the Senate, which with little or no opposition passed both houses and was signed by President Lincoln on June 30, 1864.[23]

The Act of Congress, however, was not alone sufficient to effect the transfer of Yosemite Valley to the State of California; it required acceptance, including agreement to the conditions. Governor Frederick F. Low issued a proclamation, citing the Act, and appointed the Commissioners required. But it was nearly two years before the Legislature accepted the Grant with its provisions and ratified the appointments. The Commissioners appointed were Frederick Law Olmsted, Josiah Dwight Whitney, Israel W. Raymond, William Ashburner (member of the Geological Survey), E. S. Holden (a railroad promoter), Alexander Deering (an attorney), George W. Coulter of Coulterville, and Galen Clark. The Governor was a member ex officio.[24]

Olmsted proceeded to make a thorough study of the problems involved and in August, 1865, presented a report to his colleagues.[25] "The first point to be kept in mind," he declared, "is the preservation and maintenance as exactly as is possible of the natural scenery; the restriction, that is to say, within the narrowest limits consistent with the necessary accommodation of visitors, of all artificial constructions markedly inharmonious with the scenery or which would unnecessarily obscure, distort or distract from the dignity of the scenery." "In addition to the more immediate and obvious arrangements," he continued, "are two considerations which should not escape attention. First: the value of the district in its present condition as a museum of natural science and the danger, indeed the certainty, that without care many of the species of plants now flourishing upon it will be lost and many interesting objects be defaced or obscured if not destroyed. Second: that in permitting the sacrifice of anything that would be of the slightest value to future visitors to the convenience, bad taste, playfulness, carelessness, or wanton destructiveness of present visitors, we probably yield in each case the interest of uncounted millions to the selfishness of a few individuals." In some unaccountable way this report was lost and its effectiveness greatly diminished, especially as Olmsted was called east soon thereafter to resume work for New York's Central Park. However, the Commission did not lack strength, with Whitney as chairman of an Executive Committee which included Raymond and Ashburner. They appointed Galen Clark Guardian of the Yosemite Valley and the Big Tree Grove and engaged Clarence King and James T. Gardner of the State Geological Survey to survey the boundary around the rim of the Valley.

The greatest problem that confronted the Commissioners was the matter of the claims made for title to lands under the preemption laws. In this, Hutchings played the leading part, with Lamon following along.[26] Lamon had been a bona fide settler since 1859 and had a better case than did Hutchings, who could hardly claim residence until the spring of 1864, when he brought his wife to live in the Valley.[27] The Commissioners rejected all preemption claims on the ground that they had not been completed before the State became the owner of the land. They offered ten-year leases to Hutchings and Lamon, but Hutchings would have none of it. Ejectment was ordered. Lawsuits and appeals followed. Hutchings sought remedy in Congress and in the state legislature and almost succeeded. But in the end his efforts were fruitless. The Supreme Court of the United States in 1873 upheld a decision of the California Supreme Court which had been adverse to the claimants, and that ended the legal proceedings.[28] But Hutchings had one more move; he sought compensation for his "improvements." The Commissioners were glad to get rid of him and supported his plea to the legislature, which complied with an appropriation of $60,000 to be divided between Hutchings, Lamon, and two others.[29] Hutchings was allotted $24,000, but was far from satisfied. "Thus ended," he sneered, "the unequal contest, of many

Stagecoach days in Yosemite.

years, between the Board of the Yo Semite Commissioners and the Yo Semite settlers. Comment would be superfluous, as facts not only tell their own story, but suggest their own inferences."[30] It is worthy of note that the Commissioners, in their Report, stated that "they have never heard but one expression of opinion with regard to the amounts which all the parties received, namely: that the State has dealt by them most munificently." Hutchings took out a lease and continued to operate his hotel.

Travel to Yosemite steadily increased, especially after the transcontinental railroad was opened. More accommodations were provided, trails were improved, bridges were built, and in 1874 roads for wagons and stagecoaches reached the Valley. And James M. Hutchings produced new editions of *Scenes of Wonder and Curiosity*.

NOTES AND REFERENCES

1. James Mason Hutchings (1818-1902) began monthly publication of *Hutchings' Illustrated California Magazine* in July, 1856, and continued through five volumes to September, 1860. The opening article in the first number was entitled "THE YO-HAM-I-TE VALLEY" and contained the first published illustrations of the Valley other than separate lithographs (see chap. ix, n. 10, above). In 1860 he published the first book in which Yosemite is treated at any great length, *Scenes of Wonder and Curiosity in California*, which went through a number of editions (Farquhar No. 4). *In the Heart of the Sierras* followed in 1886 (Farquhar No. 18). It is hereafter cited as *Hutchings*, 1886.

2. Thomas A. Ayers, a native of New Jersey, came to California in 1849. Biographical details are scarce, and little remains of his work other than his Yosemite drawings and the large lithograph sheet that combines a number of his drawings of the Calaveras Grove (Harry T. Peters, *California on Stone*, 1935, plate 74). Ayers was drowned in 1858 in the wreck of a ship in which he had taken passage from San Pedro for San Francisco (Jeanne Van Nostrand, "Thomas A. Ayers, Artist–Argonaut of California," *CHSQ*, September, 1941, 20:3; Elizabeth H. Godfrey, "Thomas A. Ayers, First Yosemite Artist," *YNN*, February, 1944, 23:2).

3. Hutchings says that his account was published in the *Mariposa Gazette* about July 12, 1855, but I have not been able to find a copy.

4. James H. Lawrence, "Discovery of the Nevada Fall," *Overland Monthly*, October, 1884. However, Bunnell states definitely that Nevada Fall was discovered by the Mariposa Battalion party in 1851 (see chap. ix, n. 11).

5. G. L. Pearson, "Discovery of Yosemite Valley," *Pacific Rural Press*, June 21, 1873. Lawrence cites the author as George C. Pearson and the publication date, erroneously, as May, 1873. George C. Pearson is probably correct, as given in the *Solano County Register of Voters* of that time.

6. The name of the leader is given by Lawrence as "Haughton" and so copied by Hutchings, but the roster of the Mariposa Battalion shows "Houghton."

7. Reverend W. A. Scott, "Yo-Amite Falls," *Sacramento Daily Union*, December 18, 1855.

8. *Hutchings*, 1886.

9. Ayers describes his 1856 visit to Yosemite in the *San Francisco Alta California*, August 6, 1856.

10. "There are four gentlemen—Judge B. S. Walworth, of New York; John C. Anderson, of Illinois; W. C. Walling, of Pennsylvania; and J. A. Epperson, of Indiana; all single—living here. They came last May, and took up a claim" (*The Country Gentleman*, Albany, N. Y., October 9, 1856, copied from the *California Christian Advocate;* also Ayers in *San Francisco Alta California, op. cit.*).

11. The story of hotel construction, told fragmentarily by Bunnell and Hutchings, is recounted by Russell, *100 Years in Yosemite*, 1931 and later editions.

12. "A short distance above the head of the fall on the north side, the river gives off a small part of its waters, which forms a cascade in the narrow boulder-filled channel and finally meets the main stream again a few yards below the fall. Sometime last year, the Commissioners came to regard these cascades as a waste of raw material, a damaging leak that ought to be stopped by a dam compelling all the water to tumble and sing together. Accordingly, the enterprising landlord of Snow's Casa Nevada was allowed a few hundred dollars to 'fix the falls,' as he says, and by building a rock dam he has well-nigh succeeded in abolishing the Liberty Cap Cascades, though no corresponding advantage is visible in the main fall" (John Muir, in Linnie Marsh Wolfe, *John of the Mountains*, Boston: Houghton-Mifflin, 1938).

13. Bunnell, *Discovery of the Yosemite*, Chicago, 1880, and later editions; and *Mariposa Democrat*, August 5, 1856.

14. Harriet Kirtland's diary is in CSL. Denman's account of the trip is in the *Republican Watchman*, Sullivan County, N. Y., serially in 1862 (copy in BL). James Denman (1829-1909) was born in Sullivan County. He was the father of the late Judge William Denman of the United States Circuit Court, San Francisco.

15. Galen Clark was born in New Hampshire in 1814; he died in Yosemite in 1910. He came to California in 1853 and to Mariposa in 1854. He was a charter member of the Sierra Club. John Muir, "Galen Clark," SCB, June, 1910, 7:4; same in John Muir, *The Yosemite*, New York: Century Co., 1912; the definitive biography is Shirley Sargent, *Galen Clark*, San Francisco: Sierra Club, 1964.

16. Henry R. Wagner, "The Life of Ferdinand C. Ewer," CHSQ, December, 1934, and March, 1935, 13:4 and 14:1.

17. Mr. Lamson, of Bangor, Maine, accompanied Camerer while he made some of his sketches (J. Lamson, *Round Cape Horn . . . in the Year 1852*, Bangor, 1878).

18. John Muir, *The Yosemite*.

19. The White Mountain letters were the substance of Starr King's book, *The White Hills: Their Legends, Landscape, and Poetry*, published in Boston just before King left for California in 1860. His letters about the Yosemite trip appeared in the *Boston Transcript* at intervals between December 1, 1860, and February 9, 1861. They were printed in book form by the Book Club of California in 1962, under the title *A Vacation Among the Sierras—Yosemite in 1860*, edited by John A. Hussey. (Starr King was not related to Clarence King, who came to the Sierra later on.)

20. The development of such a concept is recounted by Hans Huth, *Nature and the American: Three Centuries of Changing Attitudes*, Berkeley and Los Angeles: University of California Press, 1957, and before that, more specifically in relation to Yosemite, in his "Yosemite: The Story of an Idea," SCB, March, 1948, 33:3.

21. *Frederick Law Olmsted, Landscape Architect, 1822-1903*, edited by Frederick Law Olmsted, Jr., and Theodora Kimball, New York: Putnam's, 1922.

22. Israel Ward Raymond (1811-1887), came to California first in 1850 and again, permanently, in 1862.

23. Huth, "Yosemite: The Story of an Idea," in which Raymond's letter to Conness is given in full. The Act of June 30, 1864, is in *13 STAT., 325*, and is given in full in *Laws and Regulations Relating to the Yosemite National Park, California*, 1908.

24. *Report of the Commissioners to Manage the Yosemite Valley and the Mariposa Big Tree Grove*, for the years 1866-1867, Sacramento, State Printer.

25. "The Yosemite Valley and the Mariposa Big Trees: A Preliminary Report (1865) by Frederick Law Olmsted," with an introductory note by Laura Wood Roper, *Landscape Architecture*, October, 1952, 43:1; also, "The Lost Report by Frederick Law Olmsted," *The Living Wilderness*, Winter, 1952-1953.

26. *Hutchings*, 1886, while factually reliable, is nevertheless self-serving and should be read in conjunction with the *Reports of the Commissioners to Manage Yosemite Valley*.

27. James M. Hutchings was married to Elvira B. Sproat in San Francisco, February 2, 1860, by the Reverend Ferdinand C. Ewer (*San Francisco Bulletin*, February 3, 1860).

28. Low vs. Hutchings (1871) 41 Cal. 634; Hutchings vs. Low (1872) 15 Mall (US) 77, 21 L.ed 82.

29. *Report of the Commissioners for 1874-75*.

30. *Hutchings*, 1886.

XIV

THE WHITNEY SURVEY

When the legislature of California established a Geological Survey, most of those who voted for it undoubtedly thought they were setting up an agency that would point out with scientific accuracy just where gold was to be found; nothing thereafter would be left to chance and everyone would quickly become rich. That was not the intention of the Act, however, and nothing in its wording gave any such implication. It was definitely scientific, not utilitarian in purpose, as expressed in its opening section: "to make an accurate and complete Geological Survey of the State, and to furnish maps and diagrams thereof, with a full and scientific description of the rocks, fossils, soils, and minerals, and of its botanical and zoological productions, together with specimens of the same." If this led to a knowledge of the mineral resources of the state, so much the better, but an understanding of the *entire* resources must come first. To achieve the desired results the sponsors of the Survey knew that experienced, scientific direction was required, and this meant the elimination of patronage and politics. The extraordinary thing about the Act is that it did just this, by naming the Director in the Act itself and giving him authority to appoint his assistants. The Act, approved on April 21, 1860, states at the very beginning, "J. D. Whitney is hereby appointed State Geologist."[1]

How did this come about? Someone with high ideals and unusual influence must have been behind it. Such a one was Stephen J. Field, a former member of the state legislature and in 1860 Chief Justice of the State Supreme Court, later a Justice of the U. S. Supreme Court. His motives were beyond suspicion, even when he insisted in putting Whitney's name in the Act. He had long known the Whitney family and had confidence in the integrity as well as in the scientific qualifications of J. D. Whitney. Others played a part in devising the Survey—John Conness, afterwards United States Senator, steered the bill through the legislature—but it was Field's prestige and influence that secured its passage.[2]

Josiah Dwight Whitney, a native of Massachusetts and a graduate of Yale, was forty-one years of age at the time. He had received some European education and had been engaged in geological surveys in New Hampshire and in Iowa and Wisconsin, and already enjoyed a high reputation among men of science. He was well aware of the importance of securing competent men to

The California State Geological Survey, 1863:
Averell, Gabb, Ashburner, Whitney, Hoffmann, King, and Brewer.

assist him in carrying out his new task. His first selection was an especially
fortunate one: William H. Brewer, thirty-two, a native of New York State,
had graduated from the Scientific School at Yale, and he, too, had studied in
Europe. For four years he was Whitney's right-hand man and leader of the
field parties. His letters, composed on the spot from his pocket notebooks,
furnish a day-by-day account of the experiences of the Survey and give a
vivid picture of California in the years 1860-1864.[3] Whitney's second appointment was William Ashburner, whose European education in mining proved
useful in the mineral aspects of the Survey. He became one of the original
group to be appointed Commissioners to Manage the Yosemite Valley and
Mariposa Big Tree Grove. A later appointment, which was to carry forward
the influence of the Whitney Survey for many years, was that of Charles F.
Hoffmann, a young German engineer with a talent for mapmaking.

The Survey began its field work in December, 1860, under Brewer, but it
was not until the summer of 1863 that the group directed its attention to the
Sierra. In May of that year, Brewer and William More Gabb, "our paleontol-

ogist, young, grassy green, but decidedly smart and well posted in his department," made an examination of the Walker Pass region, then moved north
along the foothills, via Millerton, to Hornitas, where Gabb left for San Fran-
cisco to write his report. Brewer went on to Murphys to join Whitney for a
visit to the Calaveras Big Trees. It was now June, and a survey of the High
Sierra was begun that was to continue intensively for the next two summers.
Whitney and Brewer, joined by Hoffmann with horses and mules, entered
Yosemite Valley by way of Big Oak Flat and camped at the foot of Yosemite
Falls. After a general exploration of the Valley, they went up to Porcupine
Flat. From there they climbed a peak about five miles away which they named
Mount Hoffmann, first of the Sierra peaks to be named for a member of the
Survey.[4]

Proceeding by way of Lake Tenaya, they made camp at the Soda Springs
in Tuolumne Meadows. "The river valley here forms a flat nearly a mile wide,
green and grassy, while around is the grandest alpine scenery. It is a most
lovely spot. Several mineral springs are here—cold water charged with car-

Unicorn Peak from Tuolumne Meadows, drawn by Charles F. Hoffmann in 1863.

bonic acid gas, pleasant to the taste." They moved on toward Mono Pass.
Brewer and Hoffmann climbed a high mountain nearby and brought back
such a glowing description that Whitney was inspired to return the next day
with Brewer. They called it "Mount Dana, believing it to be the highest
mountain in the state, except Mt. Shasta." Following the ascent of Mount
Dana, Whitney returned to San Francisco, leaving Brewer and Hoffmann to
make further explorations. First they went to the head of the Lyell Fork of
the Tuolumne. "Picturesque, romantic," Brewer writes in his journal, "but
prosy truth bids me to say that mosquitoes swarmed in myriads." Early in the

Summit of Mount Lyell, as sketched by Charles F. Hoffmann in 1863.

morning they essayed the peak above them. "We cross great slopes all polished like glass by former glaciers. Striking the last great slope of snow, we have only one thousand feet more to climb. In places the snow is soft and we sink two or three feet in it. We toil on for hours; it seems at times as if our breath refuses to strengthen us, we puff and blow so in the thin air. After seven hours of hard climbing we struck the last pinnacle of rock that rises through the snow and forms the summit—only to find it inaccessible. As we had named the other mountain Mount Dana, after the most eminent of *American* geologists, we named this Mount Lyell, after the most eminent of *English* geologists." It seems to us today incredible that two able-bodied men after reaching a point within a few hundred feet of the summit should fail to complete the climb of Mount Lyell. In the history of mountaineering, however, the *appearance* of difficulty in a novel situation has again and again brought about defeat. In this case the explanation seems to be that, in addition to the unaccustomed effects of altitude, the men were tired from slogging through the soft snow and things looked worse than they really were. Since their day hundreds of climbers, many of them quite inexperienced, have made the ascent.

From Tuolumne Meadows Brewer and Hoffmann went over Mono Pass and down to Mono Lake. They found the route a well-traveled one. Trains of pack mules were passing over it nearly every week on the way from Mariposa and Coulterville to Aurora and the mines of the Esmeralda District. After an inspection of the boomtown of Aurora the two continued north to Walker River and returned across the Sierra by Sonora Pass, thence down to the town of Sonora, examining the country on the way, noting particularly the extensive lava formations. Hoffmann, not feeling well, went on to San Francisco, while Brewer joined Whitney, who was staying at Calaveras Grove Hotel with his family. Whitney and Brewer now set out to examine the reputed discoveries of silver that were causing heavy travel over the Ebbetts Pass road. They visited the new town of Silver Mountain, then returned to the Big Trees. Brewer went back into the mountains, this time to Carson Pass. He noted Tragedy Springs and Carson Spur, and climbed a peak from which he could see Lake Tahoe. "I descended," says Brewer, "by getting on a steep slope of snow, down which I came a thousand feet in a few minutes where it had taken two hours' hard labor to get up." Instead of going on down to the Carson Valley, Brewer now decided to go directly to Pyramid Peak. It was but a short distance to Lake Valley and the Placerville Road. He spent a night at Slippery Ford and started alone on the morning of August 20 for the peak. In four hours he reached the top, "with barometer, bag with thermometer, hammer, lunch, and botanical box," and remained for over three hours. "The view is the grandest in this part of the Sierra—on the east, four thousand feet beneath, lies Lake Tahoe, intensely blue; nearer are about a dozen little alpine lakes, of very blue, clear snow water; far in the east are the desolate mountains of Nevada Territory, fading into indistinctness in the blue distance; south are the rugged mountains along the crest of the Sierra, far south of Sonora Pass—a hundred peaks spotted with snow."

Brewer next visited Lake Tahoe. "We are camped in a pretty grove near the Lake House a few rods from the lake," he writes. "It is a quiet Sunday, the first we have observed for four weeks." Quiet! What would he say to today's horrors? He passed around the lake on the Nevada side and at the north came to "a new mining district which is just starting—a new excitement, and people are pouring in." "We passed through the town of Centerville," he continues, "its streets all staked off among the trees, notices of claims of town lots on trees and stumps and stakes, but as yet the *town* is not built. One cabin—hut, I should say—with a brush roof, is the sole representative of the mansions that are to be. Three miles below is Elizabethtown, a town of great pretensions and more actual houses, boasting of two or three." Knoxville, on the Truckee River, was much the same. "A shanty, in the shade of a tree, with roof of brush, has a sign out, 'Union Clothing Store.' I dined today at the 'Union Hotel'—part of the roof was covered with canvas, but most of it with bushes." Over a pass at the head of Squaw Valley (years later to be known to the world for its Olympic ski runs), through forest and across canyons, Brewer came to Michigan Bluff, Forest Hill, and Auburn, and on to Sacramento. He was out of the Sierra, at least for a while.

There now occurred one of those remarkable chance meetings that determine not alone men's careers, but events of considerable importance. It was of very considerable importance in the history of the Sierra, for it marked the

entry of one of its notable figures, Clarence King. Brewer describes the meeting: "On the Sacramento River steamer I noticed two young men conversing
together in low tones, and curiously glancing from time to time at me. Presently they drew near and one of them asked, 'Is your name Brewer?' 'Yes,' I
replied. 'Belong to the California Geological Survey?' 'Yes.' 'Well; I had a
letter of introduction to you, but it was burned up the other day.' He went
on to say that his name was King, that he had been at the Yale Scientific
School and that he and his friend had crossed the plains and the Sierra since
leaving New Haven."[5] The upshot was that King volunteered to join the
Survey as an assistant to Brewer on an exploration of the northern part of the
State. His friend Gardner[6] was temporarily employed by the Army Engineers
for work in San Francisco. The following year he, too, joined the Whitney
Survey and took part in the memorable exploration of the High Sierra in 1864.

The summer of 1864 was indeed a memorable one. For the first time the
high country at the head of the Kern, the Kings, and the San Joaquin was explored and mapped. Brewer, now well-seasoned, was in charge, assisted by the
skilled topographer Hoffmann and the young and vigorous neophytes, King
and Gardner. Hired as packer was Dick Cotter, who didn't know much about
packing, but caught on quickly and proved a tower of strength. Early in June
they headed for the Sierra across the San Joaquin plain, which they found dry
and desolate. "No green thing meets the eye," writes Brewer, "and clouds
of dust filled the air." It was a year of drought, one of the severest recorded
in California. The party entered the mountains from Visalia. At Thomas' Mill
(now Millwood) young sequoias were being cut for fence posts, which is
about all that Sequoia lumber is good for, as the larger trees shatter when
felled. A little higher up they came to great numbers of the Big Trees in what
is now called the General Grant Grove. Brewer describes a horseback ride
even more remarkable than the one in the Calaveras Grove. "We rode into
the fallen tree seventy-six feet and turned around easily. Most of the cavity
is nine feet high and as wide." They came to Big Meadows, climbed a peak to
which they gave the name of Mount Silliman, and descended Sugarloaf Creek
to Roaring River, which they called the South Fork of the Kings. They
camped at the base of a fine conical peak. "Hoffmann and I [Brewer] climbed
this cone. The view was wilder than we have ever seen before. Such a landscape! A hundred peaks in sight over thirteen thousand feet—many very sharp
—deep canyons, cliffs in every direction, sharp ridges almost inaccessible to
man on which human foot has never trod—all combine to produce a view the
sublimity of which is rarely equaled, one which few are privileged to behold."
Brewer's associates insisted on naming the peak for him, Mount Brewer.
Higher peaks were seen not far away to the east and south. One of these they
named Mount Tyndall, "in honor of the distinguished physicist and Alpine
explorer." Another peak "so far as known the culminating peak of the Sierra"

The field party of 1864: Gardner, Cotter, Brewer, and King.

was named Mount Whitney. Still another was named "in honor of Major R. S. Williamson, of the United States Engineers."

All were naturally excited over the discovery of such a group of high peaks —the highest in the land, they felt sure. King begged to be allowed to try to reach the highest of them. Brewer consented, and on July 4 King and Cotter made up their packs for a six-day attempt. Brewer and Gardner accompanied them up to thirteen thousand feet, helping carry their packs, then bade adieu to the adventurers and climbed to the summit for a second visit. The adventures of King and Cotter are left for another chapter, along with King's subsequent efforts to attain the summit of Mount Whitney.

At the end of a week King and Cotter were back and all assembled at Big Meadows, where they were joined by seven soldiers from an army post at Visalia as an escort in case they should encounter Indians, with whom there had been serious trouble in Owens Valley. Brewer and King made a trip to Visalia, where King left the party for another try at Mount Whitney. Upon Brewer's return, the augmented party, now eleven, resumed its explorations. Soon they came upon a camp of prospectors from Owens Valley. "Never before," says Brewer, "were so many white men in this solitude. Three of them were going back, and luckily for us, showed us the way into the canyon of Kings River." There follows the first description of the great Kings Canyon, amplified in the Whitney *Geology* report from the notes of both Brewer and Gardner: "The canyon here is very much like the Yosemite. It is a valley from half a mile to a mile wide at the bottom, about eleven miles long and closed at the lower end by a deep and inaccessible ravine like that below the Yosemite, but deeper and more precipitous. It expands above and branches at its head, and is everywhere surrounded and walled in by grand precipices, broken here and there by side canyons, resembling the Yosemite in its main features. The Kings River canyon rivals and even surpasses the Yosemite in the altitude of its surrounding cliffs, but it has no features so striking as Half Dome, or Tutucanula [El Capitan], nor has it the stupendous waterfalls which make that valley quite unrivalled in beauty."

Several attempts were made to find a way toward the north, but the steep descent into the canyon of the Middle Fork of the Kings was deemed too much for their animals. From a ridge above Granite Basin they could see a huge mass which they named Mount Goddard, "in honor of a Civil Engineer who has done much to advance our knowledge of the geography of California, and who is the author of *Britton & Rey's Map.*" They also saw and named The Palisades, and two nearby peaks which were named for King and Gardner. They turned back to the South Fork canyon and sought a way out toward the east. Following the trail of the Owens Valley prospectors, they worked their way over Kearsarge Pass. "The summit is a very sharp granite ridge, with loose boulders on both sides as steep as they will lie. It is slow, hard work getting animals over such a sliding mass. It is 11,600 feet high, far above trees, barren granite mountains all around, with patches of snow, some of which were some distance below us—the whole scene was one of sublime desolation. Before us, and far beneath us lay Owens Valley." Brewer gives a description of the valley as it was before the days of the Los Angeles Aqueduct: "It lies four thousand to five thousand feet above the sea and is entirely closed in by mountains. On the west the Sierra Nevada rises to over fourteen thousand feet; on the east the Inyo Mountains to twelve thousand or thirteen thousand feet. The Owens River is fed by streams from the Sierra Nevada, runs through a crooked channel through this valley, and empties into Owens Lake. This lake is the color of coffee, has no outlet, and is a nearly saturated solution of salt and alkali. The Sierra Nevada catches all the rains and clouds from the west—to the east are deserts—so, of course, this valley sees but little rain, but where streams come down from the Sierra they spread out and great meadows of green grass occur."[7]

For three days the Brewer party trudged up the Owens Valley in heat that nearly used them up. Copious hot springs are mentioned, and a lava table nearly spanning the valley. At Round Valley they turned left and climbed up to a pass, now known as Mono Pass (not to be confused with the one farther north near Mount Dana), that led to the San Joaquin. It was a blind trail, but they were piloted by one of their soldier escort who had been there a year earlier pursuing hostile Indians. They crossed the pass by a little side canyon, invisible at first. "It is very high," writes Brewer, "nearly or quite twelve thousand feet on the summit. Horses cross over on the snow." They continued down to Vermilion Valley, where they were glad to lay over in pleasant surroundings for a few days while four of the soldiers went down by an obscure trail to Fort Miller for supplies. But Brewer could not remain idle and decided to have another try at Mount Goddard. "It was very desirable to get on this, as it commands a wide view, and from it we could get the topography of a large region." They got as far as horses could go, and then, from a ten-thousand-foot camp, Brewer and Hoffmann, with Cotter and one of the soldiers named Spratt, started for the mountain. After nine hours of hard going, Brewer and Hoffmann resigned and turned back. That night they made a bivouac by a burning stump, with a scanty supper of dry bread and drier jerked beef. Back at the Vermilion Valley camp next day, they found Cotter, who, at double their pace, had arrived ahead of them. Spratt did not come in until nightfall. The two climbers had come within three hundred feet of the top before time ran out on them. They traveled all night, without food, as they had eaten it all the first day, an experience that I seem to recall has been repeated on later occasions.

The soldiers came back from Fort Miller with an abundance of provisions and, after a brief rest, the whole party packed up and started across rough country for the North Fork of the San Joaquin. There they noted a remarkable dome, likened by Brewer to "the top of a gigantic balloon struggling to get up through the rock." Hoffmann had developed a very sore leg, Brewer himself began to feel run down, it rained hard all one night—miseries and discomforts were piling up. On August 23 they reached Clark's ranch at Wawona. There they met Mr. and Mrs. Ashburner and Olmsted. "You can imagine the joyous meeting. We were a hard-looking set—ragged, clothes patched with old flour bags, poor—I had lost thirty pounds—horses poor." The first great exploration of the High Sierra had been accomplished; a way had been opened for pack trips and knapsackers for generations to come.

The indomitable Brewer, leaving Hoffmann in care of the others, accompanied Olmsted to Yosemite and on up to the high country of the Tuolumne. They rode horseback nearly to the summit of the peak just south of Mount Dana and named it for their friend Professor Oliver Wolcott Gibbs of Harvard. "Strange enough," says Brewer in his notebook, "we saw a group of persons on Mount Dana, clear against the sky. These turned out to be the party of a Mr. St. Johns, including a little girl six years old and a man sixty-two years old and lame. We met them at the Soda Springs next day."[8] On returning to Clark's they found Hoffmann no better. Brewer, King, Gardner, and Cotter carried him on a litter to Mariposa, whence by carriage and river steamer he got to San Francisco.

The work of the Survey was by no means completed, but the ambitious program of the early days could not be carried out. Funds were provided by the legislature only intermittently. Whitney wrote to his brother in February, 1866, "It is terribly up-hill work to drag this concern which I have been pulling at for five years, up the hill of difficulty. It is hard enough work to do to carry on the Survey even if it were appreciated and no obstacles were placed in my way. While I could not help being secretly gratified, or at least relieved, if the Survey were stopped, yet my scientific instincts make me fight for its continuance." For a few more years money was provided and the work went ahead, but with a changing personnel. Brewer went East to become Professor of Agriculture at Yale; King and Gardner did a little more work for the Survey, then engaged in other surveys in the West; Cotter, after another summer with King, went to Alaska before settling permanently in Montana; Hoffmann recovered and produced a series of maps that set a new standard and influenced cartography in America for years to come. Whitney continued to be the titular head of the California Geological Survey and supervised its publications, the final ones printed at his own expense. Most influential of these were the series of Yosemite Guide-Books, which became the source of quotations in other books about Yosemite and in the letters of tourists for many years. The guidebooks were preceded by a handsome "gift book" in an edition of 250 copies, which contained original photographs by

W. Harriss, 1867

Summit of Mount Hoffmann: Charles F. Hoffmann with transit.

W. Harriss, 1867

State Geological Survey party at Tuolumne Soda Springs.

W. Harriss, 1867

Cathedral Peak from Tuolumne Soda Springs.

C. E. Watkins of Yosemite scenes and four by W. Harriss of the upper country. One of the latter, taken near the summit of Mount Hoffmann, shows Hoffmann appropriately on the mountain that had been named for him. The Harriss photographs were taken during a continuation of the Survey under direction of Hoffmann in the summer of 1867. The final fieldwork of the Survey was conducted under Hoffmann and W. A. Goodyear and involved an ascent, in 1870, of Tower Peak, north of Yosemite, as well as the hot contest over the ascent of Mount Whitney, of which we will say more later. The breach between Professor Whitney and the California legislature, coupled with the antagonism of Governor Newton Booth, brought the Survey to an end in 1874. The fault was not all on one side, for Whitney was a stubborn man, often opinionated. Nevertheless, he performed a great service in providing a survey free from politics and venality and up to the best scientific standards of the time. Despite his scientific training, perhaps because of it, Whitney made some very positive statements that were very positively wrong. We can excuse his premature statement about Half Dome, that it was "perfectly inaccessible, being probably the only one of all the prominent points about the Yosemite which never has been, and never will be trodden by human foot," but when he declares that it had been "split in two, one-half having been engulfed at the time of the formation of the chasm at its base," he was jumping to a conclusion based on insufficient evidence. The "chasm" was an erroneous assumption. One of the most controversial of Whitney's assertions relates to the "Calaveras Skull" and the question of the antiquity of man in the Sierra Nevada.[9] In July, 1866, Whitney wrote to his brother from San Francisco: "The great excitement now at the office is the discovery of a human skull at a depth 153 feet below a series of volcanic beds with intercalated gravels. I have just returned from the locality, and we have the skull at the office. It is a bona fide find of the greatest interest, all the particulars of which I shall work up with the greatest care." But was it a bona fide find? And did the particulars worked up so carefully by Professor Whitney prove anything? Whitney read a paper before a meeting of the California Academy of Natural Sciences in which he gave an account of the skull's provenance.[10] "It was taken from a shaft," he said, "sunk on a mining claim at Altaville, near Angel's in Calaveras County, by Mr. James Matson. By him it was given to Mr. Scribner, of Angel's, and by Mr. Scribner to Dr. Jones." A lawyer, bearing in mind the rules of evidence, might at least raise an eyebrow at this sequence. Notwithstanding initial skepticism, a number of noted scientists made exhaustive examinations both of the provenance and of the testimony of the skull itself.[11] The general conclusion seems to be that the skull that came into Professor Whitney's hands was not that of a man of Tertiary times, but more likely was that from a cave burial, ancient perhaps, but not from a remote geologic age. It may have come from Matson's mine shaft, but whether it got there by accident or as a hoax cannot be determined. It may be that the skull Whitney received was an accidental or even intentional substitution. In short, Whitney's elaborate presentation has failed to convince modern paleontologists that man existed in the Sierra in Tertiary times.

Before taking leave of Professor Whitney let us revert to an incident in which he appears in a better light, if not on firmer ground. At about half-past two o'clock on the morning of March 26, 1872, there was felt over nearly all of California a severe earthquake shock. As reports came in it was found that the heaviest shock and greatest damage seemed to be in the neighborhood of Lone Pine at the eastern base of the Sierra. Whitney proceeded at once to join a field party that was operating in that area and to gather all the data he could about the earthquake. He interviewed many people and examined the fissures and subsidences that were evident for many miles along the base of the Sierra. "In one place," he reported, "an area of ground two to three hundred feet wide has sunk to a depth of twenty or thirty feet, leaving vertical walls on each side." There were marked displacements of roads and fences and there were evidences of slides and rockfalls on the face of the mountain escarpment.[12] Whitney's thorough investigation of the phenomena and his deductions therefrom were among his most useful contributions to earth science. The earthquake itself was a clear demonstration of the forces that served to raise the Sierra to its great height.

NOTES AND REFERENCES

1. Complete text of the Act is in Whitney Survey, *Geology*, vol. I, 1865 (*Farquhar* No. 6).

2. Edwin Tenney Brewster, *Life and Letters of Josiah Dwight Whitney*, Boston: Houghton Mifflin, 1909.

3. *Brewer Journal*.

4. This chapter is based principally on the *Brewer Journal* and on the publications of the Whitney Survey (*Farquhar* Nos. 6 and 7); and occasionally on Brewer's notebooks (in BL).

5. Letter from Brewer quoted by Rossiter W. Raymond, *Clarence King Memoirs*, New York, published for the Century Association by G. P. Putnam's Sons, 1905.

6. At the time of the Whitney Survey, James Terry Gardner spelled his name as given here. In later life he adopted an earlier family spelling, "Gardiner." Biography in *American Journal of Science*, 1912.

7. Owens Valley is Mary Austin's "Land of Little Rain" (Mary Austin, *The Land of Little Rain*, 1903; new edition, illustrated by Ansel Adams, Boston: Houghton Mifflin, 1950).

8. Lawyer St. John, of Big Oak Flat, with his family and others (Brewer letter to Whitney, November 29, 1868, in BL).

9. Whitney's final account is in his *The Auriferous Gravels of the Sierra Nevada of California*, 1880, which contains a double-page engraving of the skull.

The skull itself, or at least the one that Whitney thought was the original find, is now in the Peabody Museum at Harvard.

10. *Proceedings*, July 16, 1866. The name of the organization was later changed to the California Academy of Sciences.

11. William H. Holmes, "Review of the Evidence Relating to Auriferous Gravel Man in California," *Smithsonian Institution Report for 1899*; William J. Sinclair, "Recent Investigations Bearing on the Question of the Occurrence of Neocene Man in the Auriferous Gravels of the Sierra Nevada," *University of California Publications in American Archaeology and Ethnology*, 1908, 7:2.; John C. Merriam, "The True Story of the Calaveras Skull," *Sunset Magazine*, February, 1910; and not forgetting *The Pliocene Skull* by Bret Harte.

12. J. D. Whitney, "The Owen's Valley Earthquake," *Overland Monthly*, August and September, 1872. (Whitney consistently, and erroneously, puts an apostrophe before the *s* both in *Owens* and in *Kings*.)

View from Mount Brewer
across Kings–Kern Divide to Mount Tyndall and Mount Whitney.

XV

CLARENCE KING'S MOUNTAINEERING

When Clarence King and Dick Cotter bade good-bye to their companions on the shoulder of Mount Brewer they began a new era in American mountaineering. Never before had anyone attempted to traverse such a complex maze of ridges and canyons as those that confronted them. To venture into such unknown country, scantily equipped and without experience on steep snow and precipitous rock, required more than ordinary courage. Two important factors were in their favor, however; they were in splendid physical condition, and they had unbounded determination. There are two accounts of the five-day trip that followed. Best known is the one in King's *Mountaineering in the Sierra Nevada*,[1] but there is an earlier account in the Whitney Survey, *Geology*,[2] stated to be "nearly in King's own words." Taken together, the two accounts afford a fairly clear indication of King's route. In *Mountaineering*, actualities are frequently obscured by thrills. A few examples: "The summit of the ridge continued to be broken by fantastic pinnacles, leaving us no hope of making our way along it—We continued more than half the afternoon in descending a thousand feet of broken, precipitous slope—The gorge below us seemed utterly impassable—From this cruel dilemma the cross divide seemed our only hope—As we advanced, the snow sloped more and more steeply up toward the crags, till by and by it became quite dangerous." The finale is most exciting. "There was no foothold above us—to turn back was to give up in defeat—About thirty feet directly over our heads was another shelf which seemed to offer at least a temporary way upward—On its edge were two or three spikes of granite—I thought of but one possible plan, to lasso one of these blocks, and to climb hand-over-hand up the rope—At last I made a lucky throw—I drew the noose close and began to climb very slowly—A few pulls brought me to the edge of the shelf, when, throwing my arms around the granite spike, I swung my body upon the shelf and lay down to rest—Cotter came up the rope in his very muscular way without stopping to rest." They came out upon a thin blade of a ridge, where they dared not walk, but got astride, "now and then holding our breath when loose masses rocked under our weight." They descended to the basin at the head of the Kern by a series of rope-downs, with very inadequate belaying, saved at one point by a fortuitously placed gooseberry bush.[3]

The "official" account, given in the *Geology* report and stripped of the stage effects, is more comprehensible. They climbed down the eastern slope of the ridge that extended from Mount Brewer, reached the bottom of a cliff, and went rapidly down a snowslope to a frozen lake in an amphitheater above which were inaccessible crags. For six hours they climbed down over polished granite beside a shallow current of water that flowed from the lake into Kings River Canyon. Then, up over a long debris slope and across snowfields into another amphitheater, the southern wall of which was the divide between the Kings and the Kern rivers. Next morning they cut steps for three hours, then climbed on rocks to "a very bad ravine," where their "reata came into play." They took turns in climbing the length of the rope and reached the top about noon. They walked along the ridge until they discovered some shelves that offered a way down. "I tied the reata firmly about my body," King says, "and Cotter lowered me down to the first shelf; he then sent down the precious barometer and our packs. Next, he made a fast loop in the lasso, hooked it over a point of rock and came down hand-over-hand, whipping the rope off the rock. This operation was repeated, not without considerable danger, until at last the bottom was safely reached. At the foot was a beautiful lake, half a mile long."

Whether there are sufficient clues to determine King's route is a question we leave to future inquisitive and active mountaineers. After all, the important point is that King and Cotter succeeded in crossing the divide into the Kern River basin and that they succeeded in reaching the mountain that was their goal.

Let us, then, accompany them on their next great adventure, the ascent of Mount Tyndall. Here it is not difficult to follow their route, even if one remains skeptical about King's adjectives. Starting before dawn, they clambered over blocks of enormous size until they reached smaller ones, which served as a sort of stairway. They came to a long snowslope, whose surface was pierced by knobs of granite. They took a look farther to the east, but found it too precipitous for climbing, so they headed straight up for the summit.[4] They climbed up alternately smooth faces of granite and "fearfully steep slopes of ice." After various fearsome encounters with steepness, they reached a point where they could pause to enjoy the view. "The wall of our mountain sank abruptly to the left, opening for the first time an outlook to the eastward. The summit peaks to the north were piled in titanic confusion. Clustered upon the shelves and plateaus below were several frozen lakes, and in all directions swept magnificent fields of snow." They were now not more than five hundred feet from the summit. "But if Nature had intended to secure the summit from all assailants, she could not have planned her defences better; for the smooth granite wall which rose above the snowslope continued, apparently, quite round the peak, and we looked in great anxiety to see if there was not one place where it might be climbed." There appeared to be one, "a great ice-column frozen in a niche of the bluff." Up this they cut toe-holds, "in constant dread lest our ladder should break off." At last King was able to roll out upon a smooth surface of granite and watch Cotter climb up to join him. They now had an easy slope to the summit, where King rang his hammer on the topmost rock and "reverently named the grand peak *Mount Tyndall*." No question about it, this is "literature," and in the *Atlantic Monthly* and in King's perennially popular book it has provided thrills for thousands of readers. But, lest it should give a false impression of climbing in the Sierra Nevada, the parallel account from the *Geology* report, "nearly in King's own words," must be cited: "The summit was reached, without serious diffi-culty, after some risky climbing."

It was at once apparent that they were not on the highest peak in the range. Two slightly higher peaks stood not far away. "That which looked highest of all was a cleanly cut helmet of granite, lying about six miles south. Mount Whitney, as we afterwards called it in honor of our chief, is probably the highest land within the United States. The summit looks glorious, but inaccessible." Provisions were low, and, since there was no hope of reaching the great peak at this time, they packed up the instruments and started down. To their consternation they found their ice ladder broken to pieces. Forced to look for another way down, they decided to try the southwestern side. It seemed to them to resemble the inner curve of a great horseshoe. The diffi-culties of the descent, as described by King, are hard to account for.[5] Per-haps one should accept the offer King once made to a friend who challenged some of his statements, that he would "throw off five degrees for a flat ac-ceptance, or, otherwise he would conduct him personally to the scene."[6] Those who have been on the scene would, I believe, demand more than five degrees. Even after the descent, the way back to the Brewer camp across the Divide was not without its adventures, but, dangers and difficulties overcome, they received a hearty welcome from their comrades. Brewer gave an ac-colade: "It was by far the greatest feat of strength and endurance that has yet been performed on the Survey." We may well forgive Clarence King his literary trimmings and voice our concurrence.

King was not content, however, to leave matters as they stood. On his journey to Visalia with Brewer he pleaded for another opportunity to try for the highest peak. Brewer consented and helped him obtain an escort of two soldiers from the cavalry post. They rode over a trail recently con-structed by a cattleman named Hockett which led up the South Fork of the Kaweah and on eastward. "Where the trail crosses the main Kern," according to the *Geology* report, the river is twenty-five or thirty yards wide; the water is clear and cold, and abundantly supplied with trout." The trail had not been completed beyond that point, and "it was necessary to continue the exploration without any other guides than the eye and the compass."

Without map or place names to go by it is not easy to determine King's route toward Mount Whitney. A bare granite peak is mentioned, "called Sheep Rock, from the great number of mountain sheep found in this vicinity," evidently the Sheep Mountain that seven years later was to cause King so much embarrassment. It was, in his opinion, about eight miles south of Mount Whitney and "the termination of this high portion of the Sierra." By some unidentified pass King crossed the main crest and "worked for three days before he could reach the base of the mountain, whose summit he was endeavoring to attain." "The highest point reached by King," continues the account in the *Geology* report, "was between 300 and 400 feet lower than the culminating point of the mountain." It is fruitless to speculate upon the exact spot at which King turned back. Had he not been so obsessed with the notion of inaccessibility he might then and there have made the first ascent of Mount Whitney. But he seems to have had a genius for finding the wrong routes. What became of the two soldiers and the animals is not related. Presumably they did not cross the crest, but remained on the west side where there was plenty of good grass, and, ah, the trout!

There is no record of King's return trip to Visalia. There he enjoyed two days' rest and accustomed himself to "such articles as chairs and newspapers, and to watching with unexpected pleasure the few village girls who flitted about." His ride to Mariposa, subject of the chapter, "Kaweah's Run," in *Mountaineering*, may be passed over as amusing fiction, except that there actually was a horse named "Kaweah." In one way or another King reached Mariposa, where he was presently joined by Brewer and the rest of the field party.

As soon as they had returned from taking the ailing Hoffmann to San Francisco, King and Gardner assumed the task of running a boundary survey around Yosemite's walls for the newly established Yosemite Grant. The reliable Cotter was with them. In *Mountaineering* King gives some vivid and perceptive descriptions of Yosemite's outstanding features as seen first from the north side, then from the south. But, of all the objects that inspired King's enthusiasm, the one that attracted him most was a peak which Whitney and his men called "The Obelisk" from its peculiar shape as seen from the north rim. It was shortly afterwards named Mount Clark. He longed to climb it, and made up his mind to attempt it "at all hazards." The boundary survey completed, he set out with Cotter on the climbing adventure. But this time they were not to test their strength and courage upon high-angle rocks. It was November, and the first winter storm struck with full force. They retreated. The field season of 1864 was at an end.

After an interval in the East and a surveying assignment in Arizona, King returned to Yosemite early in the summer of 1866, eager to renew his explorations. The "Obelisk" still fascinated him, and one afternoon in July he and

Ansel Adams

Mount Clark.

Gardner made camp "in the self-same spot where Cotter and I had bivouacked in the storm." "There was in our hope of scaling this point." he says, "something more than a mere desire to master a difficult peak. It was a station of great topographical value, the apex of many triangles, and, more than all, would command a grander view of the Merced region than any other summit." The story, told in King's best manner in *Mountaineering*, is condensed as follows: "At gray dawn Gardner and I were up and cooking our rasher of bacon, and soon had shouldered our instruments and started for the top. At last we struggled up to what we had all along believed to be the summit, and found ourselves only on a minor turret, the great needle still a hundred feet above. From rock to rock and crevice to crevice we made our way up a fractured edge until within fifty feet of the top, and here its sharp angle rose smooth and vertical. One step more and we stood together on a little detached pinnacle, where, by steadying ourselves against the sharp, vertical Obelisk edge, we could rest. About seven feet across the open head of a cul-de-sac (a mere recess in the west face) was a vertical crack riven into the granite not more than three feet wide, but as much as eight feet deep; in it were wedged a few loose boulders; below, it opened out into space. At the head of this crack a rough crevice led to the summit. Summoning nerve, I knew I could make the leap, but the life and death question was whether the debris would give way under my weight, and leave me struggling in the smooth recess, sure to fall and be dashed to atoms. Two years ago we had longed to climb that peak, and now within a few yards of the summit no weak-heartedness could stop us. There was no discussion, but planting my foot on the brink, I sprang, my side brushing the rough projecting crag. The debris crumbled and moved. I clutched both sides of the cleft, relieving all possible weight from my feet. The rocks wedged themselves again, and I was safe. Gardner followed, and we sprang up the rocks like chamois, and stood on the top shouting for joy."

It is interesting to compare Gardner's account of the same episode: "Passing the instruments up from one to another, we slowly worked our way up to within a short distance of the summit; then the face we were climbing became perfectly smooth and vertical. We moved along on a little shelf about three inches wide till we got to the edge round which we could look onto the other side of the thin flat wall of granite. Here was our only chance of reaching the summit. A little smooth knob protruded from the precipice face, and beyond it, but out of stepping distance, was a crack in an angle of the rock, and in it two or three loose stones had become jammed. One might possibly step on the knob and by a strong sure jump get half of one foot into the crack and then climb up. We looked at the smooth little knob and wondered if we should slip, and we looked at the trifling foothold at the other end of the perilous leap, and we looked for one instant down the fifteen hundred feet which it overhung. Then we looked at our instruments and thought of the results if we succeeded. It was, I think, duty's call that nerved us. That leap, like most dangers, seemed more perilous after it was made than before; it was not the length of the spring—that was easy—but to light in exact balance on a projecting rock that scarcely held half of one foot, while the remainder of the body hung over a precipice 1500 ft. deep, was a thing requiring most exact judgment. Another winter's frost may break those stones caught in the crack and then Mt. Clark is inaccessible."[7]

Gardner took note of the view in more detail than did King. "Our view of the southern Sierra," he continued, "was very fine. In the extreme distance, yet clear and prominent, was the double-peaked summit of Kaweah Mountain, always most easily distinguished of the southern group." Mount Goddard was visible, and several dark peaks east of it, almost as high. But the peak that seems to have attracted most attention was Mammoth Mountain, which Gardner calls "one of the most striking peaks in the Sierra, from its great size and from the needle-like pinnacles that rise from a mountain at its southern end. King names them the Minarets."[8]

On the descent the perilous leap was accomplished without mishap. King reported, "We sprang strongly, struck firmly and were safe. We worked patiently down the east face, wound among blocks and pinnacles of the lower descent, and hurried through moraines to camp, well pleased that our Obelisk had not vanquished us."

From their base camp on Illilouette Creek they explored further among the Merced Peaks, then crossed to the San Joaquin and followed up the North Fork of that river. They made an attempt to climb Mount Ritter, but failed on account of unfavorable weather.[9] King said that he "climbed to a point about as high as Mount Dana, and had still above him an inaccessible peak some 400 or 500 feet high." Inaccessible, again! Whitney records that "Messrs. King and Gardner discovered a bed of ice on the east slope of Mount Ritter. But it is doubtful," he adds, "whether these residual masses of ice can with propriety be called glaciers; they have no geological significance as such at the present time, however interesting they may be as possible relics of a once general glaciation of the highest part of the range."[10] Thus both the ascent of Mount Ritter and the identification of glaciers had to wait for John Muir.

Before concluding his work with the Whitney Survey at the end of the summer of 1866, King conducted a surveying party to Tuolumne Meadows. They climbed Mount Dana twice and spent a cold night in their blankets near the summit of Mount Conness.[11] King followed the canyon of the Tuolumne as far as he could, "to where the river precipitated itself down in a grand fall, over a mass of rock so rounded on the edge, that it was impossible to approach near enough to look over into the chasm below, the walls on each side being too steep to be climbed."[12]

Mount Langley ("False Mount Whitney") at left, from Lone Pine.

Ansel Adams

Although no longer with Whitney's California Survey, but engaged in initiating his own Survey of the Fortieth Parallel, Clarence King's mountaineering in the Sierra Nevada was not quite ended.[13] In June, 1871, leaving his field party to carry on their work in Wyoming, he entrained to San Francisco to purchase supplies. On his way back to Wyoming he made a detour. He had never relinquished the hope that he might be the first to stand on the summit of Mount Whitney, and now thought he saw his opportunity. He took the stage through Carson Valley and on through Owens Valley, arriving at Lone Pine the second day. "For two days storm-curtains hung low about the Sierra base," then the sun came through the clouds and he could see "the sharp terrible crest of Whitney." He remembered "the impossibility of making a climb up the northern precipices and at once chose the more southern gorge" for his approach. In the morning, with Paul Pinson, a man whom he engaged at Lone Pine as a companion, and a boy to take care of the horses, he rode to where the climbing began. All day they toiled up, with heavy packs, to a bivouac in an alpine grove. The next morning began with a clear sky, but before long mist began to float around "the brow of Mount Whitney, forming a gray helmet." Up over snow and rocks they climbed until "above us but thirty feet rose a crest, beyond which we saw nothing. I dared not think it the summit till we stood there, and Mount Whitney was under our feet." This was all very dramatic, but Clarence could not resist the temptation to top it with an additional touch: "Close beside us a small mound of rock was piled upon the peak, and solidly built into it an Indian arrow-shaft, pointed due west."

It was perhaps an unwarranted assumption on King's part that because of the presence of an arrow his predecessor must have been an Indian. It was not at all in character for an Indian to make a pile of rocks and put an arrow in it. Actually, the pile of rocks was almost certain proof that a white man had been there before Clarence King. Indeed, Hoffmann had told Brewer that same year that he had met a man who claimed that he had been on Mount Whitney and offered to pilot him up.[14] But for King this was the crowning achievement of his mountaineering adventures. His description of the view from the summit is superb and undoubtedly reflects what he saw, even if his identifications were at fault. "Sombre storm-clouds and their even gloomier shadows darkened the northern sea of peaks. Only a few bars of sudden light flashed in upon granite and fields of ice. The rocky tower of Mount Tyndall, thurst up through rolling billows, caught for a moment the full light, and then sank into darkness and mist." But it was not Mount Tyndall that he saw, but, ironically, the true Mount Whitney. For he was not on Mount Whitney at all, as will be shown in a subsequent chapter.

NOTES AND REFERENCES

1. Clarence King, *Mountaineering in the Sierra Nevada*, 1872 and later editions (*Farquhar* No. 12). Some of the chapters, including those on Mount Tyndall, were published in the *Atlantic Monthly* in 1871.

2. Whitney Survey, *Geology*, vol. I, 1865 (*Farquhar* No. 6). The passages cited are substantially the same in the subsequent Whitney Survey, *Yosemite Guide-Book*, 1869 (*Farquhar* No. 7).

3. This is the earliest record in the Sierra of the practice of roping-down.

4. The Sierra Club *Climber's Guide* lists five routes up Mount Tyndall. The one climbed by King and Cotter is rated Class 3, "some exposed climbing requiring the use of hands." The northeastern route, rejected by King, was first climbed in 1935, by William F. Loomis and Marjory B. Farquhar.

5. I once traversed the mountain by approximately the same route as King's. I do not recall any particular difficulty.—F. P. F.

6. James D. Hague, *Clarence King Memoirs*, New York: published for The Century Association, by G. P. Putnam's Sons, 1905.

7. Copy of Gardner's journal, supplied by Mrs. Charles T. Fayerweather, of New Lebanon, N. Y. (in BL).

8. "Mammoth Mountain" is not the one presently so called. It probably refers to the Ritter–Banner–Davis–Rodgers group as seen from Mount Clark, before Ritter was singled out for a separate name.

9. *Yosemite Guide-Book.*

10. J. D. Whitney, "The Climatic Changes of Later Geologic Times," *Contributions to American Geology*, vol. II, Cambridge, Mass.: Museum of Comparative Zoology, 1882.

11. Notes in the Whitney papers, Museum of Comparative Zoology, Cambridge, Mass.

12. *Yosemite Guide-Book.*

13. The definitive biography of Clarence King, is by Thurman Wilkins, New York: Macmillan, 1958.

14. Manuscript note by William H. Brewer (in BL).

XVI

JOHN MUIR AND THE RANGE OF LIGHT

Then it seemed to me the Sierra should be called not the Nevada or Snowy Range, but the Range of Light. And after ten years spent in the heart of it, rejoicing and wondering, bathing in the glorious floods of light, seeing the sunbursts of morning among the icy peaks, the noonday radiance on the trees and rocks and snow, the flush of the alpenglow, and a thousand dashing waterfalls with their marvelous abundance of irised spray, it still seems to me above all others the Range of Light, the most divinely beautiful of all the mountain chains I have ever seen.

JOHN MUIR

To Muir[1] all was order and beauty, from the grandest features of the sculptured mountains to the minutest flowers. Instead of theorizing about origins and processes he examined the results in all their smallest detail, following streams upward to their sources, looking critically into the structure of rocks. His conclusions were based on observed phenomena, which led him to declare: "In the beginning of the long glacial winter, the lofty Sierra seems to have consisted of one vast undulated wave, in which a thousand separate mountains, with their domes and spires, their innumerable canyons and lake basins, lay concealed. In the development of these, the Master Builder chose for a tool, not the earthquake nor lightning to rend asunder, not the stormy torrent nor eroding rain, but the tender snow-flowers, noiselessly falling through unnumbered seasons, the offspring of the sun and sea."[2]

With allowance for the exuberance of discovery and the exalted vision of a poet, Muir's concept of the development of the Sierra by orderly process and predetermined forms was far nearer the truth as now conceived than the pronouncements of the learned scientist, Professor Whitney, who declared that "a more absurd theory was never advanced than that by which it was sought to ascribe to glaciers the sawing out of these vertical walls and the rounding of the domes. This theory, based on entire ignorance of the whole subject, may be dropped without wasting any more time upon it. The theory of erosion not being admissible to account for the formation of Yosemite Valley, we have to fall back on one of those movements of the earth's crust to which the primal forms of the mountain valleys are due." In short, "the bottom of the Valley sank down to an unknown depth, owing to the support being withdrawn from underneath, during some of those convulsive movements which must have attended the upheaval of so extensive and elevated a chain." Muir was called "a mere sheepherder, an ignoramus."[3]

But the "sheepherder" had eyes to see and vision far beyond that of the pedant. His was no superficial geology, but a patient, persistent search for truth evolved from the evidence before him. There were no imaginary cataclysms, no catastrophes of Nature. Everything that Muir saw testified to orderly processes that exemplified eternal Principle. "Such is Yosemite," he wrote, "the noblest of Sierra temples, everywhere expressing the working of Divine harmonious law, yet so little understood that it has been regarded as an 'exceptional creation,' or rather *exceptional destruction* accomplished by violent and mysterious forces."[4]

How did it come about that John Muir, the "sheepherder," attained such insight? He was indeed momentarily a sheepherder, but that occupation was merely a fortuitous excuse for reaching a desired goal. The young Scotsman— he was then thirty years old—had made a brief visit to Yosemite immediately upon his arrival in California in 1868 and could hardly wait for an opportunity to return to the Sierra. The following year the opportunity occurred when a sheep rancher, Pat Delaney, offered Muir the job of taking a band of sheep to the high country to escape the summer drought. He had merely to act as a supervisor; an experienced sheepman and a good sheepdog would take care of the daily routine. It was agreed that Muir should have plenty of time for studying plants and rocks and scenery.

Most of the months of June and July were spent in the region of Yosemite Creek, with climbs of Mount Hoffmann and North Dome, and a quick trip to Yosemite Valley. There was an experience at the brink of Yosemite Fall not recommended for neophytes of less nerve than Muir: "I took off my shoes and stockings and worked my way cautiously down alongside the rushing flood, keeping my feet and hands pressed firmly on the polished rock. The booming, roaring water, rushing past close to my head, was very exciting." He wanted to get down farther where he could see the full length of the fall. "The slope looked dangerously smooth and steep, and the swift roaring flood beneath, overhead, and beside me was very nerve-trying. I therefore concluded not to venture farther, but did nevertheless. Tufts of artemisia were growing in clefts of rock nearby, and I filled my mouth with the bitter leaves, hoping they might help to prevent giddiness. Then, with a caution not known in ordinary circumstances, I crept down safely to the little ledge. Here I obtained a perfectly free view down into the heart of the snowy, chanting throng of comet-like streamers, into which the body of the fall soon separates."[5]

He moved on with the sheep to the Tuolumne Meadows. He climbed Mount Dana and descended Bloody Canyon to Mono Lake. The climax was an ascent of Cathedral Peak, during which he seems to have taken equal in-

John Muir.

terest in the abundance of flowers and the structure of the peak. "The body of the Cathedral is nearly square and the roof slopes are wonderfully regular and symmetrical, the ridge trending northeast and southwest. This direction has apparently been determined by structure joints in the granite. The gable on the northeast end is magnificent in size and simplicity. The front is adorned with many pinnacles and a tall spire of curious workmanship. Here too the joints in the rock are seen to have played an important part in determining their forms and size and general arrangement." And in contrast, "here at last in front of the Cathedral is blessed cassiope, ringing her thousands of sweet-toned bells, the sweetest church music I ever enjoyed."[6] Thus did Muir characteristically mingle the senses, rejoicing in whatever expressed order and beauty.

Muir summarizes the results of his first summer: "The best gains of this trip were the lessons of unity and inter-relation of all the features of the landscape revealed in general views. The lakes and meadows are located just where the ancient glaciers bore heaviest at the foot of the steepest parts of their channels, and of course their longest diameters are approximately parallel with the belts of forests growing in long curving lines on the lateral and medial moraines, and in broad outspreading fields on the terminal beds deposited toward the end of the ice period when the glaciers were receding. How interesting everything is! Every rock, mountain, stream, plant, lake, forest, garden, bird, beast, insect seems to call and invite us to come and learn something of its history and relationship."[7] Although at the moment he did not see how he could accept this invitation, nevertheless, so strong was the call that he did find a way and spent the next six years continuously and intensively studying these rocks and plants and birds, even insects, so enthralling were the lessons they taught him.

Yosemite drew Muir as if by a magnet. In November of that year, 1869, he made his way to the Valley and applied to Hutchings for a subsistence job, as he expressed it, "to feed sows and turkeys, build henroosts, laying-boxes, etc. Also to take charge of the ladies and to build a sawmill."[8] The ladies that first year seem to have consisted of young Mrs. Elvira Hutchings, in whom Muir found a companionate lover of flowers; Florence, five-year-old daughter of the house (she was the first white child born in Yosemite), "a little black-eyed witch of a girl," whom he nicknamed "Squirrel"; and Mrs. Sproat, Elvira's mother, "nurse, cook, and domestic manager of hotel and home," who made "memorable muffins." In such company John passed a glorious snowbound winter with enough time off from his duties to explore the Valley and its walls and to build for himself a cabin on Yosemite Creek. "Near where it first gathers its beaten waters at the foot of the fall, I dug a small ditch and brought a stream into the cabin, entering at one end and flowing out the other with just current enough to allow it to sing and warble in low, sweet tones, delightful at night while I lay in bed."[9]

Spring came slowly, interrupted by snowstorms now and then, which only served to expand the falls to greater grandeur when the sun shone again. Soon Muir was making quick excursions to the heights. On June 27 he writes in his journal, "Arose betimes and walked to the top of Sentinel Dome. Had a fine view of the ever-glorious Sierra crest. I walked to Starr King, passing the old moraine on the banks of Illilouette Fall. And I walked above Nevada Fall into Little Yosemite. I made a memorable descent of the Nevada cliff on the left."[10] Two days later he again went to Sentinel Dome, with Judge Colby,[11] and camped and saw the sunrise. And now came the tourists, to whom he expounded his glacier theories, in contradiction of the pronouncements of the State Geologist. One extraordinary tourist came that summer and saw so much in humans as well as scenery that she settled down to write a novel. Thérèse Yelverton, who claimed with good sanction to be Viscountess Avonmore, saw so much that was unusual and romantic in the persons of John Muir and little Florence Hutchings that she made them the hero and heroine of her novel, which she called "Zanita" (an improvised contraction of *manzanita*), raising her heroine to a maturity far beyond her years and an endowment beyond plausibility. "Kenmuir," the hero, was a curious blend of fact and distortion. She describes him, "with open blue eyes of honest questioning, and glorious auburn hair. His figure was about five feet nine, well knit, and bespoke the active grace which only trained muscles can assume." A few snatches of conversation throughout the novel indicate that Muir was avidly preaching his glacial doctrines, but for the most part the depiction of life in Yosemite in 1870 is obscured and distorted by insufferable absurdities that make the book almost unreadable. An episode outside the novel, however, brings us back to real life. The *Mariposa Gazette* of November 10, 1870, reports: "The Hon. Mrs. Yelverton met with a serious misfortune on Sunday last in attempting to leave Yosemite Valley unattended." Two men traveling the Wawona trail noticed a woman's tracks in the snow leading away from the trail. Mrs. Yelverton was finally found, "wet, chilled, bewildered and exhausted about a quarter of a mile from where she had left the trail. It is supposed Mrs. Yelverton became bewildered in the snow storm of Sunday afternoon, and she could no longer manage her horse, and dismounted and tried to walk back, but lost her way, and wandered till exhausted." Not long afterward, when she had recovered, she was escorted to Mariposa and went on to San Francisco. She wrote to Muir, who had temporarily left the Valley, chiding him for not waiting to guide her out. Muir felt "a kind of guiltiness in not doing so," but it may be that the wary Scot had fled in embarrassment, as is suggested by a later letter from far away, in which she wrote, "My dear

Kenmuir, how I wished for you, and sometimes longed for you avails me not to say. It is sufficient to make you comprehend that I never see a beautiful flower or a fine combination in nature without thinking of you and wishing you were there to appreciate it with me. One of the critics of *Zanita* says that your character is all 'bosh' and exists in my imagination. I should like to tell him that you had an existence in my heart as well!"[12]

Of greater significance in the history of the Sierra Nevada, and more in keeping with John Muir's nature, was the arrival in August of the "University

LeConte's Journal of Ramblings, *1875*

"The University Excursion Party" in Yosemite, 1870, with Joseph LeConte.

Excursion Party," a group of young men from the University of California who had invited their geology professor, Joseph LeConte, to accompany them on a camping trip.[13] While exploring the Valley, they stopped a moment at the foot of the Yosemite Falls, at a sawmill, to make inquiries. "Here we found a man in rough miller's garb, whose intelligent face and earnest, clear blue eyes excited our interest. After some conversation, we discovered it was John Muir, a gentleman of whom we had heard much from Mrs. Professor Carr and others. We urged him to go with us to Mono, and he seemed disposed to do so." A few days later Muir joined the party, affording many opportunities for sympathetic discussions about glaciers and rock formations. At Tenaya Lake one evening there took place a tableau of supreme piquancy: "After supper," writes LeConte, "I went with Mr. Muir and sat on a rock jutting into the lake. It was full moon. I never saw a more delightful scene. The deep stillness of the night; the silvery light and deep shadows of the mountains; the reflection on the water, broken into thousands of glittering points by the ruffled surface; the gentle lapping of the wavelets upon the rocky shore—all these seemed exquisitely harmonized with one another and the grand harmony made answering music in our hearts. Gradually the lake surface became quiet and mirror-like, and the exquisite surrounding scenery was seen double. For an hour we remained sitting in silent enjoyment of this delicious scene, which we reluctantly left to go to bed." They continued to Tuolumne Meadows, made a climb of Mount Dana, and went down Bloody Canyon to Mono Lake and the Craters, where Muir left the party to return to Yosemite. The professor shortly afterwards published several articles in which he expressed views substantially in agreement with those of Muir about glaciation and rock structure. In neither does there appear to have been any thought of rivalry; no doubt each contributed to the development of the other's ideas and together they spread a doctrine that gained wider acceptance than the theories so stubornly maintained by the Whitney school.

John Muir was by now thoroughly committed to his wilderness life. Yosemite was his home. Hutchings had taken over his cabin, so he constructed a "hang-nest" high on the side of the sawmill, where he could keep his personal things and at the same time tend the mill. Here he could enjoy "the piney fragrance of the fresh-sawn boards and be in constant view of the grandest of all the falls." But he did not spend all his time at the mill, nor all his nights in his hang-nest; he was not what could be called a steady workman. He found a ledge high up beside Yosemite Fall, where he established a comfortable perch after a preliminary drenching from the swaying column. There, and on brief excursions to the upper country, he continued to muse upon glaciers.

One day in May, 1871, the distinguished poet and essayist, Ralph Waldo Emerson, arrived in the Valley with an escort of Bostonians who hung upon his every word. There had been letters of introduction, but Muir was too diffident to present himself in person, so left a note at Hutchings' hotel. Next day Emerson sought out the writer and found him at the sawmill. Cordiality was immediate. Muir invited him to his hang-nest, "not easy of access, being reached only by a series of sloping planks roughened by slats like a hen ladder; but he bravely climbed up and I showed him my collection of plants and sketches, which seemed to interest him greatly." Emerson invited Muir to accompany him to the Mariposa Grove of Big Trees, and Muir accepted with the urgent stipulation that they camp out beneath the giant trees. Emerson was enthusiastic, but his friends "would have none of it, and held Mr. Emerson to the hotels and trails. 'It would never do to lie out in the night air—Mr. Emerson might take cold.' Sad commentary on culture and the glorious transcendentalism." They did visit the Grove, however, and Emerson was impressed, "but he was past his prime, and was now in the hands of his affectionate but sadly civilized friends, who seemed as full of old-fashioned conformity as of bold intellectual independence. The party rode away in wondrous contentment. I followed to the edge of the grove. Emerson lingered, turned his horse, took off his hat and waved me a last good-by. After sundown I built a great fire, and as usual had it all to myself."[14]

For some time Muir and Hutchings had not been getting along together, nor could it have been otherwise. Their daily objectives as well as their concepts of life were completely divergent. So Muir quit the sawmill work, left Hutchings, and moved his small store of personal things down the Valley to Black's Hotel. But the confines of the Valley would no longer contain him and from now on he began to move in ever-widening circles. During the summer of 1871 he was constantly among the higher mountains. His first objective was a search for evidences of ancient glaciers in the region of Yosemite Creek, up to its sources under Mount Hoffmann; then, evidences of the ancient Tuolumne Glacier in the region of mounts Lyell and Dana. In all this he was abundantly rewarded. In September he made a thrilling descent into the heart of the great Tuolumne Canyon.[15] He then turned his attention to the other side of the Valley. He climbed Mount Clark, where he beheld a glorious sunset. And now came his greatest reward.[16] "On one of the yellow days of October, 1871, when I was among the mountains of the 'Merced group,' following the footprints of the ancient glaciers that once flowed grandly from their ample fountains, reading what I could of their history as written in moraines, canyons, lakes and carved rocks, I came upon a small stream that was carrying mud of a kind I had never seen. Then I observed that this muddy stream issued from a bank of fresh quarried stones and dirt. This I at once took to be a moraine. When I had scrambled to the top of the moraine, I saw what seemed to be a huge snow-bank, four or five hundred yards in length, by half a mile in width. Imbedded in its stained and furrowed surface were stones and dirt like those of which the moraine was built. Dirt-stained lines curved across the snow-bank from side to side, and when I observed these curved lines with the curved moraine, and that the stones and dirt were most abundant near the bottom of the bank, I shouted, '*A living glacier!*' " He made a thorough exploration of his new-found glacier, finding at its head a crevasse of clear, green ice. The following year he returned to Mount Lyell, and with Galen Clark's assistance made measurements of the movement of the Lyell and Maclure glaciers. He was then satisfied to publish announcements of his findings. Professor LeConte went to Mount Lyell and observed the evidences and concurred that there was true glacial motion. But acceptance of Muir's discovery was not immediately unanimous. Whitney continued obdurate. "It may be stated," he says in his ultimate publication on the Sierra, "that there are no glaciers at all in the Sierra Nevada,"[17] and Clarence King gave what he considered a final verdict: "In the dry season of 1864-'65 the writer examined many of the regions described by Mr. Muir in the Sierra Nevada, and in not a few cases his so-called glaciers had entirely melted away. The absurdity of applying the word 'glacier' to a snow-mass which appears and reappears from year to year will be sufficiently evident. Motion alone is no proof of a true glacier."[18] There is nothing here to show that King examined the same places that Muir did, or if he did, that he gave them the same careful attention. The conceited "scientist" had actually no more claim to that designation than had John Muir, if as much, and he was certainly not justified in the sneering remark he appended to his statement: "It is to be hoped that Mr. Muir's vagaries will not deceive geologists who are personally unacquainted with California, and that the ambitious amateur himself may divert his evident enthusiastic love of nature into a channel, if there is one, in which his attainments would save him from hopeless floundering." These patronizing words, coupled with the "sheepherder" appellation, may be consigned to burial in glacial mud. Modern geologists agree substantially with John Muir and recognize him as the discoverer of living glaciers in the Sierra Nevada.[19]

It is not easy to follow John Muir's movements from his writings, nor even from his notebooks. He was not much concerned with calendars and dates. There are indications that he climbed Mount Lyell in the fall of 1871, and he has been credited with making the first ascent. But his time that fall is quite well accounted for until the glacier discovery in October, and before that others had reached the summit. Hutchings states that he had found the card of a Mr. Tileston, of Boston, on the summit some ten days after it had been left.[20] The solitary climber proved to be a young man named John Boies Tileston, whose letters, printed long afterwards, contain the following passage: "On Monday, the 28th August, 1871, we moved camp to the foot of Mt. Lyell. After dinner I decided to begin the ascent on that day, so as to be on the snow in the morning before it should be softened by the sun. So I took my blankets and provisions, and set out at four. I walked up till it was

nearly dark, when I found a comfortable place to sleep. I found some dry
wood not far off, where some stunted pines grew in crevices of the rock,
made some tea in a tin cup, and enjoyed the strange and savage scene around
me. Immense precipices, great masses of snow, from which rose the black
peaks of the summit, the roar of water descending by many channels and cascades over and among the rocks, and occasionally the rattling down of loosened stones, and the novelty of my situation, alone in that wild place, made
a scene which impressed itself on my mind. I was up early the next morning,
toasted some bacon, boiled my tea, and was off at six. I climbed the mountain,
and reached the top of the highest pinnacle ('inaccessible,' according to the
State Geological Survey), before eight. I came down the mountain, and
reached camp before one, pretty tired."[21]

John Muir seems to have climbed Mount Lyell in 1872, but whether for
the first or second time is not clear. He spent some time measuring the Lyell
and Maclure glaciers. On his return from one of his trips he found three
artists waiting for him at his new cabin at the foot of the Royal Arches. One
of the artists was William Keith. Did Muir know of any place in the high
mountains suitable for a picture? He knew just the place. "I saw it only yesterday," he said. "The crown of the Sierra is a picture hung in the sky, and
mind you, it needs none of your selection, or 'composition.' I'll take you there
tomorrow."[22] It was late in the season, so they lost no time. Muir led them
out of the Valley by way of the Nevada Fall trail and the Merced–Tuolumne
divide. "The general expression of the scenery—rocky and savage—seemed
sadly disappointing; and as they threaded the forest from ridge to ridge,
eagerly scanning the landscapes as they were unfolded, the artists said, 'all
this is sublime, but we see nothing as yet at all available for effective pictures.'
'Never mind,' I said, 'only bide a wee.' At length, toward the end of the
second day, the Sierra crown began to come into view and the whole picture
stood revealed in the full flush of the alpen glow. Now their enthusiasm was
excited beyond bounds. Here, at last, was a typical Alpine landscape." While
the artists settled down happily at the Lyell Fork to sketch and paint, Muir
decided to make an "excursion to the untouched summit of Ritter." He
warned the artists not to be alarmed if he failed to appear before a week or
ten days.

"My general plan," writes Muir,[23] "was to scale the canyon wall, cross over
to the eastern flank of the range, and then make my way southward to the
northern spurs of Mount Ritter. My first day was pure pleasure; crossing the
dry pathways of the grand old glaciers, tracing happy streams, and learning the
habits of the birds and marmots." Mount Ritter was still miles away when night
came. He made his bed in a "nook of a pine thicket, where the branches were
pressed and crinkled overhead like a roof, and bent down around the sides." He
had to creep out to the fire often during the night, "for it was biting cold and I

Glacier on Mount Ritter,
drawn by Thomas Moran from a sketch by John Muir.

had no blankets." "Breakfast of bread and tea was soon made. I fastened a hard durable crust to my belt and set forth free and hopeful. Immediately in front loomed the majestic mass of Mount Ritter, with a glacier swooping down its face nearly to my feet, then curving westward and pouring its frozen flood into a dark blue lake. I began instinctively to scrutinize every notch and gorge and weathered buttress of the mountain, with reference to making the ascent. I succeeded in gaining the foot of the cliff on the eastern extremity of the glacier, and discovered the mouth of a narrow avalanche gully. Its general course is oblique to the plane of the mountain-face, and the metamorphic slates of which it is built are cut by cleavage planes in such a way that they weather off in angular blocks, giving rise to irregular steps that greatly facilitate climbing. The situation was becoming gradually more perilous, but, having passed several dangerous spots, I dared not think of descending. At length, I found myself at the foot of a sheer drop in the bed of the avalanche channel, which seemed to bar all further progress. The tried dangers beneath seemed even greater than that of the cliff in front; therefore, after scanning its face again and again, I commenced to scale it, picking my holds with intense caution. After gaining a point about half-way to the top, I was brought to a dead stop, with arms outspread, clinging close to the face of the rock, unable to move hand or foot either up or down. My doom appeared fixed. I *must* fall. When this final danger flashed in upon me, I became nerve-shaken for the first time since setting foot on the mountain, and my mind seemed to fill with a stifling smoke. But the terrible eclipse lasted only a moment, when life burst forth again with preternatural clearness. I seemed suddenly to become possessed of a new sense. The other self—the ghost of by-gone experiences, Instinct, or Guardian Angel—call it what you will—came forward and assumed control. Then my trembling muscles became firm again, every rift and flaw was seen as through a microscope, and my limbs moved with a positiveness and precision with which I seemed to have nothing at all to do. Had I been borne aloft upon wings, my deliverance could not have been more complete. Above this memorable spot, the face of the mountain is still more savagely hacked and torn. But the strange influx of strength I had received seemed inexhaustible. I found a way without effort, and soon stood upon the topmost crag in the blessed light."

Muir gazed down upon "giant mountains, valleys innumerable, glaciers and meadows, rivers and lakes, with the wide blue sky bent tenderly over them all, and in contemplation of Nature's methods of landscape creation. But in the midst of these fine lessons and landscapes, I had to remember that the sun was wheeling far to the west, while a new way had to be discovered, at least to some point of the timber-line where I could have fire; for I had not even burdened myself with a coat." After a look at the western side, he scrambled back to the head of a glacier flowing northeast. Down this he found a way. "Night drew near before I reached the eastern base of the mountain, and my camp lay many a rugged mile to the north. Darkness came on, but I found my way by the trend of the canyons and the peaks projected against the sky. All excitement died with the light, and then I was weary. But the joyful sound of the water-fall across the lake where I had camped was heard at last. I discovered the little pine thicket in which my nest was, and then I had a rest such as only a mountaineer may enjoy." In one long day he made his way back across the divide and rejoined his artist friends, to their great relief.

Muir's interest was highly excited by the glaciers he had seen in the Ritter region. Here was a field from which he could learn much. A second visit was inevitable. The following year he wrote to his sister, "I have just returned from the longest and hardest trip I have ever made in the mountains, having been gone over five weeks."[24] On this trip, after visiting the Merced peaks, he crossed the divide to the San Joaquin into what he calls the "slate Yosemite." He took the Ritter Fork, which "comes down the mountain here in a network of cascades, wonderfully woven, as are all slate cascades of great size near summits, where the slate has a cleavage well pronounced. The mountains rise in a circle, showing their grand dark bosses and delicate spires on the starry sky." He pushed on, up to the glaciers of Mount Ritter. He "thought of ascending the highest Minaret, which is one farthest south, but after scanning it narrowly, discovered it was inaccessible." Was Muir becoming cautious? He came presently to a glacier with a "mass of yawning crevasses." "It ought not to be set foot upon by solitary explorers, as many of the most dangerous crevasses are slightly snow-covered even this late in the season." He worked along the margins and found a narrow pass through the Minarets, by which he reached his camp "after a rich day." Before leaving the region he scaled two peaks, then crossed the familiar divide to the Tuolumne and camped near the Lyell glacier. "Bread about gone. Home tomorrow or next day."[25]

Glaciers and their effect upon mountain landscape were not the only objects of John Muir's excursions. Other aspects of nature soon absorbed him even more: living things—birds, flowers, and above all trees. Before quitting the Sierra temporarily for other great primitive areas, notably Alaska, he made three long expeditions southward from Yosemite that laid the foundation for what was his major lifework, the preservation of at least part of our heritage of forest lands and the interpretation of their value as an essential factor in a wholesome national life. These expeditions were of quite different character from his solitary coverage of the Yosemite region. On the first two he was accompanied by others who could both absorb his teachings and assist him in his observations. So, at the end of the summer of 1873, he left the Mariposa Grove bound for the canyons of the San Joaquin in the unwonted posture of riding a horse. With him were Dr. Albert Kellogg, botanist, of the California Academy of Sciences, and a young man named Billy Sims, who aimed to be an artist. Galen Clark also came along for the first part of the trip. They crossed the branches of the San Joaquin, descending and climbing vast canyon walls, then went up to the headwaters of the South Fork. There Muir left his companions and his horse and ran (doubtless at times literally) up to the summit peaks. He mentions an ascent of "Mount Humphreys or the mountain next south,"[26] but more important than any mountain was the discovery of a band of wild sheep. "Eagerly I marked the flowing undulations of their firm, braided muscles, their strong legs, ears, eyes, heads, their graceful rounded necks, the color of their hair, and the bold upsweeping curves of their noble horns. Presently they came to a steep, ice-burnished acclivity, which they ascended by a succession of quick, short, stiff-legged leaps, reaching the top without a struggle. This was the most startling feat of mountaineering I had ever witnessed."[27] He continued to watch their progress with admiration and keen sympathy.

Muir returned to his companions and together they took a lower route across the basin of the North Fork of Kings River, down to the main river and up the south bank to Thomas' Mill. Here they encountered the Sequoias again, and Muir grieved at the vandalism and destruction among them. But a little higher, on the Kings–Kaweah divide, prospects were brighter. "The yosemite[28] scenery about the many forks of Kings River presents sublime combinations of cliff and canyon and bossy dome, with high, sharp peaks in the distance." One black peak with a small snow patch he thought was Mount Goddard. They descended into Kings Canyon, where he found many comparisons with the Merced Yosemite. Leaving Kellogg and Sims with the animals, Muir again set out alone for the high peaks. Snatches from his notebook describe his experiences: "Hard traveling along this portion of the stream, the avalanche material planted with poplars and chaparral—ascended two peaks in the afternoon—the moon is doing marvels in whitening the peaks with a pearly luster—I have leveled a little spot on the mountain-side where I may nap by my fireside—I am blanketless—set out early for Mount Tyndall and reached the summit about 9 A.M.—descended and pushed back to the main camp—arrived about noon to find Billy and Dr. Kellogg gone—pushed on after them, following their trail toward Kearsarge Pass—scenery at the summit is grand—overtook the runaway train at sunset, a mile over the divide—in a few hours passed from ice and snow to the torrid plain."[29] In Owens Valley, Muir left his two companions again for a ten-day trip to Mount Whitney,[30] and then rejoining them went north through Owens Valley to Lake Tahoe.

Muir's climactic year in the Sierra was in 1875, when he made two memorable trips southward from Yosemite. The first was in July, accompanied by George B. Bayley and Charles E. Washburn, "with 'Buckskin Bill' as mule master, all well mounted on tough, obstinate mules."[31] Avoiding the canyons of the San Joaquin, they angled down through the foothills and crossed the Kings at Centerville, almost in the Valley. They climbed up to the forest again and meandered through the Sequoia groves, "where they heard the sound of axes, and soon came upon a group of busy men engaged in preparing a butt section of a Giant Sequoia they had felled for exhibition at the Quaker Centennial. Many a poor defrauded town dweller will pay his dollar and peep, and gain some dead arithmetical notion of the bigness of our Big Trees, but a true and living knowledge is not to be had at so cheap a rate. As well try to send a section of the storms on which they feed." They went on and up among the Giant Sequoias to the rim of Kings Canyon, where they noted the close resemblance to Yosemite as seen from Inspiration Point. "Bayley's joy usually finds expression," writes Muir, "in a kind of explosive Indian war whoop, and wild echoes were driven rudely from cliff to cliff, as the varied landscapes revealed themselves from the more commanding points along the trail." They camped on the river-bank "near a small circular meadow, that is one of the most perfect flower-gardens I have ever discovered in the mountains. It was filled with lilies and violets, and orchids, and sun-loving golden rods and asters, and ceanothus, with a hundred others all in bloom. Here I lived a fine unmeasured hour 'considering the lilies,' warming among the mellow waving golden rods and gazing into the countenances of small white violets." But in all this beauty there was a tragic warning. A sign was posted claiming the land for private ownership. For John Muir it was a signal for beginning a campaign to save these parklike lands for all the people, a campaign that was to dominate his life in the years to come.

The little party kept on up to Kearsarge Pass and down to Owens Valley, whence Muir led them to Mount Whitney ("Buckskin Bill" excepted), an excursion which, as before, needs the explanation given in the next chapter.

The last of Muir's long trips through the Sierra was a solitary one, that is, if we except his "little Brownie mule." The purpose of the trip was to learn what he could of the "peculiar distribution of the Sequoia and its history in general."[32] From the Mariposa Grove he came to the Fresno Grove, where he met a friendly hermit, relic of the gold-hunting era, named John A. Nelder, who helped him find the best examples of Sequoias. In crossing the wide basin of the San Joaquin he took note of the complete absence of Sequoias until he came to Dinkey Creek, a tributary of the Kings. "Down into the main Kings River canyon, a mile deep, I led and dragged and shoved my patient, much-enduring mule, until in a day and a half we reached old Thomas' mill flat. Thence striking off northeastward I found a magnificent forest. Here five or six days were spent, and it was delightful to learn from countless trees, old and young, how comfortably they were settled down in concordance with climate and soil and their noble neighbors." Muir was now enjoying one of the supreme experiences of his life. "Day after day," he continues, "from grove to grove, canyon to canyon, I made a long, wavering way, terribly rough in some places for Brownie, but cheery for me, for Big Trees were seldom out of sight. We climbed into the noble forest on the Marble and Middle Fork divide. After a general exploration of the Kaweah basin, this part of the Sequoia belt seemed to me the finest, and I then named it 'the Giant Forest.'"[33]

Here Muir encountered the patriarch settler of the region, Hale Tharp, who had visited the Giant Forest as early as 1858 and for some years had used it as a cattle range. Tharp had adapted a hollow Sequoia log as a cabin and invited Muir to stay with him in what Muir described as "a spacious loghouse of one log, carbon-lined, centuries old, yet sweet and fresh, weather proof, earthquake proof, likely to outlast the most durable stone castle, and commanding views of garden and grove grander far than the richest king ever enjoyed." But Muir could not linger for long; there was still much to explore. "There are ways across the Sierra graded by glaciers, well marked, and followed by men and beasts and birds, and one of them even by locomotives; but none natural or artificial *along* the range. My own ways are easily made in any direction, but Brownie, though one of the toughest and most skillful of his race, was oftentimes discouraged for want of hands, and caused endless work." Nevertheless, they kept on, "Sequoias on every ridge-top beckoning and pointing the way." Muir encountered a forest fire, which he described in great detail. And then, "toward sundown two thousand sheep beneath a cloud of dust came streaming through the grand Sequoias." "All the basin," Muir adds, "was swept by swarms of hoofed locusts." The southernmost range of the Big Trees was not far away, and Muir pursued them to the end, at the South Fork of Deer Creek and just over a pass to the east side of the Kern River divide.

Muir's biographer, Linnie Marsh Wolfe, sums up: "From this autumn journey stemmed two important results: a first-hand knowledge of land-and-water monopoly, and a greatly strengthened resolve to lead men back to the healing powers of nature."[34] From that time on, scientific inquiry, although not by any means extinguished, was dimmed by his devotion to the cause of Conservation.

Notes and References

1. John Muir was born at Dunbar, Scotland, 1838. He came to America with his family when he was eleven years old. He attended the University of Wisconsin 1860-1863. After a walking trip to Florida in 1867 he came to California, which was his home until his death in 1914. In conferring on him the degree of LL.D. in 1913, University of California President Benjamin Ide Wheeler cited him as "widely traveled observer of the world we dwell in, man of science and of letters, friend and protector of Nature, uniquely gifted to interpret unto other men her mind and ways." Muir's published writings are extensive, and writings about him equally so. His principal works relating to the Sierra are: *My First Summer in the Sierra*, 1911; *The Mountains of California*, 1894; *Our National Parks*, 1901; *The Yosemite*, 1912; *Letters to a Friend*, 1915; and *Studies in the Sierra*, 1950 (reprinted from articles in *Overland Monthly*, 1874-1875). Selected writings: *John of the*

Mountains, edited by Linnie Marsh Wolfe, 1938; and *The Yosemite and the Sierra Nevada*, edited by Charlotte Mauk, photographs by Ansel Adams, 1948. Many chapters of his earlier books were first published in magazines. Biographical works, which contain letters and extensive quotations, are: William Frederic Badè, *The Life and Letters of John Muir*, 2 vols., Boston: Houghton Mifflin, 1923-1924; Linnie Marsh Wolfe, *Son of the Wilderness*, New York: Knopf, 1945; and Edwin Way Teale, *The Wilderness World of John Muir*, Boston: Houghton-Mifflin, 1954.

There is much duplication in the writings of John Muir, and it is also frequently necessary to combine two or more versions in order to produce a complete account. Perhaps an index, or concordance, of all Muir's writings will some day be made.

2. Muir, "Studies in the Sierra," *Overland Monthly*, serially in 1874.

3. Whitney Survey, *The Yosemite Guide-Book*, 1869.

4. Muir, "Studies in the Sierra," *Overland Monthly*, June, 1874. A summary of the conflicting theories is in François E. Matthes, "Geologic History of the Yosemite Valley," U.S. Geological Survey *Professional Paper 160*, 1930; also M. E. Beatty, "A Brief Story of the Geology of the Yosemite Valley," *YNN*, April, 1943.

The final demolition of Whitney's "convulsive" theory and the verification of Muir's glacial theory came through a series of seismic explorations conducted by John P. Buwalda, Professor of Geology at California Institute of Technology, in 1934-1935, in which it was found that Yosemite was a glacial U-shaped valley far deeper than the present floor of alluvial deposits would indicate. Buwalda, "Form and Depth of the Bedrock Trough of Yosemite Valley," *YNN*, October, 1941; and Beno Gutenberg, John P. Buwalda, and Robert P. Sharp, "Seismic Explorations on the Floor of Yosemite Valley, California," *Bulletin of the Geological Society of America*, August, 1956.

5. Muir, *First Summer*.   6. *Ibid.*   7. *Ibid.*

8. Wolfe, *John of the Mountains*.   9. Badè, *Life and Letters*.

10. Wolfe, *John of the Mountains*.

11. Judge Gilbert W. Colby, of Benicia, father of William E. Colby, the great Sierra Club leader and disciple of John Muir.

12. For the Yelverton story see her *Zanita, A Tale of the Yosemite*, 1872 (*Farquhar* No. 11), and her *Teresina in America*, 1875; also Charles Warren Stoddard, *In the Footprints of the Padres*, 1902 (the chapter, "A Mysterious History," is omitted in the 1911 edition); Mary Viola Lawrence, "A Summer with a Countess," *Overland Monthly*, November, 1871; Badè, *Life and Letters*; Wolfe, *Son of the Wilderness*.

13. Joseph LeConte (1823-1901), a native of Georgia, a pupil of Agassiz, was invited to a professorship in the newly founded University of California in Berkeley. "In the summer of 1870, at the end of the first session of the University, eight of the students invited Professor Frank Soulé, Jr., and me to join them in a camping trip to the Sierras, and we joyfully accepted. This trip was almost an era in my life —perfect health, the merry party of young men, the glorious scenery, and, above all, the magnificent opportunity for studying mountain origin and structure" (*The Autobiography of Joseph LeConte*, edited by William Dallam Armes, 1903). See also LeConte's *A Journal of Ramblings through the High Sierra of California by the "University Excursion Party,"* 1875, and subsequent editions (*Farquhar* No. 14).

14. James Bradley Thayer, *A Western Journey with Mr. Emerson*, Boston,

1884; Badè, *Life and Letters*; Muir, *Our National Parks*; Samuel T. Farquhar, "John Muir and Ralph Waldo Emerson," *SCB*, June, 1934, 19:3.

15. Muir, "Explorations in the Great Tuolumne Canyon," *Overland Monthly*, August, 1873; reprinted in *SCB*, 1924, 12:1.

16. Muir, "Living Glaciers of California," *Overland Monthly*, December, 1872; also *Harper's New Monthly Magazine*, November, 1875.

17. Whitney, "The Climatic Changes of Later Geologic Times," in *Contributions to American Geology*, vol. II, Cambridge, Mass.: Museum of Comparative Zoology, 1882.

18. Clarence King, *Systematic Geology*, 1878.

19. Israel C. Russell, *Glaciers of North America*, 1897; Andrew C. Lawson, "The Sierra Nevada," *University of California Chronicle*, April, 1891, 23:2; François E. Matthes, "John Muir and the Glacial Theory of Yosemite," *SCB*, April, 1938, 23:9.

20. J. M. Hutchings, *In the Heart of the Sierras*, 1886.

21. *Letters of John Boies Tileston*, Boston, privately printed, 1922; Mountaineering Notes, *SCB*, 1926, 12:3.

22. Wolfe, *Son of the Wilderness*.

23. Muir, "In the Heart of the California Alps," *Scribner's*, July, 1880; Muir, *Mountains of California*.

24. Badè, *Life and Letters*.

25. Wolfe, *John of the Mountains*. The two peaks may have been Banner and either Davis or Rodgers.

26. Probably not the peak now known as Humphreys; more likely Darwin.

27. Muir, *Mountains of California*.

28. Muir uses "yosemite" as a generic term for Yosemite-like canyons.

29. Wolfe, *John of the Mountains*. Muir was probably mistaken about the identity of Mount Tyndall; it seems unlikely that even Muir could have reached Mount Tyndall in the time stated.

30. The account of Muir's climb of Mount Whitney is reserved for the next chapter.

31. Muir, "Summering in the Sierra," *San Francisco Daily Evening Bulletin*, August 13, 1875; reprinted in *SCB*, 1941, 26:1.

32. The September, 1875, trip is described in Muir, *Our National Parks*.

33. This appears to be the earliest mention of the name "Giant Forest" (*San Francisco Bulletin*, August 22, 1875).

34. Wolfe, *Son of the Wilderness*.

XVII

MOUNT WHITNEY

We left Clarence King in June, 1871, standing on the summit of the peak that he supposed to be Mount Whitney, immensely pleased with himself. For two years he enjoyed the satisfaction of believing that he had reached the highest point in the United States. Neither he nor anyone else doubted that Mount Whitney had been climbed. Then came a shock. At a meeting of the California Academy of Sciences, August 4, 1873 (Professor J. D. Whitney in the chair), a paper was read by W. A. Goodyear "On the Situation and Altitude of Mount Whitney."[1] He came directly to the point: "On the 27th day of July, 1873, Mr. M. W. Belshaw and myself rode our mules to the highest crest of the peak southwest of Lone Pine, which for over three years has been known by the name of Mount Whitney and which was ascended and measured as such by Mr. Clarence King. I know this peak well, and cannot be mistaken in its identity." Moreover, he found King's record on the summit. "I do not mention the fact that Mr. Belshaw and myself reached the summit in the saddle as being one of any new or special interest, for Mr. Sheriff Mulkey, of Inyo County, accomplished the same thing on the 6th day of August, 1872, with his wife and daughter, and since that time it has also been done by several other parties." Then came the astonishing statement: "*This peak is not Mount Whitney.*" Goodyear went on to prove that another peak five or six miles away, and considerably higher, was the one named by the Brewer party in 1864. "Certain it is," he said, "that the peak which for over three years has borne the name of Whitney, has done so only by mistake, and that a new name must be found for it; while the name of Whitney must now go back to the peak to which it was originally given in 1864, and which is, in reality, the highest and grandest of this culminating cluster of the Sierra Nevada. It is safe to say that no man will ever ride a horse or mule to the summit of *that* peak, unless it be by a costly as well as dangerous trail.[2] Whether the peak is utterly inaccessible or not, is still a question. I am disposed to think that it can be climbed; but it will certainly involve a great deal of hard and, very possibly, some dangerous work for anybody who shall attempt to reach its gigantic crest."

When Clarence King received this disconcerting news in the East he was naturally greatly surprised and disappointed. He hastened to California, engaged two men at Visalia to accompany him, and was soon riding over the familiar Hockett Trail to the Kern. At eleven o'clock in the morning of September 19, 1873, he stood at last on the summit of the true Mount Whitney. But, alas for him, he was too late for the first ascent. On the summit he found a monument and the records of two preceding parties, "the first, Messrs. Hunter and Crapo, and afterwards Rabe, of the Geological Survey. The former were, save Indians hunters, the first, so far as we know, who achieved this dominating summit."[3] This statement sounds definite and final. But it was not correct, Unfortunately it became imbedded in King's *Mountaineering in the Sierra Nevada*, with its wide and enduring circulation, and it took years to set the record straight. King at that time was in a position to ascertain the facts, and it seems rather unfair that he should have passed so lightly over the matter of the first ascent, especially since he had attached some importance to the honor while he himself was seeking it.

To whom, then, should the honor go? It is not easy to say, for one has to evaluate the claims, counterclaims, and accusations that for several months scorched the pages of the local newspaper, the *Inyo Independent*.[4] There emerges, however, what seems to be the true story of the first ascent of Mount Whitney. In the summer of 1873 a jolly party of residents of Lone Pine was encamped at Soda Springs in Kern Canyon, to "recuperate from the heat of Owens Valley" and indulge in fishing and other sports. Sheriff Mulkey and his wife and daughter Mattie were among those present. Three members of the party, Charley Begole, Johnny Lucas, and Al Johnson "took a trip to the summit of the highest mountain in the range, and christened it Fisherman's Peak," wrote the *Independent's* correspondent. "Some people are now trying to take the credit of their being the first there away from them, but they won't succeed. Prof. Whitney's agent finds fault with the people here for their lack of romance in calling it 'Fisherman's Peak.' Ain't it as romantic as 'Whitney'? The fishermen who found it looked mighty romantic on their return to Soda Springs. Wonder who the old earthquake sharp thinks is running this country, anyhow?"

The ascent can be followed fairly well from the newspaper accounts. The Fishermen, Begole, Johnson, and Lucas, rode up from the Soda Springs camp in Kern Canyon to the base of the false Mount Whitney and climbed it on August 17. From the summit they could see that the other peak was the higher, and they resolved to go to its top. Returning to their horses, they rode down Rock Creek for several miles, then up a steep ravine to the north, with a bald peak (Mount Guyot) on the west. They followed the right-hand ravine for a mile or two, then rode up the northeast fork to "Ramshorn Springs," where they camped. At daylight next morning they left their horses and took a northeasterly direction to the top of a ridge. Finding no way to get down, they followed the ridge to a pass that brought them down and around a lake. They made for a red streak crossing the next ridge and at the foot of this pass came to another lake. The route to their goal was now in front of them. Up the southwestern side of the mountain they climbed, over serrated crests of rocky "ribs," and at noon of August 18, 1873, the three Fishermen stood on the summit of the true Mount Whitney. They built a monument to commemorate the event and named it "Fisherman's Peak."

The story of the Fishermen was promptly challenged by Tom McDonough, of Cerro Gordo, who asserted in a letter to the *Independent* that "they was never on the mountain and that Abe Leyda, Wm. Crapo, Mr. Rabe, W. L. Hunter and myself are the only persons that ever were on the summit." Crapo also attacked the Fishermen's story. He declared that the Fishermen's peak and the true Mount Whitney could not be the same. He called them "itinerant climbers" and "the inimitable three." Crapo claimed that he and Abe Leyda were on the summit August 15 and had made barometer observations at that time. The date is certainly wrong, and it is most unlikely that they had a barometer. It does seem likely, however, that Crapo and Leyda were on the summit soon after the Fishermen and that they may be credited with the second ascent.

A fully authenticated account now appears in the record. Belshaw, who had been with Goodyear on the false Mount Whitney the preceding July, organized an expedition to determine the facts about the situation and altitude of the true Mount Whitney. Crapo offered his services as guide; Hunter and McDonough joined the party; and Carl Rabe, a German employed by the Geological Survey as cook, was entrusted with the barometer. Rabe had learned to read the instrument and to perform other duties as assistant to the surveyors while with Hoffmann. For the rest of his long life he took pardonable pride in considering himself a man of science. To him we owe a very circumstantial account of the first "scientific" party to climb Mount Whitney.[5] They took the Hockett Trail from Lone Pine over Cottonwood Pass to "Long Valley" (Whitney Meadows), and after some twenty miles camped at the base of the true Mount Whitney, "a very hard day's work for our animals." Next morning, September 6, they made an early start. "Following my companions in silence," says Rabe, "and keeping a sharp lookout ahead, I at last spied a crevice going up among the crags which seemed to offer a way. This crevice appeared to be about ten feet wide, with a slope of some 45 degrees. Keeping to the larger boulders, I slowly worked my way through it. I found the ascent, though not particularly dangerous, extremely laborious and slow. The light atmosphere at the height of over 13,000 feet was beginning to tell upon my lungs, and I had to stop every fifteen or twenty minutes to rest and breathe. But after an hour and a half of very hard climbing, we stood at last on the crest of Mount Whitney, and I hung my barometer on the monument which had been erected by our predecessors a few days before. Shortly after 2 P.M. we left the summit. In the descent I took a slightly different route from the one I had followed in the morning, and after an exhausted tramp of two hours and a half reached our camp, where I found my companions awaiting my return."[6]

Controversy over the Fishermen's ascent continued to rage. McDonough again came to the support of Crapo and Leyda, asserting that the "celebrated Fishermen" could not have done what they said they did in the stated time and were on the wrong mountain. His concluding argument rather weakens his case. "When we were coming home," he says, "Mr. Charley Johnson told and showed Mr. Hunter a different peak altogether, that Al showed him was the one they were on." This merely says that Mr. McDonough learned from Mr. Hunter that Al's brother Charley told Mr. Hunter what Al had told Charley. Verdict for the Fishermen. Case dismissed.

The matter of the name was argued with even greater vehemence. Professor Whitney had made himself unpopular in Owens Valley when he came there in 1872 to examine the scars of the recent earthquake. Consequently, when the mountain which for several years had been known as Mount Whitney proved to be a comparatively inconsequential peak, the local anti-Whitney people were only too glad of an excuse to fix his name permanently on the lesser peak. Further to insure this, when the right of the Fishermen to place their name on the higher peak was challenged, the local press proposed the name "Dome of Inyo." The Fishermen magnanimously acquiesced. But "The Dome" never got beyond local usage and soon died out. Meanwhile Hoffmann corrected the error on his map that had caused all the trouble and moved the name "Mount Whitney" to its rightful position a little farther north. And there it has remained. Not without further threats of dislodgement, however, for when "Dome of Inyo" failed to take hold, the local people went back to "Fisherman's Peak"—anything to get rid of "Whitney." And then, in 1881, an Inyo County assemblyman, Moffat, introduced a bill in the State Legislature to make the name "Fisherman's Peak" official. The bill passed the Assembly, but it reached the Senate on April Fools Day and the jolly senators amended it to read "Fowler's Peak" in honor of one of their colleagues. But neither fish nor fowl prevailed, for the Governor vetoed the bill as frivolous. The name "Mount Whitney" has become an integral part of the mountain, and few people today are concerned about the merits of the old controversy.[7]

At the end of September 1873 the record of ascents of Mount Whitney stood: (1) August 18—Charles D. Begole, Albert H. Johnson, John Lucas; (2) late August—William Crapo, Abe Leyda; (3) September 6—William Crapo, William L. Hunter, Tom McDonough, Carl Rabe; (4) September 19—Clarence King, Frank Knowles. These ascents were made from the southwest, coming north from the Hockett Trail; King and Knowles from Visalia, the others from Lone Pine by way of Cottonwood Pass.

A new epoch begins with the coming of John Muir in October of that year. When Muir left his companions at the foot of Kearsarge Pass, he rode alone southward along the foot of the range and took the usual route from Lone Pine over Cottonwood Pass. Leaving his horse in a meadow, he climbed the false Mount Whitney and from there saw, as others had done, the higher peak a few miles away. Without delay he ran down, moved his horse to another meadow, and by a very rough way up and down ridges and canyons reached the base of the true Mount Whitney at sunset the same day. As there was no wood for a fire, he made up his mind to spend the night climbing. "I was among summit needles by midnight or 11 o'clock," he writes in his diary.[8] "Had to dance all night to keep from freezing. Was feeble and starving next morning and had to turn back without gaining the top. Was exhausted ere I reached horse and camp and food." He returned to Independence, ate, and slept all next day; then, not to be defeated, "set out afoot for the summit by direct course up the east side." He camped in the sagebrush the first night and next morning made his way up the North Fork of Lone Pine Creek and camped at timberline.[9] On the morning of October 21, at eight o'clock, he was on the summit of Mount Whitney. There he found Clarence King's record and a memento left by Rabe with a note, "Notice Gentleman however is the looky finder of this half a Dollar is wellkom to it Carl Rabe Sep 6th 1873." Muir sketched, gained glorious views, left the half a Dollar where he found it, and descended to the foot of the mountain by the way he came. He was back at Independence next day. Many years later Muir wrote, "For climbers there is a canyon which comes down from the north shoulder of the Whitney peak. Well-seasoned limbs will enjoy the climb of 9000 feet required for this direct route, but soft, succulent people should go the mule way."[10] Should someone of the present generation of mountain climbers feel inclined to make light of John Muir's exploit, let him endeavor to duplicate it, starting from Independence (not Lone Pine) on foot, with or without sleeping bag and modern concentrated foods—Muir had neither.

Muir's second visit to Mount Whitney came two years later. This time he took his two companions with him to the top. He knew the way and could proceed unerringly. He followed his former route up the North Fork of Lone Pine Creek until he came to the final climb. There he made a variation, crossing the main crest a little to the north, and descended to a lake on the western side.[11] They passed along the rocky shores, "gradually climbed higher, mounting in a spiral around the northwest shoulder of the mountain, then directly to the summit." Their arrival was "duly announced by Bayley as soon as he was rested into a whooping condition.[12] Undemonstrative Washburn examined the records of antecedent visitors, then remarked with becoming satisfaction, 'I'm the first and only student visitor to visit this highest land in North America.' "[13] The descent is described by Muir in one sen-

Mount Whitney from Lone Pine.

tence: "We left the summit about noon and swooped to the torrid plains before sundown, as if dropping out of the sky."

Another ascent the same year is worthy of note in that it included the first photographer known to have climbed Mount Whitney, W. E. James, of New York. The leader was James M. Hutchings, of Yosemite. Dr. Albert Kellogg, botanist, left behind by Muir two years before, this time reached the top.[14] Al Johnson went along as guide. The *Inyo Independent* took due note of the climb, especially of Hutchings' adventures on the return. "He proposed to take a short cut across the country (if such gigantic, awe-inspiring mountains of rock can be called a country), with a view of intersecting the Kearsarge trail, and a possible ascent of Mount Williamson. Two others of the party volunteered to accompany him. Taking a small supply of 'grub,' but no blankets, the three started afoot, the main party taking the back track. It was expected the three across country gentlemen would reach here (Independence) on the second day." When they did not arrive, a rescue party was sent out. "By the time it had fairly reached the mountains the missing ones came tramping in, weary, footsore, and, oh, how hungry. Instead of a practical route for even expert footmen, they found sheer precipices thousands of feet high cutting square across the proposed line of travel, so that it was simply impossible to proceed in the desired direction. The mountains around appeared to tower as high above them as from this valley. By this time the party were looking for a way to reach the foot, not the top of the mountains."[15]

Although Mount Whitney had been climbed in the first few years of its history by fishermen and others from Inyo County, by Clarence King, by John Muir, by a "scientist," a botanist, a photographer, by Hutchings of Yosemite, and by a college student, it does not appear that any woman reached the top until 1878. In the summer of that year a group of men and women from Porterville, Tulare County, made an expedition to the mountain. One of the four women in the party, Miss Anna Mills (later, as Mrs. Johnston) wrote a reminiscent account of the trip.[16] At the Soda Springs in Kern Canyon they found over thirty people from Inyo County, "as jolly a crowd as one would wish to meet." William Crapo was there and offered to guide the Porterville party to Mount Whitney. They followed the usual route to the base. "Just before reaching camp," writes Mrs. Johnston, "my horse took a notion to jump over a small stream, very unexpectedly to me, and my back was so severely injured that I could hardly step without experiencing severe pain. Having been lame from early childhood, everybody said it would be utterly impossible for me to climb to the summit of Mt. Whitney. But I was not easily discouraged, and had always held to the idea that I could do what other people could—my surplus of determination making up for what I lacked in the power of locomotion. But now at the eleventh hour, like Moses, I had gotten where I could see the promised land, but the chances for getting there were indeed few. In that hour of anguish I remembered my sins, and carefully walking to an obscure place, away up there so near heaven, where none but God could hear, I knelt, facing the great mountain, and prayed—prayed as I had not for years; prayed with the spirit and the understanding also. When I had finished, the mountain-top seemed closer, and I returned to camp with a much lighter heart." The following day, August 3, 1878, the pain nearly gone, she started on alone ahead of the party in order to rest before the steep portion of the climb. All reached the top without too much difficulty, including the other women, Miss Hope Broughton, Miss Mary Martin, and Mrs. Redd. "The supreme joy I felt," writes Anna Mills Johnston, "when I realized that my prayer had been answered, and that I was at last really standing on the summit of Mount Whitney, knew no bounds. For the time being I forgot that I ever was tired; one glance was enough to compensate for all the trials of the trip."

Not many women climbed mountains in those days, but in August of that year three women were included in a party of eight that made the climb from Lone Pine. They followed substantially the route of the present trail up Lone Pine Creek and over Whitney Pass to Crabtree Meadows, thence up the usual route to the summit.[17]

The year 1881 was important in the annals of Mount Whitney, for it saw the first of a series of expeditions that occupied the summit for scientific observations. Professor Samuel Pierpont Langley, at that time Director of the Allegheny Observatory, near Pittsburgh, Pennsylvania, later Secretary of the Smithsonian Institution and pioneer in airplane development, selected Mount Whitney, on the advice of Clarence King, as a site for conducting observations to determine the amount and quality of the heat sent to the earth by the sun. Professor Langley was assisted by James E. Keeler of the Allegheny Observatory, William C. Day of Johns Hopkins University, and Captain Otho E. Michaelis of Army Ordnance, temporarily detailed to Signal Service. William Crapo was engaged as guide. "Near the upper extremity of Owens Lake (a small dead sea), we got our first sight of Whitney, and in a few miles more reached the little hamlet of Lone Pine, built on a small patch of green.— The outline of Whitney and the neighboring peaks seen from Lone Pine is very extraordinary, the serrated edge and the snow, justifying the name of 'Sierra Nevada'—reaching at nightfall a small meadow whose altitude must have been 8,000 or 9,000 feet—A little farther we found the woods burning over many acres, the fire having been apparently wantonly set by some sheepherders, who are the great destroyers of the timber in this upper region—we finally rose above the entire timber-belt, and reached camp at an elevation of about 12,000 feet, for which an excellent site had been chosen by Mr. Crapo." The pack train with the instruments was delayed, seriously shortening the time available for observations. Professor Langley went to the summit for the first time on August 22. "The sky," he noted, "is of the most deep violet blue, such as we never, under any circumstances see near sea-level. It is an incomparably beautiful sky for the observer's purposes, such as I have not seen equaled elsewhere." "The top of Whitney," he remarks, "is an area of perhaps three to four acres, nearly level, or with a slight downward slope toward the west. Stone for the erection of permanent buildings is here in unlimited quantity." On the descent he noticed "parts of great tree-trunks, some eight or ten feet long, evidently very old, lying on the naked boulders, without the slightest trace of vegetation within a mile or any sign to show how they came there. I afterward found these isolated trunks elsewhere, and it seems clear that they are relics of a remote day, when the forest grew 2,000 feet higher than it does at present."[18]

On September 2 Captain Michaelis and two or three others carried supplies and a tent to the summit, intending to stay for several days, but early the next morning they made their appearance back in camp, "reporting that they had passed a sleepless night, without shelter or warmth, the wind being so high that they could not pitch the tent, while the quarter-cord of wood, carried up with great difficulty, had been all burned up in a vain effort to keep warm." In this manner was passed the first overnight occupancy of Mount Whitney. Notwithstanding the hardships involved, the summit was occupied again on the night of the 4th and valuable observations were made. But the season was too far advanced, and at the end of a week Langley decided to break camp. "We had, by hard struggling, and in spite of adverse circumstances," he writes, "secured what seemed most essential to our purpose, and though we had not done all we had hoped to do, we had done more than at one time seemed possible." So, with Michaelis, Keeler, and Day, and with Johnson (presumably Al, of the first ascent) as guide, Langley set out on foot for Lone Pine "by the direct descent down Lone Pine Creek." "This day," says Langley, "will always live in my memory. We first ascended for over two hours, past snow-cliffs and along the frozen lakes in the northern shadow of Whitney Peak, and then passing through a defile in the rocks, so narrow that only one person could traverse it at a time, we suddenly found ourselves on the other side of the ridge—so suddenly that we were startled as we looked down as through a window from our wintry height, to the desert, and the bright green of the oases far below, in a climate where it was still summer." This was unmistakably the route that Muir had used six years earlier with Bayley and Washburn, joining his other route, the "Mountaineer's Route" of Clyde, at what is now known as East Face Lake.

In conclusion, Langley says, "I hope I have made plain my own belief that Mount Whitney is an excellent station for the purpose for which it was chosen. The great drawback in our case was the inability to remain at the very summit, for to do this requires a permanent shelter. It is most earnestly hoped that something more than a mere ordinary meteorological station will be finally erected here, and that the almost unequaled advantages of this site will be developed by the Government."

It was a good many years before Professor Langley's hopes were realized. In the summer of 1903 Dr. Alexander G. McAdie, of the United States Weather Bureau, visited the summit and reported to the chief of the Bureau that "Mt. Whitney, of all the extremely high peaks of the Pacific Coast is probably most suited for a meteorological observatory."[19] Although McAdie's recommendations were not acted upon by the Weather Bureau, his report led ultimately to a series of expeditions under the auspices of the Smithsonian Institution. Meanwhile the people of Lone Pine realized that a pack-train trail to the summit was necessary. On July 22, 1904, G. F. Marsh, of Lone Pine, wrote to Dr. McAdie, "I'm glad to inform you that we completed the pack trail to the summit of Mt. Whitney last Sunday. We had three pack-trains loaded with wood, and one saddle horse. We had a large fire at night, and fireworks which were plainly seen at Lone Pine. The pack-train had no difficulty in climbing the mountain. The trail is in good shape and parties are going over it every day."[20]

One of the first parties to use the western portion of the new trail was that of Dr. Barton Warren Evermann, at that time chief of the Division of Scientific Inquiry, United States Bureau of Fisheries, engaged in investigating the Golden Trout of the Kern River region. While they were on the summit on July 26, 1904, a thunderstorm gathered and lightning began to flash. As they were eating their luncheon, three of the party were knocked down by an electrical discharge. Dr. Evermann and Dr. Jenkins were not injured, but the third, Byrd Surby, whose feet were apparently wet from the snow, was killed outright. So far as the records show this was the first and only fatality on the summit of Mount Whitney.[21]

A curious by-product of the Langley expedition was the establishment of the Mount Whitney Military Reservation, on September 26, 1883, setting aside land which included Mount Williamson on the north, Sheep Mountain on the south, and the eastern slope of Whitney almost as far as Lone Pine. There the matter stood for twenty years, until some prospectors who were denied access to the foothills pressed an inquiry by the Army General Staff to determine the need of the reservation for military purposes. It turned out that the tract had been set aside "ostensibly for military, in reality for scientific purposes," while the Weather Bureau was attached to the Signal Corps in the War Department. When the Weather Bureau was transferred to the Department of Agriculture, the military reservation was forgotten and no one in Washington seemed to be aware of its existence. The War Department, having assured itself of the safety of the country without the aid of the reservation, relinquished it.[22]

In due time the summit of Mount Whitney was again sought as a site for observations. Dr. William Wallace Campbell, of the University of California's Lick Observatory, on Mount Hamilton, had long been interested in the spectrum of Mars, "for the purpose of detecting the presence of water vapor." "I realized," he says, "that the water in the Earth's atmosphere is the greatest obstacle in the way of success." An altitude of over 14,000 feet would reduce this substantially. In August and September, 1909, Mars would be near the Earth and high above the horizon. Dr. Charles G. Abbot of the Smithsonian Institution was also interested in the summit of Mount Whitney for the purpose of continuing Professor Langley's studies of solar radiation. So, late in August, 1908, Campbell and Abbot climbed the mountain to make preparations for the following year. They remained all night on the summit, and "because of physical fatigue, reduced vitality, mountain sickness, and exposure to wind, the night was not spent in comfort." Dr. Campbell decided that before any extended residence could take place it was necessary to have a building of some kind as a shelter in case of a storm. He proceeded to draw up plans and specifications for "a three-room hut with stone walls and steel roof and doors, to be used not primarily as an observatory, although it might be convenient to use a part of it occasionally as a dark-room for photography, but rather as a shelter and living quarters for observers in any branch of science."[23]

Before construction could begin it was necessary to rebuild the trail, which had become badly out of repair since 1904. Marsh undertook the job once more. A ball was held in Lone Pine which netted a considerable sum. Work was begun as early in the spring as conditions permitted. On July 28, 1909, the first mule train of the season reached the top and work was begun on the stone house, for which Marsh was also the contractor. In spite of difficulties the work was practically completed by the end of August, when the scientific party arrived. Dr. Abbot writes, "Marsh worked at all kinds of jobs himself—cooking, breaking stone, carrying stone, carrying snow for water, riveting and cementing, as well as general bossing. He will never get paid in this world for the work he did on that house."

The results achieved by all parties were eminently satisfactory, although Dr. Abbot was unable to complete his observations on account of storms, and was obliged to come back the next year. Dr. Campbell reported perfect atmospheric conditions on the nights of September 1 and 2. He reached the conclusion that "the quantity of any water vapor existing in the equatorial atmosphere of Mars at the time these observations were made was too slight to be detected by present spectrographic methods." Dr. McAdie obtained continuous records of pressure, humidity, and temperature for the entire period. Reminiscing some years later, McAdie wrote: "The season was a rainy one. We had some five out of seven rainy days. We had thunderstorms *below*

Observatory cabin on summit of Mount Whitney.

us. On one occasion the hairs on the burros stood out straight, I think if the storm had been a trifle more intense there would have been four or five dead astronomers on the summit."[24]

In 1913 the shelter was again put to use by a Smithsonian expedition, under Anders Angström, of Uppsala, Sweden, for the purpose of studying the radiation of the atmosphere. W. R. Gregg, of the U. S. Weather Bureau, made explorations of the upper air by means of captive balloons, "probably the first that have been carried on by captive balloons at altitudes exceeding 4000 meters."[25] Still another group of scientific observations was conducted in the Mount Whitney region from 1922 to 1925, under Dr. Robert A. Millikan, for the study of cosmic rays, but the stations were not at the summit.[26]

Finally, what is the altitude of Mount Whitney? Over the years many attempts have been made to arrive at a precise figure. Clarence King, in 1864, estimated that it was somewhat over 15,000 feet, later using the figure 14,887. Rabe, with his barometer, in 1873, computed it at 14,898. The Wheeler Survey, in 1875, gave it at 14,471, and Langley, in 1881, produced the figure of 14,522, which was long in vogue. Then, in 1903, McAdie computed it at 14,515. The latter figure was used until 1905, when the U. S. Geological Survey substituted 14,502, or 14,501. That remained the official figure until careful leveling in 1928 produced 14,495.811. Even then there was no finality. An adjustment became necessary to bring Owens Valley levels into agreement with the U. S. Coast and Geodetic Survey's general transcontinental network. On this basis the official figure became 14,495 feet, approximately 4418 meters. The question naturally arises, do we stop there? The successive corrections have been due chiefly to improvements in instrumental accuracy. The instruments have now reached such precision that there is slight chance of error. But is it really necessary to ask the question? For all practical purposes we have known for a long time that the altitude of Mount Whitney is approximately 14,500 feet or 4420 meters.[27]

NOTES AND REFERENCES

1. *Proceedings of the California Academy of Sciences*, vol. V.

2. A rough trail was constructed in 1881 from the southwestern base to the summit, and loaded mules were taken to the top. In 1904 a trail was completed direct from Lone Pine over Whitney Pass just south of the summit. (Shown on U.S. Geological Survey, Mt. Whitney Quadrangle, 1907). It was rebuilt in 1928-1930. These trails were indeed costly, but can hardly be called dangerous.

3. In a new edition of *Mountaineering*, published in 1874 (*Farquhar* No. 12d), King added several pages to his chapter on Mount Whitney, in which he gives credit to Goodyear, with rather labored pleasantries, "for having so clearly pointed out my mistake."

4. The *Inyo Independent* was published weekly at Independence, Inyo County,

California, P. A. Chalfant, editor. It was later moved to Bishop, edited by W. A. Chalfant, son of P. A., who owned a file of the earlier numbers from which he had copies made for me a number of years ago of the Mount Whitney items. (Now in BL.)—F.P.F.

5. Rabe's account appeared in *San Francisco Daily Evening Bulletin, Supplement*, September 27, 1873; also, Carl Rabe, *The Ascent of Mount Whitney*, Berkeley, 1888 (in BL); in part, in *SCB*, 1911, 8:2.

6. Hundreds of people have made this climb by the same route since Rabe's day, and not a few have stopped "every fifteen or twenty minutes to rest and breathe."

7. "False Mount Whitney" or "Old Mount Whitney," alias "Sheep Mountain," had an even harder time acquiring a permanent name. Capt. George M. Wheeler, in U.S. Geographical Surveys West of the One Hundredth Meridian, *Geographical Report*, vol. I, 1889, states, without explanation, "This peak has since been called Mount Corcoran by the artist Mr. Albert Bierstadt." The explanation is not difficult to conjecture. There is today in the Corcoran Gallery of Art, Washington, D.C., a painting entitled "Mount Corcoran in the Sierra Nevada," by Bierstadt, dated 1878. It is large, handsome, and romantic, but it bears no recognizable resemblance to good old Sheep Mountain. It is known that Bierstadt visited Owens Valley in the 1870's, and he doubtless made sketches and notes for paintings to be finished in his studio. What more natural than that the artist should put the name of the wealthy patron of art on his picture when selling it to him at a good price? And what more natural than that Wheeler when making his map should, to oblige a friend, put the name on the map? This is only conjecture, of course, but how else could this entirely irrelevant name have appeared simultaneously on both painting and map? To make things complete, the U.S. Board on Geographic Names in 1891 rendered a decision, "Corcoran; not Mount Whitney No. 1, Old Mount Whitney, nor Sheep Rock." There the matter rested for many years, "Mount Corcoran" in Washington, "Sheep Mountain" in California. Then, in 1905, R. B. Marshall, of the U.S. Geological Survey, unaware of the Washington decision, acceded to local recommendation and placed the name "Mount Langley" on the map where it remained until 1928, when someone in Washington dug up the old "Corcoran" decision, and the next edition of the map appeared with a name never before heard by local inhabitants or those who frequented the mountains. It took fifteen years of protest before the Board in Washington would reverse its decision and come out for "Langley, not Corcoran." For face-saving, the Board gave another peak nearby the name Corcoran. The painting in the Art Gallery remains as handsome as ever, a complete unlikeness of either mountain.

8. When John Muir's original diaries were in the hands of Dr. Badè, while he was preparing the *Life and Letters*, he kindly gave me the opportunity to copy certain passages pertaining to Muir's mountain climbs. Quotations here are partly from these direct copies, partly from L. M. Wolfe, *John of the Mountains*, Boston: Houghton Mifflin, 1938.

9. For a long time Muir's route seems to have been forgotten. until Norman Clyde rediscovered it in 1930, calling it the "Mountaineer's Route." It is the most attractive route for climbing Mount Whitney, as well as the most direct, save for the almost vertical East Face Route. Neither of these should be attempted by other than experienced climbers. (See *SCB*, 1931, 16:1; *SCB*, 1941, 26:1; and the Sierra Club *Climber's Guide*.)

10. John Muir, "A Rival of the Yosemite," *Century Magazine*, November, 1891.

11. The Whitney–Russell Pass (*SCB*, 1941, 26:1; *Climber's Guide*).

12. Muir describes Bayley as "A firm, condensed, muscular little man who comes aclimbing in the mountains every year. His love of alpine exercise seems to suffer no abatement, notwithstanding he scrambles most of the year among the dangerous heights and hollows of the San Francisco stock market. He is a short man, or even shorter" (*San Francisco Evening Bulletin*, September 6, 1876; reprinted in *SCB*, 1932, 17:1). Bayley is credited with the first ascent of Mount Starr King and was a pioneer on Mount Rainier. On April 30, 1894, he was caught by an elevator in his office building and instantly killed (*SCB*, 1894, 1:4).

13. Charles Edward Washburn, of San Jose, attended Cornell, transferred to University of California, class of 1876; sang first bass in Glee Club and was a member of "The Temple of Ease" (*Blue & Gold* '76); died November 21, 1884.

14. Albert Kellogg, M.D. (1813-1887), "the first botanist who became a resident of California," and one of the founders of the California Academy of Sciences. "All who have known Dr. Kellogg will remember him as a man who, without asserting any claims to rank as a great botanist, was nevertheless one of the most ardent lovers of plant life, especially of those forms of it which make the forest, grove and thicket" (Edward L. Greene, in *Pittonia*, 1887, vol. I.)

15. *Inyo Independent*, October 9, 1875.

16. Anna Mills Johnston, "A Trip to Mt. Whitney in 1878," *Mt. Whitney Club Journal*, Visalia, 1902, 1:1.

17. A. W. de la Cour Carroll, in *SCB*, 1896, 1:7. A party from Bakersfield in 1883 included two women, according to Ella Roper Landers, in *SCB*, 1947, 32:5.

18. S. P. Langley, "Report of the Mount Whitney Expedition," in "Researches on Solar Heat," *Professional Papers of the Signal Service*, XV, 1884.

19. A. G. McAdie, "Mount Whitney as a Site for a Meteorological Observatory," *Monthly Weather Review*, November, 1903; reprinted in *SCB*, 1904, 5:2.

20. *Monthly Weather Review*, September, 1904; reprinted in *SCB*, 1905, 5:3.

21. B. W. Evermann, "Experiences in an Electrical Storm on Mount Whitney in 1904," *SCB*, 1932, 17:1. Dr. Evermann was afterwards head of the California Academy of Sciences.

22. Col. E. H. Crowder, Judge Advocate, First Division General Staff, U.S. Army, Memorandum, September 23, 1903; W. A. Langille, "Report on the Mt. Whitney Addition to the Sierra Forest Reserve," Bureau of Forestry, Department of Agriculture, 1904.

23. Quotations are from W. W. Campbell, "On the Spectrum of Mars," *Publications of the Astronomical Society of the Pacific*, October 10, 1909, 21:128; and *Lick Observatory Bulletin*, 1910, no. 169; C. G. Abbot, "A Shelter for Observers on Mount Whitney," *Smithsonian Miscellaneous Collections*, 1910, 52:4; Alexander McAdie, "The Observatory on Mount Whitney," *SCB*, 1910, 7:4. Dr. Campbell was subsequently President of the University of California.

24. McAdie to Farquhar, November 5, 1935, quoted in *SCB*, 1936, 21:1.

25. Anders Angström, "A study of the Radiation of the Atmosphere," *Smithsonian Miscellaneous Collections*, 1915, 65:3; F. P. Brackett, "The Smithsonian Expedition to California for Measurement of Nocturnal Radiation," *Publications of the Astronomical Society of Pomona College*, October, 1913, 3:1.

26. R. A. Millikan, "High Frequency Rays of Cosmic Origin," *Proceedings of the National Academy of Sciences*, January, 1926, 12:1.

27. F. P. Farquhar, "The Story of Mount Whitney," *SCB*, 1936, 21:1.

Ansel Adams

"Monolith."

XVIII

FURTHER EXPLORING AND CLIMBING

Although Brewer, King, and Muir may well be considered the foremost of early explorers of the High Sierra, there were others, both before and after, who deserve recognition. Information about some of them is meager, and there were undoubtedly many pioneers whose exploits have never been recorded. The sheepmen left no records other than the devastation wrought by their flocks, except occasionally a little pile of rocks or a carved stick. We do know a little about the prospectors from Owens Valley who showed the Brewer party the way into Kings River canyon in 1864 and whose trail led over Kearsarge Pass. One of the members of this party many years later told of their experiences.[1] From the South Fork of Kings River they made their way to the upper regions of the San Joaquin and eventually left the mountains by Taboose Pass. Although no useful information about the High Sierra resulted from this trip, it is cited as evidence that even the remotest parts of the mountains were being visited. But the time was at hand when published accounts began to appear which stimulated a great deal of interest in the mountains among the growing communities on both sides of the Sierra. Such was the account of a very thorough exploration of Kings canyon in 1868 by Judge E. C. Winchell, a pioneer of Fresno County.[2] A neighbor and friend of his, Frank Dusy, not only made explorations in the Kings River country, especially in the North Fork region, but presently offered his services as a guide. From his summer home, which he called "Dinkey," he made extensive trips far up the Middle Fork of Kings River.[3] He had earlier discovered Tehipite Dome and Valley, and in 1879 brought bulky camera equipment into the Valley and took the first photograph ever taken of Tehipite Dome. Lil A. Winchell, twenty-four-year-old son of Judge Winchell, assisted Dusy on that occasion, and went on to explore farther up the Middle Fork and make the first ascent of Mount Goddard.[4]

One of the most active of the Government surveys during the decade of the 1870's was the Wheeler Survey (Geographical Surveys West of the One-Hundredth Meridian), conducted by Lieutenant (later Captain) George M. Wheeler, of the U. S. Army Engineers. Although most of its work was east of California, a considerable amount of triangulation was done in the Sierra. Mount Whitney was surveyed in September and October, 1875, but with no important results save a computation of altitude at 14,471, nearest to present figures obtained up to that time.[5] Of greater interest was the work of the Wheeler Survey under Lieutenant M. M. Macomb in the three years that followed.[6] In 1876 Macomb and his assistants operated in the Tahoe region. They made camp at Glenbrook, "very prettily situated on a small bay about the middle of the east shore of the lake. A brook flowing through a deep and shady glen empties into this bay and gives the place its name. Settled in 1860, it is the center of the Lake Tahoe lumber trade and possesses four sawmills and a planing-mill." Macomb describes the operation by which the sawed lumber was carried to the summit east of Glenbrook by a narrow gauge railroad, built in 1875, and thence sent down to the Carson Valley by flume.[7]

From Glenbrook, Macomb and his party moved south along the lake shore to Rowland's.[8] With his topographer, Frank Carpenter, he climbed Freel's Peak, highest point in the Tahoe area, where they found records of a party of the U. S. Coast Survey, left there the previous year.[9] They continued surveying around the southern and western sides of the lake, including Fallen Leaf and Cascade lakes and Emerald Bay. Pyramid Peak and Mount Tallac were occupied. Of the latter Macomb writes, "This peak is a most interesting one, not only on account of its own beauty as seen from the lake, but because of the beautiful view from its summit. The little steamer, a white speck upon the blue expanse, was seen making its daily rounds." The geologist, Alfred R. Conklin, reported on many features of the region. "Echo Lake," he says, "lies between two rocky ridges on top of the Western Summit, about one mile from the Placerville Road. It is about one and a half miles long and one-fourth mile broad. The southern bank of the lake is lined with conifers and a few alder bushes. Elsewhere the shores are very barren and rocky.[10] There are at least twenty other lakes of minor importance throughout the Western Summit. These mountain lakes usually lie in cup-shaped depressions in the granite."

At the beginning of the field season of 1877 Lieutenant Macomb's party made a brief excursion in the vicinity of the Central Pacific Railroad north of Lake Tahoe, in the course of which Castle Peak was occupied. They then turned their attention to the area farther south. While surveying on the divide between the Carson and the Stanislaus a serious accident occured to topographer Cowles—an example of what may happen, and indeed has happened, among the huge loose blocks of rock on Sierra ridges. "We had finished a very successful day's work," writes Macomb, "and were completing our labors by putting up the usual monument, experiencing considerable difficulty in finding suitable material, the peak being composed of large fragments of heavy magnetic rock. In attempting to detach a small piece, Mr. Cowles loosened a heavy mass, which, slipping from its bearings, precipitated him some fifteen feet upon the jagged rocks below, passing over his legs as it rolled on. Mr. Vail (the meteorologist) and myself, on hastening to his assistance, were inexpressibly shocked to find that both legs had been broken below the knee, but were immensely relieved to find that he had escaped with his life. We carried him in our arms as best we might over the uncertain footing afforded by the loose rock, until we reached a spot level enough to put him down." With the help of other members of the survey party and some nearby woodcutters he was brought down to the foot of the mountain. A doctor, summoned from Genoa fifty-five miles away, found that both bones in each leg had been broken in several places, but he thought that both could be saved as the flesh had been protected by high boots.[11]

"Another misfortune," reports Lieutenant Macomb, "was the scarcity of feed in the mountains. This was due to the fact that the country was completely overrun with vast herds of sheep, which utterly denuded the mountain valleys of grass, and in fact of nearly every green thing within their reach. This unusual influx of sheep was caused by the drought throughout Central and Southern California, the water-supply having failed on account of the light rain and snow fall of the previous winter, the average being one of the smallest on record for years. All through the mountain country visited there are fine summer ranges, with abundance of wild grasses, on which the right to drive sheep and stock is claimed by original discovery or purchase. The men who are in the habit of summering their flocks here are known to one another, and, as a general rule, respect each other's rights. But this year there were many interlopers from the south, who, rendered desperate by circumstances, respected no one's claims, and, in consequence, numerous feuds resulted whenever they came in contact with the original occupants, sometimes resulting in loss of life. There is much bitter feeling among the cattle-owners against the shepherds, since it is impossible for their herds to feed where the sheep are, the latter invariably driving them off. There is no doubt that if the sheep continue to be driven up into these mountains in such vast numbers the grasses will eventually be killed out and great injury inflicted on the country." This damage by sheep continued for many years throughout the Sierra and in some areas, notably the headwaters of the Kern, did permanent damage. Not until the establishment of the National Parks and the Forest Reserves was there any effective regulation.

For one more season the Wheeler Survey operated in the Sierra Nevada, principally in the Yosemite region. Lieutenant Macomb and his topographer J. Calvert Spiller in September, 1878, occupied Mount Dana and Mount Conness and "the highest one of the Cathedral Peaks." They climbed Mount Lyell, "but all our trouble was rendered fruitless by the clouds and chilling mists which hung about the summit." But although it was the first of October, Macomb was not to be defeated. From Yosemite Valley he returned to Mount Lyell, apparently alone, and suceeded in getting the necessary angles. Next day, by a forced march of thirty-five miles, he returned to the Valley. In spite of a heavy snowstorm work was continued to the end of the month. Triangulation was completed by the occupation of Mount Hoffmann and finally Mount Clark and Merced Peak. Although Macomb and his assistants carried out their assignments faithfully and efficiently, the work of the Wheeler Survey in the Sierra Nevada was of very little permanent value. An exception was the map of Yosemite and its immediate surroundings, issued in 1883, prepared largely from Macomb's surveys and for many years the standard map of the region.

The great Half Dome in Yosemite Valley had been pronounced by Professor Whitney in his most pontifical manner to be "perfectly inaccessible." "It never will be trodden by human foot," he added. He weakened a little, however, when an attempt to climb it nearly succeeded, and introduced "perhaps" in a new edition of his *Yosemite Guide-Book*.[12] John Muir gives a lively account of this attempt.[13] "John Conway, a resident of the Valley, has a flock of small boys who climb smooth rocks like lizards. He sent them up the Dome with a rope, hoping they might be able to fasten it with spikes driven into fissures, and thus reach the top. They took the rope in tow and succeeded in making it fast two or three hundred feet above the point ordinarily reached, but finding the upper portion of the curve impracticable without laboriously drilling into the rock, he called down his lizards, thinking himself fortunate in effecting a safe retreat." Sound mountaineering on the part of Mr. Conway!

It remained for another resident of the Valley, George C. Anderson, whom Muir was happy to acknowledge as a fellow Scot, to complete the climb and be the first to set foot upon the summit of Half Dome. "Anderson began with Conway's old rope," says Muir, "and resolutely drilled his way to the top, inserting eyebolts five or six feet apart, making his rope fast to each in succession, resting his foot on the last bolt while he drilled for the next above. Occasionally some irregularity in the curve or slight foothold would enable him to climb fifteen or twenty feet independently of the rope, which he would pass and begin drilling again, the whole thing accomplished in a few days." Muir himself hastened to be among the first to follow. "Our first winter storm had bloomed," he writes, "and all the mountains were mantled with fresh snow. I was therefore a little apprehensive of danger from the slipperiness of the rock, Anderson refusing to believe that anyone could climb his rope in the condition it was then in." But Muir went up, alone, and "gained the top without the slightest difficulty." In characteristic fashion he goes on to describe the view and particularly the botany. Spiraea and Pentstemon were there, and several species of grasses and sedges. There were three species of pines, "repressed and storm beaten." He never gets around to telling us how he got down, but it may be presumed that he did not spend the night there.[14]

Others soon followed, including "four English gentlemen, then sojourning in the Valley. A day or two afterwards, Miss S. L. Dutcher, of San Francisco, with the courage of a heroine, accomplished it, and was the first lady that ever stood upon it."[15] There were other early ascents of Half Dome, and there is one that deserves special mention, for it introduces an advance upon Clarence King's riata method. During the winter of 1883-1884 ice and snow had carried away most of Anderson's rope and some of his eyebolts. "Just after sunset, one evening of the ensuing summer," writes Hutchings, "every resident of the Valley, familiar with the fact of the rope's removal, was startled by the sight of a blazing fire upon the crest of the Dome." It turned out that two young men had made the perilous climb. One of them, Alden Sampson, of New

Phimister Proctor on Half Dome in 1884, drawn by him from memory in 1945.

York, a few days later gave Hutchings a vivid account of their experiences; the other, Phimister Proctor, of Colorado, writing sixty years afterwards, added some interesting details.[16] To read the whole story leaves one limp with vicarious fatigue, as may be conceived from the following abridgement: "I made the climb barefoot," says Proctor. "Sampson had nailed boots. I was a pretty fair hand with a lariat, so, tying a loop on a lash rope, I made a throw. After several false pitches I got the range. As we proceeded we found that some of the pins had been bent and were difficult to rope. Often my loop would roll over a ring twenty times before I caught it. Several of the pins pulled out when I put my weight on the rope. When I reached a pin I would climb up on it, leaning against the wall of the mountain, and hook my big toe over the pin." Now let Sampson take up the tale: "After a while we came to a clean stretch of a hundred feet where every pin had been carried away; yet at this point a difficult corner of the ledge had to be turned. In the hardest place of all, a little bunch of dwarf Spiraea, six or eight inches high, which was growing in a crevice, gave me friendly assistance." At the end of the first day they had made but half the distance. The second day was even more perilous than the first, but they made the top at last and just at sunset built the fire that was seen from below. "Reluctantly we left," writes Proctor, "slid down the cable and reached safety just at dark."

"Mount Starr King," Whitney declared, "is the most symmetrical and beautiful of all the dome-shaped masses around the Yosemite. Its summit is absolutely inaccessible."[17] Once again Whitney was wrong, for in 1876 George Bayley, the same who had been with Muir on Mount Whitney the year before, together with a young lawyer named Schuler, conquered it, "with the exception of a few branches of spirey needles, the last of Yosemite's inaccessibles."[18]

A notable excursion took place in 1881, coincident with Professor Langley's visit to Mount Whitney. Three friends from the Tulare Valley took the Hockett Trail across the Kern to Whitney Creek, "upon which we tried unsuccessfully to impress the name 'Volcano Creek,' as the stream does not rise in the vicinity of Mount Whitney."[19] They noted the phenomenon of "red snow," which when crushed looked like "red rock-candy."[20] At the base of Mount Whitney they met Captain Michaelis of the Langley party, whose invitation to spend the night with him on the summit was accepted by Wallace and Wright. There, in the moonlight, "outlines of all other great mountains in the region were visible, and the snowfields about Mount Keweah shone with subdued brilliancy." In the morning, looking across the Inyo mountains, they could see Telescope Peak overlooking Death Valley. "What a contrast," writes Wallace, "between two points! Here we stood on the highest mountain in the United States, and there, but seventy-five miles away, was the lowest land in America—280 feet below sea-level!"[21] From Mount

Whitney the three, Wallace, Wales, and Wright, made their way toward the head of the Kern and pioneered a way down to the river at Junction Meadow.[22] A few days later they mounted the Chagoopah Plateau, at the base of Mount Kaweah, and proceeded to climb the nearby peak. At noon they left their horses below the first snowfield. "Thence they moved to the west, climbing from rock to rock, upward and ever upward, soon wearied and out of breath. No one can have a conception of the extreme exertion and utter exhaustion from time to time of this rough and trackless peak climbing." It is quite apparent that Mr. Wright is speaking—he was the eldest and the heaviest of the three. His comrades reached the summit more than an hour and a half ahead of him. "After a careful examination not the slighest trace was found that any human being had ever been there before."[23]

Two government agencies now take a foremost place in the exploration of the Sierra. First of these was the United States Coast and Geodetic Survey, engaged in a vast scheme of triangulation connecting the Atlantic and the Pacific coasts. The western end was under direction of George Davidson. Signals had been exchanged in 1879, and again in 1887, between Round Top, near Carson Pass, and Mount Conness, north of Tuolumne Meadows.[24] "When we were at Round Top in 1879," writes Professor Davidson, "two of our best heliotropers were at Conness, and the difficulties and dangers were so great that they took turns in each staying at the station three days consecutively; and rather than go over the dangerous ridge below the summit they burrowed in a recess near the station, and only left in a snowstorm, or when the terrific thunderstorms played around the summit. When these men received the signal from Round Top to leave, the snow hence to Mono Lake was ten feet deep, and they had to abandon their clothes and blankets but one apiece, and leave with provisions for two days." The third, and most extended, occupation was in the summer of 1890. A temporary advance camp was established at the Soda Springs in Tuolumne Meadows, "by permission of Mr. John Lembert, the owner."[25] Difficulties were extreme that season—the river was in flood and the trail to Mount Conness was mostly under snow when they arrived, and was rendered further impassable by fallen trees. "It was, however, with great labor opened for ten miles to the old heliotropers' camp, about eighteen hundred feet below the summit of Conness. No quadruped, except the mountain sheep, had ever gone higher than this camp." A rough route was worked out to the top, and there a little shelter was built to house the instruments. "Every moment of the month of August and a week in September was utilized for observing, and more than two thousand five hundred observations were made."[26] Davidson gives a vivid account of thunderstorms: "Early in the day magnificent masses of cumulus formed along the line of the Sierra as far north and south as was visible. When forming over such masses as Mount Lyell and its neighbors, the magnificent volumes of cloud would become very black and flattened at the base, and gradually settle down enough to envelope the tops of the mountains, and heavy thunder peals would reverberate through the canyons at frequent intervals. Between the higher mountain masses there would be long breaks in the cloud volumes, and broad areas of lower mountains, valleys, and canyons would be in sunshine. Toward sunset the ominous clouds would begin to dissolve, and sometimes the most gorgeous effects of light, shadow, and color would be exhibited. By nine o'clock at night the clouds had usually disappeared and the heavens seemed filled with twice as many stars as are visible at low altitudes, and the Milky Way was a most impressive object." "After the clearing," he continues, "there is revealed a limitless sheet of snow, but the sky is deep blue, the atmosphere so remarkably clear that ranges distant one hundred and fifty miles seem to be not even fifty miles away."

The other Government agency exploring the Sierras was the United States Geological Survey, which had, in 1879, gathered into one the several independent surveys that had been operating in the West for the previous ten years. Although a systematic survey of the Sierra Nevada was not begun until several years later, an intensive study was made in 1882-1883 of the eastern slope adjacent to Mono Lake and of the region embracing mounts Dana, Lyell, and Ritter. This study was carried out by Israel C. Russell, assisted by Willard D. Johnson, under the general supervision of Grove Karl Gilbert. These men were professionals, who proceeded with scientific precision. "Existing glaciers on Mount Dana and Mount Lyell," reports Russell, "were visited by Mr. Gilbert and myself during the summer of 1883; I also examined one at the head of Parker Creek, a tributary of Mono Lake; others on Mounts Conness, Maclure, and Ritter were explored by Mr. Johnson."[27] Russell gives a fine description of the eastern escarpment of the Sierra: "After crossing Rush Creek, we begin the ascent of the sloping plain leading to the base of the Sierra. There are no foothills, but one can ride directly to the base of the great scarp. The precipitous eastern slope is determined by an immense fault. That there has been very recent movement along this fracture is rendered certain by the fresh scarps [scars?] of displacement which cross moraines, terraces, and alluvial slopes, thus proving that orographic movement has taken place since the withdrawal of the glaciers and since the evaporation of the large lake which formerly filled the valley."[28] A detailed account is given of the ascent of Mount Dana and the glacial phenomena observed. They descended to a "well constructed wagon road near the west base of the mountain, which will enable one to journey with ease through a mountain range that is among the most attractive and most instructive in the world."[29]

By the year 1890 the main features of the Sierra Nevada had became fairly well known and a few of the more spectacular regions, such as Yosemite Valley and Mount Whitney, had been intensively studied. A number of the high peaks had been climbed, and all the principal canyons had been visited. The foothill regions and the main forest belt were being actively exploited for their timber and minerals. Search for minerals in the higher parts of the range had yielded almost nothing of value—a trace of copper here and there, and a little silver. The mining booms of Mineral King, Mammoth, and Tioga had flourished for a time, then faded into memories. Only in the extreme northern end of the range was mining a continuing activity. Recreation in the high mountains had almost been extinguished by the invasion of the sheep. Trails were almost nonexistent and reliable details were not to be found on any maps. Even in Yosemite conditions were far from satisfactory. The Commissioners were under attack for alleged mismanagement of the Valley, and, whether rightly or wrongly, it can at least be said that there was confusion of policy. On one occasion the introduction of electric lights was considered, "the dynamos to be run by the ample hydraulic power furnished by the various waterfalls. Electric lights on the Yosemite trails and summits would enable effects unrivalled in their awe-inspiring beauty, and serve to carry the fame of the valley farther than ever."[30] Although this particular horror was spared us, we cannot in this age of bulldozers and concrete assume too much of an air of superiority.

But if the year 1890 may be said to mark a low point in the position of the Sierra as a permanent asset of the nation, a new epoch was about to begin. A more mature appraisal of natural beauty and a more widespread recognition of the value of living forests and unspoiled wilderness were already in the making. And in this, John Muir, as if trained for this very purpose, was to take a leading part.

Notes and References

1. Thomas Keough, "Over Kearsarge Pass in 1864," *SCB*, 1918, 10:3.

2. E. C. Winchell, "Kings River Canyon in 1868," *San Francisco Morning Call*, September 11 and 12, 1872. Reprinted in *SCB*, 1926, 12:3.

3. *A Guide to the Grand and Sublime Scenery in the Sierra Nevada in the Region about Mount Whitney*, prepared and published by W. W. Elliott, San Francisco, 1883 (*Farquhar* No. 16).

4. Memorandum of conversation with Lil A. Winchell, October, 1921.—F.P.F. (in BL.)

5. Wheeler Survey (U.S. Geographical Surveys West of the One-Hundredth Meridian), *Geographical Report*, 1889.

6. Wheeler Survey, *Annual Reports* (appendixes of the *Annual Reports of the Chief of Engineers*), for 1877, 1878, 1879 (field seasons 1876, 1877, 1878).

7. See John Debo Galloway, "Early Engineering Works Contributory to the Comstock," *University of Nevada Bulletin*, June, 1947.

8. This and other places on the shore of Lake Tahoe are fully described in Edward B. Scott, *The Saga of Lake Tahoe* Crystal Bay, Lake Tahoe, Nevada: Sierra-Tahoe Publishing Co., 1957.

9. *Ibid*. Freel's Peak (Freel Peak) was named for James Washington Freel, an early rancher. It is the highest of the three Job's Peaks, which were named for Moses Job, an early Mormon settler in Carson Valley.

10. The shores of Echo Lake have changed since 1876, when a dam raised the level of the lake.

11. The *Wheeler Survey Report for 1878* (season of 1877) is reassuring: "William A. Cowles, who received a most untimely and unfortunate fall, resulting in a compound fracture of both legs, by skillful treatment and care is about to secure the renewed use of his limbs, and hopes to be a candidate for further survey-work."

12. The 1874 "pocket edition" (*Farquhar* 7f).

13. In the *San Francisco Evening Bulletin*, November 18, 1875. The Whitney account mentions only one boy, Conway's son Major, aged nine years.

14. *Ibid*.

15. *Hutchings*, 1886. My brother-in-law, Farnsworth Currier, on seeing the name of Dutcher in my notes, recalled that he had recently seen the name in a book. He located the following passage amid other quite irrelevant subjects: "While spending an hour upon the summit, I discovered on its barren surface, a lady's bracelet. On showing it to Anderson, he said, 'I pulled up a young woman recently but she never mentioned any loss except from nausea.' Returning to Merced, I observed a vigorous young woman wearing a bracelet similar to the one I had found. The lady proved to be Miss Sally Dutcher of San Francisco, who admitted the loss and thankfully accepted the missing ornament. A letter to me from Galen Clark states that he assisted in Miss Dutcher's ascent and that she was the first woman who made the ascent" (Julius C. Birge, *The Awakening of the Desert*, Boston: Gorham Press, 1912).

16. A. Phimister Proctor, famous sculptor and artist, lived the last few years of his life at the Bohemian Club, San Francisco, where I was privileged to know him. "Phim" was writing his memoirs (alas, never completed) and showed me his chapter, "An Ascent of Half Dome in 1884." I persuaded him to let me have it printed and he drew a picture of himself as he remembered it in the act of lassoing the pins. This was printed in a small edition for private distribution by the Grabhorn Press, San Francisco, in 1945; reprinted in *SCB*, 1946, 31:6.—F.P.F.

17. Whitney Survey, *Geology*, 1865.

18. Muir, *San Francisco Evening Bulletin*, September 6, 1876. Even the "spirey needles" were ultimately climbed; see chap. xx below.

19. W. B. Wallace, "A Night on Mt. Whitney," *Mt. Whitney Club Journal*, May, 1902, 1:1.

20. In order to procure reliable information about "red snow" I consulted my long-time friend and companion on Sierra Club trips, Dr. Rimo Bacigalupi, of the Jepson Herbarium, Department of Botany, University of California, who has furnished the following references. I am also indebted to Dr. Janet R. Stein, of the Department of Biology and Botany, University of British Columbia, Vancouver, for the appended note.—F.P.F.

Gilbert M. Smith, *The Fresh-Water Algae of the United States*, New York: McGraw-Hill, 1933: "The phenomenon of red snow has been recorded a number of times from the mountains of the western part of the United States. In every case this was assumed to be due to *Sphaerella nivalis* Sommerf. Examination of red snow from Desolation Valley above Fallen Leaf, California, has shown that there are other red snow organisms in this country besides *S. nivalis*." This quotation is from the 1st edition of Smith; in the 2d edition, 1950, a footnote is added, "Since it is now known to be a *Chlamydomonas*, the generic name, *Sphaerella* is invalid."

Frederick Vernon Coville, "Botany of the Death Valley Expedition," *Contributions from the U. S. National Herbarium*. Vol. IV, Washington, 1893: "The so-called red snow of alpine regions was seen frequently about Farewell Gap and other points in the vicinity of timber-line in the high Sierra Nevada. The moist snow presents in spots a beautiful pink color, in clear contrast with the white of other portions. When examined in the hand the snow looks precisely as if it had been stained with a pale-red fluid, and does not show any red corpuscles. No microscopic examination of the minute algae could be made."

Janet R. Stein: "Red snow has been observed in melting snows in late spring and early summer. The color is the result of many millions of microscopic (10-60 microns) algal cells. The main organism considered responsible is a motile, green alga, *Chlamydomonas nivalis*, present in the non-motile, resting stage and containing red carotenoid pigments. Sometimes present are other green algae that may be non-motile and contain abundant orange carotenoid pigments in the resting cells. The algae collect around detritus. The intensity of color seems dependent upon light intensity with the color being brighter on a cloudy day than on a sunny day. The algal cells are able to withstand repeated freezing and thawing of this environment, although the temperature of the snow remains close to 0° C. In many areas, as the snow melts, the red resting cells remain on the underlying rocks and soil. These resting stages are able to withstand adverse conditions and are probably blown about by the wind, thus being dispersed throughout the snow zone."

21. Death Valley is not visible from Mount Whitney although frequently said to be—the Panamint Range intervenes. Both, however, are in Inyo County.

22. That is, they "pioneered" in the spread of information; the ubiquitous sheepherder had been there before with his devastating hoofed locusts.

23. Elliott's *Guide* (see n. 3).

24. George Davidson, "The Occupation of Mount Conness," *Overland Monthly*, February, 1892.

25. John Baptist Lembert homesteaded land in Tuolomne Meadows in 1885. The property included the Soda Springs and the meadow directly across the river. He built a log cabin and for a time lived there the year round. He later moved to a cabin below Yosemite, where he was murdered in the winter of 1896-1897. The Soda Springs property was purchased by the McCauley brothers, from whom it was acquired by the Sierra Club in 1912.

26. "The signals used in these great triangulations," writes Davidson, "are reflected beams of sunlight, which reach the observer as bright, starlike points. On lines of sixty miles a mirror of three inches diameter will reflect a bright, minute image that is readily seen with the naked eye if the intervening atmosphere is clear; and the light from a mirror eight inches square has been seen by the naked eye as a bright star at one hundred and sixty miles. These heliotrope signals penetrate the atmosphere when it is quite smoky, and the area of the mirror is computed for such emergencies" (Davidson, *op. cit.*).

27. Israel C. Russell, "Existing Glaciers of the United States," *Fifth Annual Report of the United States Geological Survey, 1883-'84*. Substantially the same in Russell, *Glaciers of North America*, Boston: Ginn, 1897.

28. Israel C. Russell, "Quaternary History of Mono Valley, California," *Eighth Annual Report of the United States Geological Survey, 1886-'87*.

29. The road referred to was the "Great Sierra Wagon Road," built in 1882-1883 to serve the Tioga Mining District. It was abandoned soon after completion when the mines closed down. It became impassable for wagons and was hardly more than a trail when, in 1915, it was acquired from the successors of the Great Sierra Consolidated Silver Mining Company by Stephen T. Mather and a few friends and donated to Yosemite National Park. The story of the mining district and the Tioga Road is told by Carl P. Russell, "Early Mining Excitements East of Yosemite," *SCB*, 1928, 13:1, and in his *One Hundred Years in Yosemite*, Berkeley: University of California Press, 1931, and later editions; also, Douglass Hubbard, *Ghost Mines of Yosemite*, Fresno: Awani Press, 1958. The old Tioga Road has since been rebuilt, and in part relocated, as a modern highway.

30. *Biennial Report of the Commissioners to Manage Yosemite Valley and the Mariposa Big Tree Grove for the Years 1891-92*. It was further suggested that a searchlight operated from Glacier Points "could be made to illuminate, in various colors, the Yosemite Falls, Vernal and Nevada falls, Mount Starr King, Clouds Rest, and the various domes and cliffs; and could be used to illuminate a fountain at night with its various rainbow colors, and to produce most novel effects in Mirror Lake."

XIX

NATIONAL PARKS AND FORESTS

▼▼▼

When California became a state in 1850 practically all the land in the Sierra remained in federal ownership. Most of it was unsuitable for cultivation or for homesteads, the only uses for which existing laws provided. There was no provision for the potential uses of grazing and lumbering. This did not deter the owners of sheep and cattle from bringing their stock into the mountains in search of summer pasturage, regardless of any legal right. The cutting of timber was another matter. There had long been a law prohibiting depredations of timber on the public domain. Acquisition of enough land to make economical lumber operations possible could only be brought about by the purchase or pooling of individual 160-acre tracts. This led to subterfuge, frequently abetted by laxity, or even venality, on the part of government agents. When it became apparent that this was going on, the public began to demand new policies. The first step was to obtain withdrawal from entry of forest lands thought to be in jeopardy. But withdrawal was at the discretion of individuals and could be reversed. Legislation was needed. Threatened encroachments upon the Big Trees and other species in the great Tulare County forests brought into action a group of citizens who conducted a vigorous campaign, with appeals to Washington.[1] At their head was George W. Stewart, editor of the *Visalia Delta*. He was ably supported by Frank J. Walker, also of Visalia, and Tipton Lindsey of Tulare. They were making good progress toward effective reservation when a new kind of organization appeared, more difficult to deal with than lumber companies. This caused them to alter their plans.

One day in October, 1885, a group of forty or fifty people arrived by train from San Francisco and filed claims in the Visalia Land Office for 160-acre tracts along the Kaweah River and in Giant Forest. Out of these claims there grew the Kaweah Co-operative Colony, which proposed to establish a modern Utopia.[2] They had an elaborate plan for pooling their tracts after their claims were allowed. When all was in order they would build a road to Giant Forest, set up a sawmill, and begin lumbering operations. The economy of the Colony was predicated upon the sale of lumber, the proceeds to provide funds for outside purchases such as provisions and other supplies. Members of the Colony would do the work, receiving, instead of cash, time checks at a uniform rate per hour for laborers and administrators alike. The time checks would be the medium of exchange at the Colony store. For a few years all went well. After some uncertainties, the claims in the Giant Forest were allowed. The road was built, although it did not get quite to Giant Forest; it was near enough, however, that a mill was set up and lumber was produced, mostly from small trees. The largest tree in Giant Forest was renamed "Karl Marx."[3] But in the course of time weaknesses began to appear and dissension arose. Nevertheless, for a while the almost religious zeal of the founders kept the enterprise going. By 1891 there was no doubt that the socialistic plan of the Colony had failed. Proceeds from the lumbering operations did not come up to expectations. The time checks ceased to be valid currency and became mere curiosities. "Karl Marx" reverted to "General Sherman." Nevertheless, effects of the enterprise lasted for many years. Many of the colonists and their descendants remained as highly regarded citizens of the Kaweah region, and their tracts in Giant Forest continued to be occupied as summer homes.

The advocates of forest reservation found that they had to modify their plans, for there was considerable sympathy with the colonists throughout the community. Stewart himself, through the *Delta*, recommended the exclusion of the Giant Forest region. So, when a bill was introduced in Congress for forest protection, in the summer of 1890, that area was not included. There has long been uncertainty about the source and weight of influence that produced this bill and obtained its remarkably prompt passage. General William Vandever, who introduced it into Congress, had not been a member of the Tulare County group—in fact he was a representative of another district—but he was certainly in close touch with them. However, the movement for preserving the Big Trees was growing. The American Association for the Advancement of Science was interested. So was the California Academy of Sciences, stimulated by the Swedish savant Gustavus A. Eisen, then living in Fresno, who had an extensive knowledge of the territory. But recent studies have disclosed that probably the most effective influence was that of the Visalia group headed by Stewart, supplemented by another Visalian, Daniel K. Zumwalt, a land agent of the Southern Pacific Railroad, who was in Washington during the summer of 1890.[4] There seems to have been little or no organized opposition to the bill. It passed both House and Senate without dissent and was signed by President Benjamin Harrison on September 25, 1890. The Sequoia Act provided that two townships in Tulare County, plus four adjacent sections, be "reserved as a public park, or pleasure ground, for the benefit and enjoyment of the people." In this, and in other phrases, it followed closely the precedent of the Act of 1872 that established Yellowstone National Park. Then a curious thing occured. Another bill, also sponsored by Vandever, relating to the Yosemite region, came before the House on September 30, the last day of the session. Just before it was voted upon it was amended by consent, tacking on two other areas unrelated to Yosemite. One of these areas more than doubled the size of the reservation stated in the Act of September 25, and this time Giant Forest and a large region surrounding it were included. The other area reserved four square miles not contiguous to the other reservations. Again there was no opposition, and the bill was signed by the President on October 1.

The Yosemite Act of October 1, 1890, had a different origin and, except for the amendments, a different purpose from that of the preceding Act. It was concerned not so much with forest preservation as with watershed protection. In this it was John Muir who was the activating agent. By a fortunate circumstance he had met Robert Underwood Johnson, an editor of the *Century Magazine*, who had come to San Francisco in the summer of 1889 to arrange for a series of articles on California. Muir persuaded him not only to visit Yosemite but to go on a camping trip with him to Tuolumne Meadows. Johnson was entranced. "One conversation that we had beside the campfire at Soda Springs," he wrote later in his memoirs, "had an important sequel, for it was here that I proposed to Muir that we should set on foot the project of the Yosemite National Park. Our camp on the Tuolumne was outside the limitations of the Yosemite Valley reservation. It did not by any means include the headwaters of the streams which fed the three great falls, the Yosemite, the Nevada, and the Bridalveil. On account of the denudation by sheep the winter snows, having no underbrush to hold them, melted in torrents early in the spring, so that there was comparatively little supply for the waterfalls during the summer months. This was all explained to me by Muir, whereupon I said to him, 'Obviously the thing to do was to make a Yosemite National Park around the Valley on the plan of the Yellowstone.' "[5] It was planned that Muir would write some articles for the *Century* and Johnson would further the park project through his influential friends in the East. The following summer the articles appeared, just in time to arouse popular interest in support of Vandever's bill.[6]

The almost simultaneous enactment of these two bills has posed many questions to which there are no entirely satisfactory answers. The Sequoia Act, in its original form, used the word "park"; the Yosemite Act used the term "reserved forest lands." In other respects the provisions were much the same. The lands were "withdrawn from settlement, occupancy, or sale," and placed under the control of the Secretary of the Interior, who was authorized to make regulations for the preservation from injury of "all timber, mineral deposits, natural curiosities or wonders, and their retention in their natural condition." He was to provide against "the wanton destruction of the fish and game and their capture or destruction for purposes of merchandise or profit." He was also authorized to cause all persons trespassing to be removed. These regulations were all very well, but how were they to be enforced? Nothing was said in either act about administrative personnel, and no appropriations were made. There were no penalties for trespassing or for the other offenses named. Moreover, a considerable amount of patented land was included within the boundaries of both parks, but the rights of the owners were not defined. Secretary of the Interior John Noble, to whom the administration was entrusted, met these problems as best he could. In the first place, he gave names to the reservations: Sequoia National Park (a name suggested by Stewart), General Grant National Park (for the General Grant Tree, which had been named in 1867), and Yosemite National Park (proposed by Muir and Johnson). The term "National Park" thus became established. The problem of administration and payroll was solved according to the Yellowstone precedent of requesting assistance from the Army. The Secretary of War responded by designating a troop of cavalry for each park. Thus began a service that continued for twenty-four years, marked by the outstanding character and ability of the officers and men assigned to this duty.

The first officer to become Acting Superintendent of Yosemite National Park was Captain Abram Epperson Wood, of the Fourth Cavalry. Immediately upon his appointment he visited the Park for the purpose of selecting a site for headquarters. The Yosemite Valley was still under state administration and was not subject to federal jurisdiction. The next most convenient location was found by Captain Wood to be on the South Fork of the Merced at Wawona. There he established the camp, soon to be known as Camp A. E. Wood, today a public campground bearing the same name. Almost immediately the Acting Superintendent was confronted with two major problems: trespass by sheep and cattle, and the rights of land owners in and adjacent to the Park. These problems were discussed extensively in his report at the end of the first season. "The cattle owners have generally tried to observe the law," he wrote, "but there are many small holders living in the vicinity of the Park who are too poor to hire a herder, and whose old stock will drift up the various canyons leading into the Park as the feed in the foothills gets poor. Most of the owners have told me that they would dispose of such stock before the snows melt next year."[7] The sheep owners were different. "The last days of May," Wood reported, "the sheep commenced their annual migrations to the mountain grazing grounds, and by the 10th of June there were fully 60,000 of them close to the southern and at least 30,000 near the western boundaries of the Park." "I had to adopt some plan of action," he continued, "that would thoroughly frighten the owners as well as the herders, or my men and horses would be worn out by perpetually scouring these almost impassible mountains, and even then, as soon as our backs were turned the herds would be slipped in and grazed until another patrol came along." So the Captain sent Lieutenant Davis, of his troop, to warn all herders whom he found trespassing to leave the Park, and if after a reasonable lapse of time he found any of them back he was to arrest the herders and bring them to headquarters at Wawona.

For the time being the sheepmen were scared, but when they found that they could not be penalized they returned to the Park. For two more years Captain Wood continued as Acting Superintendent, until his untimely death, in April, 1894. By his third year he had practically conquered the problem of the sheep. "When herders are arrested," he wrote, "they are marched to another part of the Park for ejectment, this march consuming four or five days; and after they are ejected it takes as long to go back to their herds. In the meantime the sheep are alone, and the forest animals are liable to destroy and scatter many of them. When the owner awakens to this fact, he takes more interest in the doings of his herders and gives them orders not to enter the Park under any circumstances. So far this season (1893) no willful trespass by the sheepmen has been discovered."

Few serious fires were reported during Captain Wood's administration, but one episode deserves mention. "Students from the various educational institutions of the State frequently make up parties to travel on foot to the different objects of interest in the Sierras during the summer vacations. Such a company of students from the University of California, whilst journeying near Hazel Green, discovered a fire, and throwing aside their knapsacks they applied themselves with such diligence and effect that, in the course of three or four hours, they subdued what might have become a very destructive fire."

It turned out in the next few years that the sheepmen were not conquered after all. They merely became more wary and brought their bands into remote portions of the Park. One superintendent wrote in his report, "The great trouble is that the sheepmen know the country thoroughly. They band together and hire men who act as scouts, and from commanding points watch the trails. When troops are seen they give warning." Year after year the superintendent would beg for legislation that would impose penalties, but vigorous and conscientious as these cavalry officers were, they seem to have made no impression on a somnolent government in Washington.

Other problems, too, continued without abatement, except where a superintendent took matters into his own hands with firmness and ingenuity. Such was the case in the summer of 1896, when a request was made on behalf of a small party for permission to carry rifles while crossing a part of the Yosemite Reservation. Lieutenant Colonel S. B. M. Young, Acting Superintendent, replied that he could not issue such a permit, but offered an escort. When informed later that the party had entered the Park by way of the Lake Eleanor trail, he ordered a detachment to go in search, "and in the event of finding them carrying arms within the limits of the Park to arrest them." They were found, arrested, and brought to headquarters at Wawona, a three-day journey. They were very indignant and filed a complaint against the Acting Superintendent. Colonel Young replied categorically to the points raised in the complaint and concluded with a burst of indignant eloquence: "The letter of Mr.

George C. Perkins, U. S. Senator from California, which accompanies this complaint, is worthy of the serious attention of the Department. There is no reason why Mr. Perkins should not vouch for the social standing and credit of these complainants in support of their own averments on that point. But when Mr. Perkins, on a statement of facts by one side only, goes so far out of his way as to denounce my conduct as 'hasty, ill-considered, and very reprehensible,' he is guilty of gross injustice. If I had any doubt as to the character of the complaint and those by whom it is preferred, it would be removed by this open and scandalous attempt to influence the judicial action of the Secretary by the official influence of a Senator in Congress." [8] The complaint was reviewed by the Department and dismissed. But what happened to a mere Lieutenant Colonel for daring to denounce a United States Senator in such terms? Within two years he was a Major General, commanding a division in the Spanish-American War, and not hesitant in calling down a certain Lieutenant Colonel of Rough Riders for the boisterous conduct of his men.[9] In 1903 he became a Lieutenant General, and President Theodore Roosevelt made him Chief of Staff of the United States Army.

The incident is recorded as an indication of the kind of men who pioneered in national park administration and the kind of thing they had to contend with. It took a lot of perseverance and firmness to make it clear that rules against trespassing and poaching were going to be enforced. Many of the Army officers assigned to this novel duty proved highly efficient and, moreover, in the course of their work became ardent devotees of the High Sierra. Such, for instance were Lieutenants Nathaniel F. McClure, Harry C. Benson and William R. Smedberg, who scouted the back country, even where no trails existed, and made excellent maps of the Park. Their names are commemorated in lakes Benson, McClure, and Smedberg; while those of the superintendents are found on Bigelow and Gale peaks and on lakes Rodgers and Young. Lieutenant Benson was especially interested in propagating trout in the lakes and streams of the Park and to that end cooperated with the State Fish and Game Commissioners, whose names were given to lakes Babcock, Emeric, Fletcher, Murdock, and Vogelsang. In later years Benson and McClure, then colonels, were wont to extol the virtues of some of their men, in particular, Arndt, Fernandez, Foerster, Isberg, for whom various features of the park are named.[10]

As the years went by the dual administration of Yosemite Valley by the state and the surrounding country by the federal government became more and more awkward. Responsibility for fires and for trespass was divided. It was fortunate that Galen Clark, with his long experience, was for a long time Guardian of the Valley and the Mariposa Big Tree Grove. But he resigned in 1896, and after that things deteriorated. John Muir, as usual, headed a movement to remedy this situation. Backed by such men as George Davidson, J. N.

LeConte, Warren Olney, and William E. Colby, he began a campaign to have the state of California recede to the federal government the lands granted in trust in 1864. When a bill for this purpose was introduced in the legislature it naturally met with opposition by the State Commissioners who would be legisled out of their jobs, which, though not salaried, carried certain perquisites. The chances of passage looked slim until the powerful railroad magnate, Edward H. Harriman, was induced by Muir, whom he greatly admired, to intervene through his associates in the Southern Pacific Company, who, for good or evil, were dominant in the political affairs of the state. Muir and Colby were indefatigable in lobbying, and at last the bill was passed by the California Assembly. But in the Senate defeat seemed inevitable until Senator Charles Shortridge, bombarded by letters and telegrams from his constituents (stimulated by President David Starr Jordan of Stanford and others), voted "aye" and the bill carried by a narrow margin and was signed by the Governor on March 3, 1905.[11] The recession, however, could not be completed until it was accepted by Congress. The opposition fought a delaying action, but at last, on June 11, 1906, the recession was accepted and Yosemite National Park became a solid entity.

While the struggle over recession of Yosemite Valley was going on a substantial revision of the boundaries set by the Act of 1890 was brought about as the result of a report by a special Commission appointed by the Secretary of the Interior.[12] The Commission was primarily concerned with the large amount of privately owned land within the western boundary, which was a source of constant dispute and which practically everyone agreed should be eliminated from the Park. By an Act of Congress on February 7, 1905, which followed, this land was, in the main, eliminated. The park's northern boundary in compensation was rectified to include the headwaters of the Tuolumne River up to the main crest of the Sierra. The Commission was also concerned with areas in which there were mining claims, and its recommendations resulted in excluding from the Park the highly scenic Mount Ritter–Minaret region, leaving a wound that is still unhealed.

A survey of existing roads was made at the same time, and proposals for new roads were made. Several years elapsed before much was done in this respect, but eventually the approach roads were improved or entirely rebuilt and tolls were abolished. Happily, a road builder's paradise that was proposed was deemed too ambitious, for which we may be eternally thankful. It consisted of a network that included a road from the Valley to the head of Nevada Fall, thence a branch to Glacier Point and another back of Clouds Rest to Lake Tenaya and on along the rim of the Valley to El Capitan.

As soon as the consolidation of the Park was complete, headquarters were transferred from Wawona to Yosemite Valley, greatly simplifying the administration. At the time of the transfer the Acting Superintendent (a term that continued to be used until a civilian Superintendent was appointed in 1915) was the same Harry C. Benson who had shown so much zeal as a Lieutenant a decade earlier, now Major of the Fourteenth Cavalry. His assignment for the next four years, followed by that of Major William W. Forsyth, of the Sixth (later the First) Cavalry, for another four years, did much to stabilize the administration of Yosemite National Park. Beginning in 1898 a few Forest Rangers (afterwards called Park Rangers) had been employed, but it was not until 1914 that a permanent ranger force was established. Among these "First Rangers" were Charlie Leidig, Archie Leonard, Henry Skelton, and Jack Gaylor, who established a fine tradition of devoted public service.[13] It took time, however, to eradicate trespassing and poaching, although Major Benson, in particular, was relentless in his efforts at enforcement of the regulations. At the very beginning of his administration he was confronted with a new problem. "The Yosemite," he writes in his Report for 1906, "has during recent years been a death trap to all game that was unfortunate enough to enter it. Practically every person living in the Valley kept a rifle, shotgun, and revolver, and any animal or bird that entered the Valley was immediately pursued by the entire contingent, and either captured or killed. It is hoped that within a short time the game will learn that the Valley is a safe retreat and not a death trap."

An event of considerable importance took place at this time: construction of a railroad, branching from the main lines at Merced up Merced Canyon to the border of the Park, where, at a terminal called El Portal, passengers and freight were transferred to horse-drawn vehicles and brought to Yosemite Valley by a narrow, and sometimes steep, dusty road. For the next thirty years many thousands of travelers came to Yosemite by this route, until a storm in December, 1937, washed out the railroad beyond repair. By that time the advent of the automobile and the All-Year Highway, via Mariposa, made reconstruction and renewal of railroad operation out of the question.[14]

The first automobile to enter Yosemite Valley had come in July, 1900. It was a Stanley Steamer, driven by A. E. Holmes and his brother F. H. Holmes, of San Jose. They came by way of Madera and Raymond and the Wawona Road. Describing the adventure many years later A. E. Holmes said, "The Wawona Road leading into Yosemite Valley gave us much difficulty, as our machine was not wide enough to bridge the regular horse-stage tracks, necessitating our making a new path over the entire length of the road. Then, too, when we encountered a stage-coach, the horses became very much frightened at the horseless carriage that moved steadily toward them in a cloud of steam. Our arrival in Yosemite Valley did not end our motoring troubles, for we found the deep sand annoying. The little automobile, however, weathered the trip, and we returned to our homes safely."[15] A year later two Locomobiles reached Yosemite by way of the Big Oak Flat Road. But the day of the automobile had not yet come, and presently a simple statement appeared in the Regulations, "Automobiles are not permitted in the Park." Not until 1913 were the barriers removed by public pressure. Automobiles were then cautiously admitted—at a price. The price was $5 for "a single round trip in and out of the Park." But a more irksome price was the speed limit, "an approximate speed of 10 miles per hour on rolling mountain country." There were rigid time schedules, and hours of entry and departure were restricted. At length, as elsewhere, the automobile became an accepted way of life.

Fortunately for Major Benson, the automobile was left for his successors to contend with. He had troubles of his own in the perennial contest with John B. Curtin and his cattle. In his Report for 1905 Benson wrote, "There is but one person, one J. B. Curtin, of Sonora, Cal., who continues to be and has been for many years a persistent trespasser upon the Park. He has fenced in, about the land which he claims, hundreds of acres of Government land. He claims that the rules and regulations as made by the Secretary of the Interior are 'nul and void,' and he has brought suit against the Department for enforcing the same." This suit was instituted in the Superior Court of Tuolumne County, but was removed to the United States Circuit Court, where the complaint was dismissed. Curtin was not to be put off so easily, however. He appealed to the Supreme Court of the United States, which held, Justice McKenna delivering the opinion, that the Secretary of the Interior or the Superintendent lacked the power "to limit the uses to which lands in the park, held in private ownership, may be put."[16] J. B. Curtin, "Constitutional John" as he was called, emerged from the conflict with the law on his side; but far away from the marble halls of justice, on the unsurveyed and unfenced meadows of the Sierra, Curtin's cattle continued to stray upon Government lands. This, however, was no longer a matter of concern to Major Benson, for long before the decision of the Supreme Court was rendered, in 1911, he had left Yosemite to become Superintendent of Yellowstone National Park, and a few years later he was retired with the rank of Colonel.[17]

The years 1909 to 1912, under administration of Major Forsyth,[18] were comparatively quiet ones in Yosemite National Park. The road from El Portal was improved, but was inadequate to take care of the increasing travel that came by rail. Other roads in and entering the Valley continued to be narrow and dusty. The total number of visitors per year averaged about 13,000, only a very few of whom visited the upper regions of the Park. Public accommodations in the Valley were divided among Camp Curry (founded in 1899), Camp Ahwahnee (at the foot of the trail to Glacier Point, operated by William Sell), Camp Lost Arrow (near the foot of Yosemite Falls, operated by William Sell, Jr.), and the decrepit Sentinel Hotel. There followed an uneventful year under Major William T. Littebrant, and in midsummer of 1914 a new regime began. Mark Daniels, with the title of "General Superintendent and Landscape Engineer of National Parks," made his headquarters in Yosemite Valley and acted as Superintendent. This lasted only briefly, for when Stephen T. Mather became Assistant to the Secretary of the Interior in 1915 a reorganization of administration was begun that was made permanent by the National Park Service Act of August 25, 1916. Under this Act, Mather became Director of the National Park Service and W. B. Lewis was appointed Superintendent of Yosemite National Park.[19]

In following the paths of history we sometimes overlook certain men, who, working behind the scenes, nevertheless make substantial contributions. This should not happen to Gabriel Sovulewski, whose work in Yosemite extended over more years than any other save Galen Clark. Like Clark he was devoted to Yosemite. Sovulewski, a native of Poland, came to the national parks as a corporal in the Fourth Cavalry, first in Sequoia and General Grant in 1891, then in Yosemite from 1895 to 1897. He returned to Yosemite in 1906 and spent the remainder of his life there. At times he acted as Supervisor, in the absence of the Superintendent, but his greatest contribution to Yosemite National Park was in the construction and maintenance of trails. He had his own methods. In a letter to the Director at the close of his career he wrote: "We forget that trail construction is more common sense than engineering. Thorough knowledge of the country, love for that kind of work, instinct of a dog to know which way to get home, and last but not least, disregard for the time of day, are the principal requisites. A man with a tripod, transit, and level has no business on trails. Personally I would consider him a nuisance. In my experience, wild animals solved many problems for me. In conclusion, I want to thank you all in the Park Service. I regret to leave you, but law must take its course and I am leaving after 42 years of service to the nation." Captain Dorst had written in his report for 1892: "Corp. Sovulewski had charge of the guard in General Grant Park and showed great tact in his relations with the numerous visitors, while he performed the duties required of him with firmness and thoroughness." When he retired in 1936 the same words might well have been said of him.[20]

Administration of Sequoia and General Grant national parks took much the same course in the beginning as did Yosemite. The grazing of sheep and cattle on park lands was even more difficult to cope with because of lack of communication between isolated portions of the parks, which were separated by canyons that cut deeply into the terrain. Private ownership of choice areas presented the added problem of summer homes and prevented for many years the full realization of a *public* park. Originally, one-quarter of General Grant National Park was privately owned. Nevertheless, the primary purpose of the legislation of 1890 was accomplished—preservation of the Big Trees. The extent of this treasure turned out to be far greater than was originally supposed.[21]

From the very beginning the Army officers detailed as Acting Superin-

White Horse Troop on a log near General Grant National Park, October, 1896. First at left on the log is Lieutenant (later General) Milton F. Davis.

tendents recognized the importance of extending the Park to include the high mountains on the east, both because of their scenic attraction and because of the need of protecting the watershed. Captain Joseph H. Dorst, first of the cavalry officers to have charge of Sequoia, reported that there were an estimated 500,000 sheep in the Kern and the Kings, adjacent to the Park. "The sheep have been crowded so closely," writes Dorst, "that pleasure parties visiting the mountains could get no grass for their horses and pack animals." Monopoly by sheep and the consequent denudation of the watershed were only part of the reason for expanding the Park boundaries. Captain James Parker, Dorst's successor, presented a plan for enlargement that would include a country devoid of inhabitants, without roads, and naturally suited for a game preserve; it would include the sources of Kern River, "a stream which is much depended on for irrigation, and what is perhaps the finest fishing ground of America." Year after year each superintendent made similar pleas for expansion; and year after year nothing happened.[22]

In Sequoia, as in Yosemite, certain officers and men stand out, among them Captain Charles Young, Negro West Pointer, and Captain George F. Hamilton. Two junior officers, who later saw service in Yosemite, deserve special mention: Lieutenants Harry C. Benson and Milton F. Davis. There were civilian rangers, too, whose services should not be overlooked, such as Charlie Blossom, Lou Davis, Ernest Britten, and Ralph Hopping. Outstanding among those connected with Sequoia National Park in its early days was Walter Fry. During the winters, when the Army Superintendents were away, he took full charge of the Park, until in 1914, he himself became Superintendent. In 1920, when Colonel John R. White (in a civilian capacity) began his long career as Superintendent, Walter Fry was made United States Commissioner for the Park. Midway in his life Walter Fry performed a feat of endurance that must rank among the great deeds of the Sierra. On August 31, 1906, he left Colony Mill on his six-year old mare "Maud" at four in the morning and rode to Giant Forest (10 miles). From there he rode to the trail construction camp on Seven Mile Hill (10 miles); then, via Buck Canyon and Timber Gap, to Mineral King (18 miles). It was his intention to camp there, but he found no feed for his horse, so he went on to Atwell Mill and Lake Canyon. There he received word of a fire on the South Fork, so he rode to Three Rivers (30 miles). He continued to the scene of the fire (6 miles), arriving at 10:45 at night. This made a continuous ride of 74 miles, over the roughest kind of trails and with enormous changes of altitude. He spent the rest of the night fighting fire.[23] Those of us who knew Judge Fry during the latter part of his long life recognized in him a man of rare spiritual qualities. He knew and loved the tender and delicate forms of nature—the small flowers, the little folk of the forest. Fawns and seedlings engaged his attention. He was kindly and gentle, and people loved him.

The first flush of a dawn that presaged better things came in 1915, when Stephen T. Mather, newly appointed Assistant to the Secretary of the Interior, brought a galaxy of influential men to Giant Forest on the first stage of a propaganda expedition, the like of which had never been seen before in the Sierra.[24] Mather believed that demonstration was far more effective than speeches, writings, or even illustrations. On this trip, as on others later, he provided (at his own expense) every conceivable camping comfort, together with delicious food prepared by the celebrated mountain cook Ty Sing. The results were more than gratifying. Not only was the project of enlarging Sequoia National Park reactivated, but the long-deferred acquisition of privately held land in Giant Forest was brought near completion. A strong plea was made to Congress and $50,000 was appropriated to buy the key portion. But by the time the money was available another $20,000 was required. Here is where Steve Mather's educational work bore fruit. Gilbert H. Grosvenor, President of the National Geographic Society, had been one of the 1915 camping party. He induced the Society's Board of Directors to come to the rescue, an act of which the Society has never ceased to be proud. A few years later most of the remaining private holdings in the Park were acquired, again with the help of the National Geographic Society and with funds raised by Stephen Mather from his friends, together with a substantial contribution of his own.[25]

To get a bill through Congress enlarging the Park was not an easy task. The story of how it was eventually achieved is long and devious, a subject for more extended treatment than is appropriate here.[26] Suffice it to say that on July 4, 1926, Superintendent White received a telegram from Congressman Henry E. Barbour saying, "Bill enlarging Sequoia National Park signed by President Coolidge late yesterday. The Greater Sequoia National Park is now a reality."[27] It was a major addition to the National Park system; it rounded out the Park in the Kaweah region and took in the entire upper Kern basin, including Mount Whitney. The Kings River region, to the north, however, had to wait for several years, until, on March 4, 1940, President Franklin D. Roosevelt signed the Kings Canyon National Park bill.

A good deal of the opposition to national park enlargement had come from the Forest Service representatives in the field, who honestly felt that the lands in question should remain under Forest Service administration. The United States Forest Service was concerned primarily with the care and use of timber resources, influenced to a considerable extent by the growth of the scientific study of forestry. The Forest Reserves were established in 1893, when President Cleveland withdrew large portions of the national domain from entry in a move to halt uncontrolled exploitation. The Sierra Forest Reserve alone consisted of over 4,000,000 acres, in which grazing and water conservation equaled, if not exceeded, timber resources in importance. The establishment

of the Forest Reserves had the legal effect of practically preventing all economic use, but actually, in the Sierra Reserve, grazing and other forms of
trespass went on much as before. Trained men were not available to patrol
the Forest, and supervision was almost totally lacking. Nevertheless, a beginning had been made, and by the end of the decade, Gifford Pinchot, a trained
forester, was at the head of the Division of Forestry, promoting unification
and successfully seeking appropriations from Congress. With the hearty support of President Theodore Roosevelt, the Forest Reserves (presently to be
renamed "National Forests") were transferred in 1905 to the Department of
Agriculture, with Pinchot as Chief Forester.[28] In 1908 a major change was
made in the administration of the National Forests in California: the Sierra
National Forest was divided into five units—the Sierra, the Sequoia, the Inyo,
the Mono, and the Stanislaus. Other changes have since been made—additions,
eliminations, combinations—so that today the National Forests in the Sierra
Nevada are, from north to south, Plumas, Tahoe, part of Toyabe, El Dorado,
Stanislaus (with the small Calaveras), Sierra, part of Inyo, and Sequoia.

The purposes for which the National Forests were established would not
have been achieved were it not for the devoted public service of the rangers
and administrators in the Forest Service. A great deal of this service was obscure and unrecorded, but there are a few connected with the National
Forests of the Sierra whose names should not be forgotten. In the earlier
days there were Charles H. Shinn and Sam Ellis; later there were super-
visors Paul G. Redington, Maurice A. Benedict, Frank Cunningham, and Roy
Boothe. Two notable engineers contributed much to the successful operation
of the Forests: Walter L. Huber, who passed on applications for water development,[29] and Frederick H. Fowler, his successor. To give proper credit a
complete roster of the Forest Service would be required: men who built
bridges and trails, men who rode for long days up and down canyon walls
and over passes (a pass has been named in their honor—Foresters Pass, from
the head of the Kern to the Kings), men who looked after the needs of
campers and rescued wanderers, and men who fought fires. These were only
a portion of the duties, and the deeds beyond the call of duty, that these
Forest Service men have performed. Their successors can indeed say with
pride that the Forest Service has lived up to the charter given them by the
Secretary of Agriculture, James Wilson: "The National Forests are for the
purpose of preserving a perpetual supply of timber for home industries, preventing destruction of forest cover which regulates the flow of streams, and
protecting local residents from unfair competition in the use of forest and
range. The timber, water, pasture, and mineral resources of the National
Forests are for the use of the people."[30]

NOTES AND REFERENCES

1. The movement to preserve the Big Trees of the Giant Forest and other groves in Tulare County is exhaustively treated by Douglas H. Strong, "A History of Sequoia National Park," dissertation for the degree of Doctor of Social Science, Syracuse University, 1964 (MS in BL). Also letter of George W. Stewart in Walter Fry and John R. White, *Big Trees*, Stanford, 1930.

2. Literature about the Kaweah Colony is voluminous, beginning with publications of the Colony, notably *The Commonwealth*, and George W. Stewart in the *Visalia Delta*, November and December, 1891. Later publications are: Burnette G. Haskell, "How and Why the Colony Died," *Out West*, September, 1902; Ruth R. Lewis, "Kaweah: An Experiment in Co-operative Colonization," *PHR*, November, 1948; Robert V. Hine, *California's Utopian Colonies*, San Marino, Calif., 1953; and Douglas H. Strong, *op. cit.*

3. The General Sherman Tree was named by James Wolverton in 1879. (Walter Fry)

4. The part played by Zumwalt is discussed by Oscar Berland, "Giant Forest's Reservation: The Legend and the Mystery," *SCB*, December, 1962, 47:9; also Douglas H. Strong, *op. cit.*

5. Robert Underwood Johnson, *Remembered Yesterdays*, Boston: Little, Brown, 1947. See also W. F. Badè, *Life and Letters of John Muir*, 2 vols., Boston: Houghton Mifflin, 1923-1924.

6. John Muir, "The Treasures of Yosemite," *Century Magazine*, August, 1890; "Features of the Proposed Yosemite National Park," *ibid.*, September, 1890.

7. *Reports of the Acting Superintendent of the Yosemite National Park* for the years 1891 and following.

8. *Complaint of John L. Howard et al. Against Col. S. B. M. Young, U.S.A., Superintendent of the Yosemite National Park, California, dated September 15, 1896;* and *Reply of Col. Young, dated November 30, 1896. In the Department of the Interior* (National Archives; copies in BL). Colonel Young's *Reply* was reprinted for private distribution, Berkeley, 1962

9. Conversation with General Young at his home in Helena, Montana, November 22, 1922.—F.P.F.

10. F. P. Farquhar, *Place Names of the High Sierra*, San Francisco: Sierra Club, 1926.

11. William E. Colby, "Yosemite and the Sierra Club," *SCB*, 1938, 23:2; and "The Recession of Yosemite Valley," *SCB*, 1962, 47:9.

12. *Report of the Yosemite Park Commission*, submitted by H. M. Chittenden, Major of Engineers, U.S. Army; R. B. Marshall, U.S. Geological Survey; Frank Bond, U.S. General Land Office, December, 1904. 58th Cong., 3d Sess., Senate Doc. No. 34.

13. John W. Bingaman, *Guardians of the Yosemite: A Story of the First Rangers*, Palm Desert, Calif., 1961.

14. Hank Johnston, *Railroads of the Yosemite Valley*, Long Beach, Calif., 1963. (The title is a misnomer—there are no railroads in Yosemite Valley.)

15. *Standard Oil Bulletin*, September, 1926; also *YNN*, August, 1943, 22:8, and Irene D. Paden and Margaret E. Schlichtmann, *The Big Oak Flat Road*, 1955.

16. Curtin v. Benson (1911), 222 US 78.

17. Francis P. Farquhar, "Colonel Benson," *SCB*, 1925, 12:2.

18. William Woods Forsyth (1856-1933). A peak and a pass were named for him; three lakes and a dome for his daughters, Dorothy, Evelyn, Helen, and Polly; and for his sons-in-law, who otherwise left no mark on Yosemite, Lake Keyes and McCabe Lakes. It may be remarked that Robert B. Marshall, topographer of the U.S.G.S., who helped make the map, was a close friend of Major Forsyth.

19. The first two decades under civilian superintendents (W. B. Lewis, 1916-1928; E. P. Leavitt, 1928-1929; C. G. Thomson, 1929-1937) were marked by construction of roads, bridges, service buildings, and hotel and camp accommodations to take care of the vast increase in the number of visitors to the Park, especially to Yosemite Valley.

20. Gabriel Sovulewski, "The Story of Trail Building in Yosemite National Park," *YNN*, April, 1928, 7:4; Francis P. Farquhar, "Gabriel Sovulewski, 1866-1938," *SCB*, 1939, 24:3.

21. Walter Fry and John R. White, *Big Trees*, Stanford, 1930.

22. *Reports of the Acting Superintendent of Sequoia and General Grant National Parks* for the years 1891 and following; see John R. White and Samuel J. Pusateri, *Sequoia and Kings Canyon National Parks*, Stanford, 1949.

23. Francis P. Farquhar, "Walter Fry of Giant Forest," *SCB*, 1942, 27:4.

24. Robert Shankland, *Steve Mather of the National Parks*, New York: Knopf, 1951.

25. *National Geographic Magazine*, January, 1917; *ibid.*, July, 1921. See also Douglas H. Strong, *op. cit.* (see n. 1 above).

26. *Ibid.* See also Holway R. Jones, *John Muir and the Sierra Club: The Battle for Yosemite*, San Francisco: Sierra Club, 1965; and Francis P. Farquhar, "Legislative History of Sequoia and Kings Canyon National Parks," *SCB*, 1941, 26:1.

27. *Ibid.*

28. Gifford Pinchot, *Breaking New Ground*, New York, 1947; and "How the National Forests Were Won," *American Forest*, October, 1930.

29. *SCB*, January, 1912, 8:3. Huber was for many years a director of the Sierra Club and its President, 1925-1927. He was later President of the American Society of Civil Engineers.

30. United States Department of Agriculture, Forest Service, *Miscellaneous Circular No. 95*, 1927.

XX

THE SIERRA CLUB AND THE HIGH SIERRA

On June 4, 1892, articles of incorporation were signed by twenty-seven residents of the San Francisco Bay area, bringing into being the Sierra Club.[1] Its purposes were declared to be: "To explore, enjoy, and render accessible the mountain regions of the Pacific Coast; to publish authentic information concerning them; to enlist the support and cooperation of the people and the government in preserving the forests and other natural features of the Sierra Nevada." John Muir was elected President. By the end of the summer there were 182 charter members. In January, 1893, the first number of the *Sierra Club Bulletin* was issued and has ever since carried out one of the primary purposes of the club, publishing authentic information and serving as a record of the club's activities.

In fulfillment of another purpose, to help preserve the forest and natural features, the club carried on the work already begun by some of its members in establishing and protecting Yosemite National Park. Efforts of this character have continued and have never been more active than they are now.[2] Other purposes stated in the Articles of Incorporation—to explore and enjoy the mountains and render them accessible—have in the course of time attained a magnitude hardly contemplated by the Club's founders. To "render accessible" became obsolete when the automobile brought almost too much accessibility, and the words were eventually deleted. Exploration and enjoyment, however, have never ceased, nor will they ever cease. There will always be something new to explore in the ever-changing life and aspects of the forests and mountains, while enjoyment continues from generation to generation.

Even before the Sierra Club was formally organized, some of its future members were engaged in opening trails to canyons and passes and in climbing peaks. Foremost among them was young Joseph N. LeConte, son of the professor who had accompanied the "University Excursion Party" in 1870. "Little Joe," as he was frequently called, while still an undergraduate at the University of California, accompanied his father in 1889 on a camping trip to Hetch Hetchy, Yosemite, Tuolumne Meadows, and the Mariposa Grove of Big Trees, in the course of which he climbed mounts Hoffmann, Dana, and Lyell.[3] Such was the effect of this trip that for the rest of his life the younger LeConte, like his father before him, remained enamoured of the High Sierra.[4] The following year, with three college friends, he visited Kings Canyon,

Kearsarge Pass, and Mount Whitney. They returned to Yosemite by way of Owens Valley, Bloody Canyon, and Tuolumne Meadows.[5] On this trip Le-Conte carried a camera and began a series of photographs which for many years were famous as the finest views of the Sierra published.[6] Year after year he continued to camp in the Sierra and climb the peaks, with various companions but more and more with Miss Helen Marion Gompertz and some of her friends.[7] A climax for the LeConte family was a trip in 1900, when the elder LeConte, then 77 years of age, accompanied the younger people on a camping trip to Kings Canyon. They spent six weeks in the mountains, and the Professor climbed to 12,000 feet at Kearsarge Pass. "I enjoyed intensely," he wrote, "every step of the journey, and in some parts, as we approached the summit, the exhilaration of spirit and the exultation of mind was such as I had not felt for ten years."[8] In June, 1901, Helen Gompertz and Joe Le-Conte were married. She, too, was a charter member of the Sierra Club and for the rest of her life continued to share with her husband an unwavering devotion to the high mountain country.

There now enters into the history of the Sierra one of its greatest figures, William E. Colby, who was to lead the Sierra Club in action and in spirit for the next seventy years.[9] He was nineteen years old in the summer of 1894 when he joined two companions in a trip to the Tuolumne country. He was the youngest of the three, inexperienced and overconfident. His education began with his first mountain, Mount Dana; after that, in his own words, he "acquired some sense and did not overdo."[10] His next climb was Mount Conness, where he and his companion spent a night on top in bitter cold. The principal objective of the trip was a descent of the Grand Canyon of the Tuolumne, about which they had heard from John Muir and Robert M. Price. The latter had been through it from Tuolumne Meadows to Hetch Hetchy in 1892.[11] Just as they were starting, at the head of the canyon, who should show up but Price himself. A combined party of five made their way through to Hetch Hetchy in spite of a few minor mishaps.[12] The experiences of this first summer were of lasting benefit to Colby in preparing him for the years to come when he planned and led the long series of outings of the Sierra Club that brought thousands of people into the mountains.

Theodore S. Solomons, another charter member of the Sierra Club, was also active in the Sierra in the summer of 1894. He followed the Colby–Price party through the Tuolumne Canyon and took the first photographs of its splendid waterfalls.[13] He had previously made some explorations at the head of the North Fork of the San Joaquin and had climbed Mount Ritter. He conceived the idea of a route from north to south nearer the crest than any that others had taken and was now ready to test it. With one companion and with food and equipment carried on a packhorse and two jacks he followed the well-known way from Yosemite and Wawona to the San Joaquin. From the

Cedric Wright.

William E. Colby, founder of the Sierra Club outings and secretary of the club for nearly half a century.

junction of the Middle and South forks they continued up to Vermilion Valley, which Solomons named, thence over the ridge to Bear Creek. There they made their only contact with the true high mountain route, which in years to come was to be called the John Muir Trail. They climbed a picturesque peak of easy slope and gave it the appropriate name of "Seven Gables." There the year's exploration ended. It was the last week of September; a snowstorm caught them; they were obliged to abandon their jacks and with packs on their backs escape to lower altitudes.[14]

Solomons continued his search for a north-south route the following year, 1895. This time he decided not to take animals, believing that by going on foot with knapsacks he could examine more territory. With one companion, he went again up toward the headwaters of the San Joaquin and came to a high basin surrounded by peaks of varied form and hue. To these peaks Solomons gave the names of philosophers in whose theories he was interested—Darwin, Huxley, Haeckel, Spencer, Wallace, and Fiske—the "Evolution Group." This was as far as the two got in their search for a high mountain route. They now took a direction that no animals could follow. First they climbed Mount Goddard, then made a very rough descent southward down Disappearing Creek and Goddard Creek to the Middle Fork of Kings River, on the way passing through what Solomons called the "Enchanted Gorge." They contined down to Tehipite Valley, made a reconnaissance of the Dome, and resumed their journey over the Monarch Divide to Kings River Canyon. Although Solomons only partially succeeded in finding a north-south route, he should be given credit for the idea and for his initial attempts.[15]

Two University of California students of the class of 1897 now took the lead in exploring the Sierra. Walter Starr tells the story: "I spent the summer of 1895 in the northern part of Yosemite National Park with Allen Chickering. Having become infected with Sierra Club enthusiasm, we determined to make a trip of real exploration during the college vacation of 1896. We met Theodore S. Solomons, who was then as afterward tireless in exploring and mapping the High Sierra region."[16] The following spring Starr and Chickering entered the Sierra by way of Lake Eleanor and at the end of June joined Solomons in Yosemite for a journey to Kings Canyon. Solomons brought along a large camera with glass plates. "Unfortunately the unusual weather we experienced," wrote Starr many years later, "prevented our getting many of the pictures we most wanted. The seasons during the eighties and early nineties were in a stormy, wet cycle. The high mountains then presented a wholly different appearance to what they do now. Huge snowfields and accumulated drifts lasted out the summer at high altitudes and the glaciers were much larger. Perhaps due to this condition, summer storms were much more frequent and more violent." The trio crossed from the Merced to the San Joaquin by way of Isberg Pass and came eventually to Mono Creek and Vermilion Valley. Chickering and Starr climbed a peak above Mono Pass; but there Solomons became ill and the others were obliged to take him to a lower altitude. They went down to Blaney Meadows and on to a beautiful lake which they named "Florence Lake," for Starr's sister.[17] There Solomons reluctantly concluded that he could not continue on the trip. Starr and Chickering went back into the mountains and came to Tehipite by way of Collins Meadow. They ascended the Dome, measured it, and took pictures. They took the Tunemah Trail[18] up the north flank of the Middle Fork Canyon to Simpson Meadow, thence over the divide, by Granite Basin, and down Copper Creek to Kings Canyon. Starr and Chickering had thus made a continuous journey with animals from Yosemite to Kings Canyon.

It would occupy more space than is appropriate here to give an account of all the exploring, climbing, and camping trips of the 1890's. Many of them are recorded in the *Sierra Club Bulletin*, and there were doubtless many others of which no record exists. A few, however, of special interest should be mentioned. Bolton Coit Brown, Professor of Drawing at Stanford University, not only made several notable ascents but added to knowledge of the high country at the head of the Kings and the Kings–Kern Divide by his descriptions, his maps, and his fine sketches.[19] He made the first ascent, solo, of Mount Clarence King in 1896 and the same year joined J. N. LeConte in the first ascent of Mount Gardner. Professor Brown and his wife Lucy then crossed the Kings–Kern Divide and climbed Mount Williamson. A little later that summer they returned to the Divide and climbed and named Mount Ericsson, after which Brown ventured out on a northward-jutting knife edge to its highest point, where he built a monument and gave the name "Mount Stanford."[20] In 1899 Professor and Mrs. Brown resumed their exploration of the headwaters of the Kings, this time with a third member in the party, their two-year-old daughter. "We put her on a burro, and wither we went she went also."[21]

Not many college presidents have stood on the summit of a high mountain named for their institution. On August 16, 1899, President David Starr Jordan, of Stanford University, did exactly that. "I have never seen a more magnificent mountain panorama!" he exclaimed.[22] Dr. Jordan was well qualified to speak of mountain panoramas; some years before he had climbed the Matterhorn in Switzerland.[23] The Stanford party, which included Mrs. Jordan and several of the University's professors, spent many pleasant days at the head of Bubbs Creek, where Dr. Jordan gave names to a number of features, including "Ouzel Basin," suggested by Muir's description in *The Mountains of California*.[24]

The rapid increase in the number of visitors to the High Sierra made the need for reliable maps more and more urgent. The Whitney Survey and Wheeler Survey maps, useful in their day, were quite inadequate, and other maps made by later explorers and by the National Park officers covered only

Mount Clarence King.

Ansel Adams

parts of the territory. J. N. LeConte recognized this at the very beginning of his Sierra experience and, with an engineer's mind, proceeded to gather all the scattered information he could find and coordinate it. The first of his maps was published by the Sierra Club in 1893, followed by an enlarged and improved map in 1896. Thereafter he kept the work up to date by a series of blueprints until the sheets of the United States Geological Survey became available. His friend James S. Hutchinson wrote in a memoir of Joe LeConte: "I helped him carry his transit and his plane table to the summits of many high peaks in the Sierra when he was making observations and rechecking locations for his valuable maps of the Sierra."[25]

The greatest of the mountains they climbed together was the North Palisade, of which LeConte, Hutchinson, and James K. Moffitt made the first ascent in 1903.[26] LeConte was indefatigable in finding observation points for his mapping, particularly at the headwaters of the Kings River. One may share his enthusiasm by reading the accounts he wrote for the *Sierra Club Bulletin* in the years 1903 to 1909. The culmination of his explorations came in 1908 when, with James S. Hutchinson and Duncan McDuffie, he pioneered the first truly high mountain route from Yosemite to Kings Canyon. It was not quite as consistently high as the route ultimately attained by the John Muir Trail, but it linked together several sections that had been separately explored, such as Donohue Pass from the Tuolumne Meadows to Thousand Island Lake, Fish Creek to Evolution Basin, and from the latter to the Middle Fork of Kings River. The last of these links had been opened for pack animals the preceding year by George R. Davis, of the United States Geological Survey. "To be sure, the Geological Survey had crossed it at a time when everything above 10,000 feet was under snow," writes LeConte. "I myself had examined the gap when free from snow in 1904, and at that time considered it impassable to pack animals on the south side."[27] The critical day's trip is described by LeConte, in part, as follows: "We were stirring by earliest dawn, and long before the sun rose over the battlements of Mount Darwin were on the way. We passed around the east side of Evolution Lake, and at its head crossed to the west side of the creek. One bad, rocky place was encountered, and soft snow bogged one animal, but the top of the divide was reached by about 9 A.M. We were twelve thousand feet above sea level. Down the other side was an awful looking gorge in the black metamorphic rock, partly choked with snow. We went straight at it, and took our mules right over the talus piles. They did splendidly and we passed down into the rocky amphitheatre and around the south side of a little black lake, the extreme source of the Middle Fork of Kings River." The pass had been named by Davis "Muir Pass"; the canyon on the Middle Fork side is known as "LeConte Canyon," a fitting memorial to one of the greatest of High Sierra explorers. Let all who visit this remote and beautiful spot be reminded of Joe LeConte, little in

J. N. LeConte

End of the 1908 trip from Yosemite to Kings Canyon: Duncan McDuffie,
Joseph N. LeConte, and James S. Hutchinson.

stature but, in the words of his friend Jim Hutchinson, "a great and good man; a man who was fond of his fellow men, who loved his friends dearly, and who was loved by all who knew him, a man whose influence for good will last long."

James S. Hutchinson, besides accompanying Joe LeConte on a number of trips and climbs, made some notable explorations on his own account. In 1920 he led a party from Giant Forest to the Roaring River country, with Ernest McKee and Onis Imus Brown as packers, and made the first traverse of Colby Pass to the Kern Canyon. On the same trip Hutchinson, Duncan McDuffie, and Onis Imus made the first ascent of the Black Kaweah.[28] With his brother Edward, Jim Hutchinson made a first ascent of Mount Humphreys in 1904.[29]

The personal experiences of the members of the U. S. Geological Survey parties are so rarely recorded that only occasionally do we get a glimpse of them. The examination of the glaciers and glacial phenomena in the Dana–Lyell–Ritter region has already been mentioned. Willard D. Johnson was a charter member of the Sierra Club and Grove Karl Gilbert a contributor to the *Bulletin*. In fact there was always close cooperation between the club and the Geological Survey. We meet Gilbert and Johnson again in the Evolution Basin in 1908, when Johnson and E. C. Andrews, of the Geological Survey of New South Wales, climbed Mount Darwin, Andrews completing the climb solo for a first ascent of the highest point, a detached pinnacle.[30] George R. Davis, Charles F. Urquhart, and others climbed many a peak in the Sierra while surveying for the maps that have been the admiration of all who have used them in planning and carrying out camping and climbing trips in the High Sierra.

Of the many independent trips that have contributed indirectly to the history of the Sierra, a few not recorded in the *Sierra Club Bulletin* are met with elsewhere. An instance is a series of articles by Theodore P. Lukens, "One Hundred Days in the Sierra Nevadas," published in a Pasadena weekly.[31] Lukens, president of a bank and former mayor of Pasadena, with Walter Richardson, visited Mineral King, Golden Trout Creek, Mount Whitney, Kings Canyon, Owens Valley, Tuolumne Meadows and Canyon, Hetch Hetchy, and Yosemite in the summer of 1896. In Lukens' account there are many interesting observations. Another and better known account of a Sierra trip is that of Stewart Edward White, in "The Pass," first published in *Outing Magazine* in 1906, and later in book form.[32] Although the story is slightly fictionalized, it presents a vivid picture of the country and the actualities of the trip, in which White and his wife Elizabeth, with a Forest Ranger called "Wes," found a way for their horses over open granite and steep ledges from Roaring River into the canyons of the Kaweah.

One of the major events in modern Sierra history took place when Will

Colby in 1901 instituted the long series of Sierra Club outings. It was very largely his idea, but he had the strong support of John Muir, who believed that people should go to the mountains and learn to be at home in them and perceive and understand the beauty and order of Nature. Colby tells of the beginning: "It was from John Muir, the President of the Club, that I received the warmest encouragement. He was highly enthusiastic, and told me that he had long been trying to get the Club to undertake just such outings. Without his support, I would not have dared to embark upon such an enterprise, with its multiplicity of new and untried problems."[33] Colby received important aid from Edward T. Parsons, who had recently come to San Francisco from Portland, Oregon. He was familiar with the outings conducted by the Mazamas and proved an invaluable second to Colby. "Pioneering on untrodden ground, the Outing Committee had much to learn, and it took several outings before the basic problems were solved." That the problems were solved and year after year the outings continued in popularity, with profound effect both upon the lives of the participators and upon the cause of Conservation, is attested by the number of Sierra Club members who experienced life in the open under most favorable conditions. One of the features was the presence of men distinguished for their knowledge of the natural sciences who generously helped others to recognize the trees, the flowers, the birds and animals and to understand the significance of glacial polish and moraines. Among such teachers, besides Muir himself on several of the earlier outings, there were C. Hart Merriam and Vernon Bailey, of the U. S. Biological Survey; John G. Lemmon and Willis Linn Jepson, botanists; Andrew C. Lawson, geologist, and many others. Campfires were made memorable, not only by discourse of instruction and inspiration, but by music of rare beauty from the flute, the violin, and voices ranging from deep bass to lyric soprano.[34]

For a number of years the Sierra Club outings rotated between the Yosemite National Park, the Kings River region, and the Kern. Later the upper region of the San Joaquin was added. At first the outings were for four full weeks; then a few people began to come for the first two weeks or the last two weeks, until finally the pattern began to be a series of two-week outings, supplemented by a "base camp" and then by burro trips and knapsack trips. In part this change was brought about by problems of packing. Instead of one packtrain accompanying the club for the whole period, smaller packtrains coming in and out over the passes became the rule. Advanced roadheads on each side of the mountains also made it easier for people to come in and out on a shorter schedule. Yet in all these changes one thing has remained constant—the opportunity for young and old, mountaineers and "meadoweers," to visit the High Sierra under conditions that give them a maximum of enjoyment at moderate expense. A "commissary" provides excellent food in unfailing supply, prepared by skilled professional cooks, with aid, both volun-

Sierra Club outing in Kings Canyon, 1902.

J. N. LeConte

teer and paid, from the membership. The main object of the outings has never been lost sight of, however. Colby constantly reiterated that he and the other leaders could not afford to spend their time and energy merely giving people pleasant vacations; the important thing was to lead them to know and appreciate the beauty and inspiration of the mountains, and to educate them to become defenders of the wilderness. The results give ample testimony to the wisdom of this program. And, almost as a by-product, the participants, through three, even four, generations, have profited in physical strength and health as well as in an educated idealism.

The leadership of the Sierra Club has never been content merely to provide means of enjoyment for its members; it is incumbent upon the members to contribute something to the general welfare. Colby was an ardent fisherman, as were many of those who went on the outings, but it was not enough for them to take fish from the streams and lakes; for many years the club's pack-train was utilized to transplant fingerlings, particularly Golden Trout, to lakes and streams known to be barren yet good breeding ground. Of late years volunteers from the club have performed heroic service in cleaning old campgrounds and removing cans and broken glass to repositories outside the choice areas of the High Sierra. Over the years, moreover, there has been much building and improvement of trails, sometimes solely by members of the club, sometimes in cooperation with the Forest Service and Park Service. In many ways the Sierra Club has endeavored to give back to the Sierra something for what it receives.

During the course of more than half a century of outings almost every peak and canyon has been visited, and in this there has been no distinction between the sexes, for women have become completely emancipated from their traditional handicaps. In the announcement of the first outing, in 1901, the following recommendation is found: "Women should have one durable waist for tramping and one light one to wear around camp. The skirts can be short, not more than half way from knee to ankle, and under them can be worn shorter dark-colored bloomers. For the women who ride horseback, divided skirts are recommended. It would be unsafe to ride otherwise than astride on portions of the trip." After ten years there was a slight modification—the bloomers under the skirt could be of the same color as the skirt! In 1914 there was a further change, this time a radical departure, a portent of the future: "bloomers or *knickerbockers*" should be worn under the skirt, as "the latter are essential for the more difficult mountain climbs where skirts are dangerous to wear." In 1920 the outing announcement went so far as to say that "many women prefer to wear the knickerbockers or trousers on the entire trip to the exclusion of skirts." Three years later the inevitable had arrived—"women usually wear knickerbockers or riding trousers." In 1925 they were called "hiking or riding breeches." After that the girls were left to do as they pleased;

skirts are now never seen, except occasionally at dinner time, and blue jeans have become the standard costume, substituted in an increasing number of instances by shorts, even at the expense of bruised knees.[35]

The climbing of mountains during the earlier years of Sierra Club outings was remarkable both for the number of people who attained the summits and the nonchalant way in which they did it. Edward T. Parsons, Colby's chief assistant, brought from his experience with the Mazamas on Mount Hood a method quite new to the Sierra. On Mount Lyell, for instance, more than half the outing party, a hundred or even more, would line up at dawn behind two or three leaders, trudging patiently over the snow until they came to the summit rocks. There, in smaller groups, they scrambled to the top with no more aid than a friendly hand or an encouraging word. It was a marvelous experience for many of the participants who never would have been able to enjoy it by any other means. It required good leaders with patience and discretion, leaders who went on to achieve more difficult climbs, such as Walter Huber and James Rennie, the durable Scot. Greatest of all mountaineers who have participated in Sierra Club outings is Norman Clyde. For over forty years he was the most ubiquitous climber in America and probably has more first ascents to his credit than anyone else in the country. Although a great many of his climbs were done alone, he was ever ready to help others. Moreover, from his residence in Owens Valley, he was called again and again to search for lost climbers, and once in a while to discover their mangled bodies. Norman in his prime was a superb climber, whose strength and endurance have hardly been equaled by any other in the Sierra.[36]

A complete innovation in Sierra climbing took place in 1931, when techniques long in use in Europe were introduced to the Sierra Club by Dr. Robert L. M. Underhill, of the Appalachian Mountain Club, who at the instance of the writer of this history had been invited to be a guest on the Sierra Club outing that year. Actually, the first properly roped climb made in the Sierra, so far as can be ascertained, took place just before his coming, when the writer led a small group directly up the face of Unicorn Peak on July 12, 1931. When Underhill arrived he organized a regular climbing school, practicing on the steep angles of Mount Ritter and Banner Peak. Progress from that time on was rapid. Half a dozen of the best climbers joined Underhill and Clyde for a postgraduate course on North Palisade, climbing from the east-side glacier. It was on this occasion that the climbers were caught on the summit of one of the peaks by a severe thunderstorm. As he was hastening to get off the crest to a place of safety, Jules Eichorn barely escaped electrocution when "a thunderbolt whizzed right by my ear," as he claimed. So "Thunderbolt Peak" was christened.[37]

The climbing party, reduced to five, went on to the east side of Mount Whitney and followed John Muir's old route up the North Fork of Lone Pine

East Face of Mount Whitney from Mount Russell.

Creek. Next day, August 16, the first ascent of the East Face of Mount Whitney was made by Underhill, Clyde, and two others, Jules Eichorn and Glen Dawson, "young natural-born rock-climbers who had never seen the mountain; but neither had they seen any up and down the Sierra that they could not climb."[38]

In this manner modern rock climbing was introduced to the Sierra Nevada. In a short time a host of young climbers acquired the necessary skills, ascending the East Face of Mount Whitney by a variety of routes, and soon the spires and sheer walls of Yosemite. In 1934 a superb climbing team, Bestor Robinson, Richard M. Leonard, and Jules Eichorn, pioneered in the use of pitons for direct aid in the first ascent of the Higher Cathedral Spire, and a few months later made the first ascent of the Lower Spire. Another ascent of the Higher Spire (the third) was made the same year by Ted Waller, Jack Riegelhuth, and Marjory Bridge.[39]

Another event of the year 1931, repeated in 1934, is in striking contrast to the vertical rock ascents. Water was low in the Tuolume River in both seasons, affording an unusual opportunity to investigate the mysterious Muir Gorge. John Muir and Galen Clark had passed through it many years before, in 1872, and a few others afterwards, but in later years powerful cascading water had blocked the entrance so that none of the current generation knew anything about it. However, in 1931 two small parties ventured into the steep-walled chasm and by swimming the pools came through to the lower end, where they met the fine trail that had been built to Pate Valley in the heart of the Canyon. Photographs were taken then and again in 1934, when another passage was made. To the few who have been there the central pool has been a goal fully equivalent to the summit of any of the highest peaks of the Sierra.[40]

It is inevitable that history should have its moments of sadness, but in one such moment the sadness is tempered by a glimpse of beauty and the immortality of youth. Walter A. Starr, Jr. ("Pete" Starr), loved the High Sierra with a devotion that led him there on every possible occasion. He usually traveled alone, for few could keep up with him on the trails and few equaled him in the agility with which he climbed. One day in 1933 he failed to return to the San Francisco law office where he worked. Inquiries were made and a search was begun, which ended when his body was found on a ledge of one of the Minarets, near Mount Ritter. In words written by his father shortly afterward, referring to the guidebook which he completed from his son's unfinished manuscript, "May the traveler feel the companionship of that eager, joyous, and generous youth who loved the beauty of the mountains and wanted others to share his love."[41]

Starr's *Guide to the John Muir Trail* has indeed served to stimulate hundreds of lovers of the High Sierra and lead them to pleasant pastures along

Cathedral Spire, Yosemite Valley, first climbed in 1934.

Marjory Bridge, 1934

Pool in the heart of Muir Gorge in the Tuolumne Canyon.

The Minarets from the air,
taken during the search for Walter A. Starr, Jr., 1933.

the high mountain route. The Trail received its name when the California legislature, in 1915, appropriated $10,000 for its construction. The origin of the idea is stated by Colby as follows: "During the 1914 outing of the Sierra Club, a suggestion was made by Mr. Meyer Lissner of Los Angeles that a State appropriation should be secured for building trails with which to make the High Sierra more accessible. After Muir's death, the happy idea occurred of making this appropriation a State recognition of his inestimable service in bringing the mountains of California to the attention of the world." The route was selected by State Engineer Wilbur F. McClure, in consultation with members of the United States Forest Service and the Sierra Club. The major part of the work was carried out by the Forest Service, with Supervisors Paul G. Redington, of Sierra National Forest, and S. W. Wynne, of Sequoia. In subsequent years additional appropriations were made, sponsored by State Senator Arthur Breed, a Sierra Club member. Successive supervisors of the national forests continued to take charge of construction. For a while temporary routes were followed until ways could be found to cross certain key passes, particularly Muir Pass from Evolution Basin to LeConte Canyon and the Middle Fork of the Kings, then Mather Pass from the Middle Fork to the head of the South Fork of the Kings, and finally Foresters Pass, completed in 1931 from the head of Bubbs Creek to the head of Kern River.[42]

With the completion of the John Muir Trail the exploration of the Sierra Nevada may be considered to have been completed. Every canyon and every pass has been made available. Moreover, every major peak has been climbed, and in Yosemite, where the "inaccessible" points had long ago been proved accessible, the "impossible" faces of El Capitan, Sentinel Rock, and Half Dome have been scaled after long sieges by the aid of mountaineering "hardware." These later achievements, however, belong under the heading of "Current Events" rather than "History."

NOTES AND REFERENCES

1. Sierra Club, *Publication No. 1*, 1892; Joseph N. LeConte, "The Sierra Club," *SCB*, 1917, 10:2.

2. The origin of the Sierra Club and its achievements are mentioned only briefly here; they are treated more fully in Holway Jones, *John Muir and the Sierra Club: The Battle for Yosemite*, San Francisco: Sierra Club, 1965.

3. "Journals of Joseph LeConte." (MSS. in BL).

4. Joseph Nisbet LeConte (1870-1950); University of California, B.S., 1891; Cornell, M.M.E., 1892. A charter member of the Sierra Club; President, 1915-1917; Honorary President, 1931-1950. (Memorial, *AAJ*, 1950, 7:4.)

5. Hubert Dyer, "Camping in the Highest Sierra," *Appalachia*, January, 1892; J. N. LeConte, "Journal of a Camping Trip Amongst the Highest of the California Sierra, Summer of 1890" (typescript in BL).

6. Many of these photographs were published in the *Sierra Club Bulletin*, in

Sunset Magazine, and in *Alpina Americana* (published by the American Alpine Club), 1907, No. 1.

7. Helen M. Gompertz, "A Tramp to Mt. Lyell," *SCB*, May, 1894, 1:4, and "Up and Down Bubb's Creek," *SCB*, May, 1897, 2:2. (In the early days of the *Sierra Club Bulletin* there seems to have been an obsession for putting an apostrophe before an *s* even though the *s* was part of the name and not a possessive.)

8. Joseph LeConte, "My Trip to Kings River Canyon," *Sunset*, October, 1900, 5:6, reprinted in *SCB*, June, 1902, 4:2.

9. William Edward Colby, born at Benicia, May 28, 1875; attended University of California and Hastings College of Law, LL.B., 1898. He became the leading practitioner of the country in the field of mining law and a lecturer on that subject at the University of California. He joined the Sierra Club in 1895. He became its Secretary in 1901 and held that position for forty-six years, except while President from 1917 to 1919. From 1950 until his death in 1964 he was Honorary President. Colby was the initiator of the Sierra Club Outings in 1901 and their leader for thirty-seven years. In 1927 he became the first Chairman of the newly established California State Park Commission.

10. Colby, "Early Days of the Sierra Club," a tape recording, 1959 (transcript in BL).

11. Robert M. Price, "The Grand Canyon of the Tuolumne," *SCB*, January, 1893, 1:1. Robert Martin Price (1867-1940); University of California and Hastings College of Law, LL.B., 1896; practiced law in San Francisco and later in Reno, Nevada. A charter member of the Sierra Club, its Secretary 1896-1900, President 1924-1925. (Memorial by William E. Colby, *SCB*, February, 1940, 25:1.)

12. R. M. Price, "Through the Tuolumne Canyon," *SCB*, May, 1895, 1:6; Colby, "Early Days."

13. T. S. Solomons, "The Grand Canyon of the Tuolumne," *Appalachia*, November, 1896, 8:2; and "Grand Canyon of the Tuolumne," *The Traveler*, December, 1896, 4:6. Theodore Seixas Solomons (1870-1947), court stenographer and writer. A charter member of the Sierra Club. (Memorial in *SCB*, March, 1948, 33:3.)

14. T. S. Solomons, "A Search for a High Mountain Route from Yosemite to the Kings River Canyon," *SCB*, May, 1895, 1:6.

15. T. S. Solomons, "Mt. Goddard and Vicinity," *Appalachia*, January, 1896, 8:1; "An Enchanted Gorge," *The Traveler*, November, 1895, 6:6; "Tehipite Valley," *The Traveler*, May, 1896, 7:5; "Unexplored Regions of the High Sierra—Tehipite Valley," *Overland Monthly*, March, 1897, 30:5.

16. W. A. Starr, "From Yosemite to Kings River Canyon, 1896." *SCB*, 1935, 20:1. Walter Augustus Starr, born in San Francisco, 1877; graduated University of California, 1897. President of the Sierra Club, 1941-1943; Honorary President, 1964. Allen Lawrence Chickering (1877-1958); University of California, A.B., 1898, LL.B., 1901; throughout his life a prominent member of the legal profession in San Francisco; a lover of the wild flowers of California, especially those of the Sierra. (Memorial in *CHSQ*, March, 1958, 37:1.)

17. Florence Lake is now enlarged by a dam and is a reservoir of the Southern California Edison Company, as is the flooded Vermilion Valley.

18. "Tunemah" is a Chinese word of vilest significance, given because of the expletives of a Chinese cook as he rode along it.

19. Brown's maps and sketches are to be found in the first three volumes of the *Sierra Club Bulletin*.

20. *SCB*, May, 1897, 2:2.

21. Bolton Coit Brown, "Another Paradise," *SCB*, May, 1900, 3:2.

22. Vernon L. Kellogg, "A Stanford Party in the Kings River Canyon," *Sunset*, November, 1899; D. S. Jordan, "The Kings River Canyon and the Alps of the Great Divide," *Sunset*, April, 1900; Jordan, *The Alps of the King–Kern Divide*, 1903 (*Farquhar* No. 19); Jordan, *The Days of a Man*, 1922; Payson J. Treat, "David Starr Jordan," *SCB*, February, 1932, 17:1. David Starr Jordan (1851-1931) was one of the founders of the Sierra Club, and Honorary Vice-President, 1905-1931. He was the author of numerous zoological works, principally on the fishes.

23. Dr. Jordan climbed the Matterhorn in 1881. Jordan, "An Ascent of the Matterhorn," a chapter in his *Science Sketches*, 1888 (reprinted 1896, and in *SCB*, February, 1940, 25:1).

24. "Here John Muir studied the water-ouzel in his home, and wrote of it the best biography yet given of any bird." Jordan, *Alps*.

25. J. S. Hutchinson, "Joseph Nisbet LeConte: Some Recollections," *SCB*, June, 1950, 35:6.

26. J. N. LeConte, "The Ascent of the North Palisades," *SCB*, January, 1904, 5:1.

27. J. N. LeConte, "The High Mountain Route Between Yosemite and the King's River Canyon," *SCB*, January, 1909, 7:1.

28. J. S. Hutchinson, "Colby Pass and the Black Kaweah," *SCB*, January, 1921, 11:2. James Sather Hutchinson, Jr. (1867-1959), attended University of California, transferred to Harvard (A.B., 1897), attended Hastings College of Law, LL.B., 1899, practiced law in San Francisco. While still in college became a charter member of the Sierra Club; editor of the *Sierra Club Bulletin*, 1903-1904 and again in 1925. (Memorial in *AAJ*, 1960, 12:1.) Duncan McDuffie (1877-1951), a graduate of the University of California, 1899, developer of fine residential districts in the San Francisco Bay area. President of the Sierra Club, 1928-1931 and again 1943-1946. (Memorial in *AAJ*, 1952, 8:2.) Onis Imus Brown was not only a good packer but a good cook, and, although packers traditionally "haven't lost anything on the tops of those mountains," Onis Imus was different—he liked to climb. For the origin of his name, see Colossians 4:9.

29. J. S. Hutchinson, "First Ascent: Mount Humphreys," *SCB*, January, 1905, 5:3.

30. E. C. Andrews, "First Ascent of Mount Darwin—1908," *SCB*, 1924, 12:1.

31. *Town Talk*, Pasadena, December, 1896–February, 1897, vol. 9, nos. 8-14 (copy in BL).

32. Stewart Edward White, *The Pass*, New York: Outing Publishing Co., 1906 (*Farquhar* No. 20).

33. William E. Colby, "Twenty-Nine Years with the Sierra Club," *SCB*, February, 1931, 16:1.

34. For nearly every year of the long sequence of Sierra Club outings there is an article by a participant in the *Sierra Club Bulletin*. Notable among them are: Bertha Clark Pope, "The High Trip of 1925," *SCB*, 1926, 12:3; Marion Randall Parsons, "The Twenty-Eighth Outing," *SCB*, February, 1930, 15:1; Ansel Easton Adams, "Retrospect—1931," *SCB*, February, 1932, 17:1; Hollis T. Gleason, "The Outing of 1932," *SCB*, February, 1933, 18:1; Ruth R. Currier, "Sierran, 1914-1934," *SCB*, February, 1935, 20:1; David R. Brower, "Tripping High—1939," *SCB*, February, 1940, 25:1; Weldon F. Heald, "High and Dry in

1940," *SCB*, February, 1941, 26:1; Charlotte E. Mauk, "The Nth Itinerary," *SCB*, August, 1942, 27:4; also articles by Charlotte Mauk in *SCB*, 1947 and 1949.

35. *Sierra Club Outing Announcements* (a set in BL).

36. Walt Wheelock, "Norman Clyde," chapter in Norman Clyde, *Close Ups of the High Sierra*, Glendale, Calif.: La Siesta Press, 1962.

37. *SCB*, February, 1932, 17:1, Mountaineering Notes.

38. Robert L. M. Underhill, "Mount Whitney by the East Face," *SCB*, February, 1932, 17:1.

39. Richard M. Leonard, "The Cathedral Spires" (Mountaineering Notes), *SCB*, February, 1935, 20:1. Bestor Robinson was President of the Sierra Club, 1946-1948, and Richard M. Leonard, 1953-1955. Marjory Bridge became Mrs. Francis P. Farquhar in December, 1934.

40. Francis P. Farquhar, "Muir Gorge in Tuolumne Canyon," *SCB*, February, 1932, 17:1; Louise Hildebrand, "Cathedral Creek and Muir Gorge, 1934," *SCB*, February, 1935, 20:1.

41. Walter A. Starr, Jr., *Guide to the John Muir Trail and the High Sierra Region*, San Francisco: Sierra Club, 1934, and subsequent editions. "The Search for Walter A. Starr, Jr." (Mountaineering Notes), *SCB*, June, 1934, 19:3.

42. "The John Muir Trail" (Notes), *SCB*, January, 1916, 10:1; Walter L. Huber, "The John Muir Trail," *SCB*, February, 1930, 15:1; Francis P. Farquhar, "Northward Over the John Muir Trail." *SCB*, January, 1920, 11:1.

XXI

UTILIZATION AND RECREATION

At the beginning of this history it was stated that the waters of the Sierra are its greatest contribution to human welfare. Without water the Sierra would be bare and bleak; without water the Central Valley of California would be a desert. Happily, the water is there. It varies in quantity from year to year, and were it not for the intervention of man its contribution would be unstable, at times even unfortunate. Man, however, has so regulated the flow by dams and reservoirs that, except in years of extreme drought, water is available for irrigation and urban supply when needed. Floods have not been prevented completely, but progress has been made and further control is in sight. Dams and reservoirs have another function, and that on a great scale—putting water to work. From the reservoirs it is made to plunge in steep descent into turbines (the modern development of the ancient waterwheel), where its power is transformed into electric current. Released from the turbines, the water continues on its way to perform other duties, although, as some wag has said, "with all the electricity taken out."

The capture and diversion of water was first undertaken in the Sierra for use in mining operations. Water has always been essential to placer mining, the medium for sorting flakes of gold from sand and gravel. The natural flow of the streams was insufficient, so ditches were dug and flumes constructed. Very soon after the discovery of gold, water was being captured and diverted to use in the goldfields all the way from the Feather River to the Mariposa Estate and the Fresno River. A little later came hydraulic mining, by which water was directed with great force upon the auriferous gravel banks, tearing them down and loosening their burden of gold. This process filled the rivers with mud and aroused storms of protest from landowners downstream until hydraulic mining was virtually stopped by legislation. Another use of water power in mining operations was to run the primitive sawmills that furnished lumber for flumes and for buildings in the mining camps. From this local and direct application of water power grew the great hydroelectric systems of the present day. This was made possible by the invention of the electro magnetic generator, which came at an opportune time to meet the requirements of rapidly expanding population and industry in California. At first, power produced by means of generators was available only for local use, but in 1895 power generated from waters of the American River at Folsom was carried by wire twenty-one miles to Sacramento.

When it was demonstrated that power generated from falling water could be conveyed by high-voltage wires to points of application far away, engineers began to explore the Sierra for power sites. Small companies sprang up; they built dams at the outlets of little lakes, making them bigger, and in canyons and meadows; the stored waters were conducted to penstocks and dropped to the generators. Then came the mergers of firms, and the little companies became subsidiaries or components of larger companies until nearly the entire power production of the Sierra became concentrated in two systems, Pacific Gas and Electric Company and Southern California Edison Company.[1]

Among the pioneer entities that became part of the P. G and E. were the San Joaquin Light and Power Corporation, which utilized waters of the San Joaquin and Merced; the Sierra and San Francisco Power Company, which utilized the Stanislaus; and the Great Western Power Company, which developed the Feather River. Other predecessors of P. G. and E. pioneered the Yuba and American rivers.[2]

Southern California Edison Company's sources of water power in the Sierra came through mergers, and later extension of their systems, with Pacific Light and Power Company and Mount Whitney Power and Electric Company.[3] A recent merger brought into the Edison system reservoirs and power plants on the eastern side of the Sierra at Bishop Creek, Rush Creek, and Lee Vining Creek. Pacific Light and Power's major contribution was the Big Creek plant, which derived its water supply from Huntington Lake. This lake, and others in the neighborhood, were eventually interlocked in a way that made it possible to regulate the seasonal and annual supply of water to the powerhouses. After the Edison Company took over the Big Creek plant, Florence Lake was enlarged by a dam, and a tunnel twelve miles long, completed in 1925, brought its water under Kaiser Ridge to Huntington Lake. Since then other reservoirs have been added to the system, notably the Thomas A. Edison in Vermilion Valley. Another pioneer system acquired by the Edison Company was that of the Mount Whitney Power and Electric Company, which utilized waters that came down from lakes on the Great Western Divide in the Middle and East forks of the Kaweah.[4] A dam on Wolverton Creek, in Giant Forest, was never utilized, and the property was later given by the Edison Company to the government for use as part of Sequoia National Park.

In addition to these two large corporations and one or two smaller ones, a number of irrigation districts and three large municipal systems use the waters of the Sierra. The development of San Francisco's Hetch Hetchy project is a long and complicated story, involving the integrity of Yosemite National Park. Permits were granted and revoked by successive Secretaries of the Interior, until finally Congress, by the Raker Act of 1913, authorized San Francisco both to construct a dam at Hetch Hetchy and convey the waters of the Tuolumne across the Central Valley for the city's domestic use and to utilize the power developed by the reservoir. Hetch Hetchy has been the source of endless controversy, and for a time it disrupted the Sierra Club, and yet in the end it has stimulated a firmer stand throughout the country against violation of the national parks. But Hetch Hetchy Valley as a campground of primitive beauty has been forever extinguished.[5]

On the other side of the Sierra the city of Los Angeles acquired nearly all the water rights in Owens Valley and concentrated the streams that came down the eastern side into an aqueduct that paralleled the range. On the west the East Bay Municipal District impounded the waters of the Mokelumne by Pardee Dam. Independent of the big companies is the Truckee River Power Company, which uses the runoff from the upper basin of Lake Tahoe as well as other tributaries of the Truckee River. "The discharge from Lake Tahoe has been under artificial control for a long while, and the present facilities operated by the United States Bureau of Reclamation permit regulation between elevations 6,224 and 6,230. Much controversy has occurred over the regulation effected, and the riparian owners around the lake shore have serious objection to any wide fluctuation of the lake level."[6]

The winter snows continue to fall upon the High Sierra. Lakes and streams are replenished, and the waters serve many purposes besides irrigation and the production of power. In some places the waters have been defiled, as in the pollution of Lake Tahoe and the besmirched shores of Hetch Hetchy Reservoir. But today the pure waters of the Sierra Nevada are more widely appreciated than ever before, and there is good hope that in the future there will be firm resistance to unnecessary impairment of their value.

Other important material contributions of the Sierra are its minerals and its lumber. Mining has been largely excluded from this history as belonging to the foothills, with an oft-told history of its own. The requirements of the mining communities for lumber, however, caused the first extensive cutting of Sierra forests, beginning with those of the Yuba. Then came the requirements of railroad construction, followed by the frantic activity of the Nevada bonanza, which stripped the forest east of Lake Tahoe in a wasteful splurge. The giant Sequoias remained comparatively untouched because they were difficult to cut, because the revenue from the brittle wood was meager, and because their value as living trees was recognized early. Sugar Pines and Yellow Pines were too great a commercial prize to be spared, and only their remoteness and the difficulties of acquiring title to enough acreage for economical operation prevented devastation before the establishment of the national forests and the national parks intervened to protect them. Recently the importance of forest cover for protection of watersheds has become recognized, and today lumbering in the national forests, and even on privately owned lands, is carried on in accordance with sound forestry practices. Substantial areas of the finest Sugar Pine are preserved in national parks, and practically all of the Sequoias are either in national or state parks or held inviolate by regulation of the U.S. Forest Service.

The grazing of livestock, once widely practiced in the Sierra, has steadily diminished. Grazing of cattle proved to be of little benefit, save perhaps to small owners, who enjoyed respite from the summer heat of the lowlands while pasturing their herds in mountain meadows. In the economics of the industry it is not an important factor. Pasturing of sheep in the Sierra has practically ceased. It is countenanced neither by the Park Service nor by the Forest Service. The damage wreaked long ago has served as a warning against uncontrolled use of natural resources, and the grazing of sheep is inherently uncontrolled.

The remaining natural resource in the economy of the Sierra is its wildlife, and that means principally deer. The few fur-bearing animals that fall into the hands of the trapper have practically no economic effect, save perhaps a slight one to the individual who captures them. Deer, however, are both a positive and a negative factor. They provide a target for the hunter and a meager supply of meat for the rancher. On the other hand, they are a nuisance to the farmer and to the housewife who cherishes her garden. As for the fish, although they have no important economic value, they serve as an enticement to countless fishermen; and a little inquiry into the economics of fisherman's supplies and sporting magazines will demonstrate that fishermen have high monetary value.

Various forms of recreation have taken an increasingly important part in the economy of the Sierra. The search for "scenes of wonder and curiosity," a form of recreation, has brought thousands of tourists to Yosemite Valley and the Big Tree groves. Every summer sees camping parties on trail and road, on horseback or on foot, in little cars, in big cars, and in buses. They crowd the public campgrounds or seek more sequestered spots. Improved roads and improved vehicles bring them from near and far to enjoy the unrivaled facilities for outdoor life that these mountains offer. The prevalence of whole families, with children of all ages, results in a holiday mood, in wholesome contrast to the deterioration of urban life. Only in a few places, such as the south shore of Lake Tahoe, has deterioration followed to the mountains. But even there, in spite of the pestilence of noisy speedboats, honky-tonks, and garish lights, beauty remains not far away. On the shores of smaller lakes and in the forests beyond are cabins—summer homes—either on plots of privately owned land or on small tracts leased by the Forest Service. The pressure of population is forcing the Forest Service to revise some of its earlier allotments of space, but in places like Huntington Lake summer homes in the National

Forests are likely to be available for some time to come. They provide ideal centers for family living and for social gatherings around a campfire, and for rambling excursions into the surrounding forests and wildflower gardens and to the tops of nearby granite ridges and peaks. They offer swimming and boating and the companionship, if cultivated, of birds and little animals, grateful for crumbs. In the national forests there are many summer camps for Scout organizations, and there are a number of municipal camps where city families can go for vacation.

More vigorous forms of recreation can be had by taking trails, with mule or donkey as burden-bearer. On one such trail there will perhaps be found the old sign, "This Trail is Jackassable—For Horses Impassable." But if one is on foot, with knapsack on back, there is no limit save one's own abilities. At the extreme of vigorous recreation is mountain climbing. Not every last pinnacle in the Sierra has been climbed, but even if it were otherwise there are new routes to be found. Whether or not it has been climbed in the past, it always offers a new view from the top, either clearer in the distance than before or with a new formation of clouds.

Other types of recreation are as numerous as the preferences of the individual. There are hunting and fishing; there are botanizing and butterfly collecting; there are painting and photography; and there is merely sitting beside a stream and listening to the music of its waters. Recreation in the Sierra is truly a re-creation of body and spirit.

Recreation in midwinter and at high altitudes is a modern development. There are two requisites: a means of getting about, and a warm lodging for retreat. Railroads and highways and the technical improvements in skis have provided the first requisite; winter resorts and ski lodges have provided the second. Skiing was practiced in the Sierra a long time ago, but under quite different circumstances. "Snow-shoe" Thompson carried the mail across the Sierra every winter from 1856 to 1876, but his exploits can hardly be called "recreation." The activities in the 1860's of Norwegian miners in Plumas and Sierra counties may have been a sort of "recreation" at times, but for them skiing was chiefly a competitive sport, stimulated by wagers. The use of "dope," a sort of patent medicine applied to the bottoms of skis, produced astonishing results. Confident in the efficacy of their "dope," they inveigled the celebrated Thompson to race with them. The results were humiliating for "Snow-shoe," who knew nothing about "dope" and whose technique was quite different from that of the Plumas County slickers, who left him far behind. He retaliated with a challenge for a return match at Silver Mountain, which included a run "from top to bottom of the highest and steepest mountain we can find," and a jump "over a precipice fifteen feet high, without use of the pole." He offered a bet of $100 that no one could follow him across country for one day without breaking his neck. The challenge was not taken up. Today "Snow-shoe" Thompson remains the unrivaled champion in some of the toughest phases of the art of skiing.[7]

There were intermittent revivals of skiing, principally by Norwegians accustomed to it from their youth, but the modern sport with all its recreational values did not begin until after the turn of the century. There were excursions by railroad to Truckee and other points along the railroad line, but few of the excursionists possessed a high degree of skill. A few individuals, who had acquired skill elsewhere, usually in Austria or Switzerland, undertook more daring sallies upon slopes not too far from the railroad. The Sierra Ski Club built a lodge near Donner Summit; a few Sierra Club members planned another nearby, which in 1934 became the Sierra Club's Clair Tappaan Lodge, now frequented by hundreds every winter.[8] The Auburn Ski Club encouraged the sport of the high-flying ski jump and promoted activities at Cisco Grove on the road to Donner Pass. Skiing was introduced in Yosemite National Park, with emphasis first on cross-country runs. Mount Hoffmann was climbed by means of skis; then a party made a wintry expedition to high altitudes and climbed Mount Lyell.[9] Ski devotees in the south began to come up Owens Valley to the eastern flanks of the Sierra; Mount Whitney was reached by skis; and presently came the development at Mammoth, now one of the most famous ski resorts in the country. Slopes were developed for all classes, from "snow bunnies" to expert downhill and slalom racers. Winter resorts increased in number, especially when, by the use of the rotary plow, the highways remained open all winter, save only when the heaviest storms prevailed over all human efforts.[10] Today there are winter accommodations in the Sierra for thousands—Yosemite, with its Badger Pass playground; Mammoth; and the Donner–Truckee–Tahoe group, Sugar Bowl, Squaw Valley. Alpine Meadows, and Heavenly Valley. The climax came with the world-wide convocation of skiers at Squaw Valley for the Winter Olympic Games in February, 1960.

NOTES AND REFERENCES

1. Sources of information on water and power development in California are voluminous. The basic document is Frederick Hall Fowler, "Hydroelectric Power Systems of California and Their Extension into Oregon and Nevada," *United States Geological Survey Water Supply Paper 493*, Washington, 1923. Another important paper is Frank T. Bonner, *Report to the Federal Power Commission on the Water Powers of California*, Washington, 1928.

2. Charles M. Coleman, *P. G. and E. of California: The Centennial History of Pacific Gas and Electric Company, 1852-1952*, New York: McGraw-Hill, 1952; James B. Black, *California—"Stored with Many Blessings Fit for the Use of Man,"* New York: Newcomen Society, August, 1948; see also "Pacific Gas and Electric Company," *Electrical West*, August, 1952.

3. David H. Redinger, *The Story of Big Creek*, Los Angeles: Angelus Press, 1949; see also "Southern California Edison Company," *Electrica! West*, August, 1962.

4. Rudolph W. Van Norden, "System of the Mt. Whitney Power and Electric Company," *Journal of Electricity*, December 27, 1913. (This company had nothing to do with Mount Whitney, which was far away on the other side of the Great Western Divide and across the canyon of the Kern; otherwise it was a good name.)

5. The story of Hetch Hetchy is fully developed in Holway R. Jones, *John Muir and the Sierra Club: The Battle for Yosemite*, San Francisco: Sierra Club, 1965.

6. Bonner, *Report*.

7. Joel H. Hildebrand, "A History of Ski-ing in California," *British Ski Year Book*, 1939; see also Robert H. Power, *Pioneer Skiing in California*, Vacaville, Calif., 1960.

8. Joel H. Hildebrand, "Ski Heil!" *SCB*, February, 1935, 20:1.

9. David R. Brower, "Beyond the Skiways," *SCB*, April, 1938, 23:2. The party was composed of Bestor Robinson, Lewis F. Clark, Boynton S. Kaiser, Einar Nilsson, and David R. Brower. They left Yosemite in February and returned in March, 1936 (but it was February 29 and March 2).

10. George R. Stewart gives a vivid description in his novel *Storm*, New York: Random House, 1941.

Envoy

Reader:

May It Be Your Good Fortune

TO WANDER AT LEISURE THROUGH THE HIGH SIERRA

TO REJOICE WITH THE LEAPING CASCADES

TO SIT BESIDE CALM POOLS AND OBSERVE THE BEAMS OF SUNLIGHT

      AS THEY FILTER TO THE DEPTHS

TO DREAM BENEATH THE TALL PINES AND WATCH THE CLOUDS

      DRIFT ACROSS THE SKY

TO FOLLOW WITH THE EYE THE QUICK MOVEMENTS OF THE SQUIRREL

TO ADMIRE THE COLUMBINE, THE GENTIAN, AND THE SCARLET PENTSTEMON

AND TO CONTEMPLATE THE UNHURRIED GROWTH OF GIANT SEQUOIAS

W. E. Dassonville

MAPS

The maps, prepared by Mrs. Nancy Fouquet, of Atherton, California, are designed to show the principal features, place names, and routes mentioned in the text. It would not, of course, be practicable to show them all. For further detail the reader is referred to *Starr's Guide to the John Muir Trail*, published by the Sierra Club; to the Adamses' *Illustrated Guide to Yosemite Valley*, also a Sierra Club publication; and to the U. S. Geological Survey topographic maps and the maps published by the U. S. Forest Service and the National Park Service.

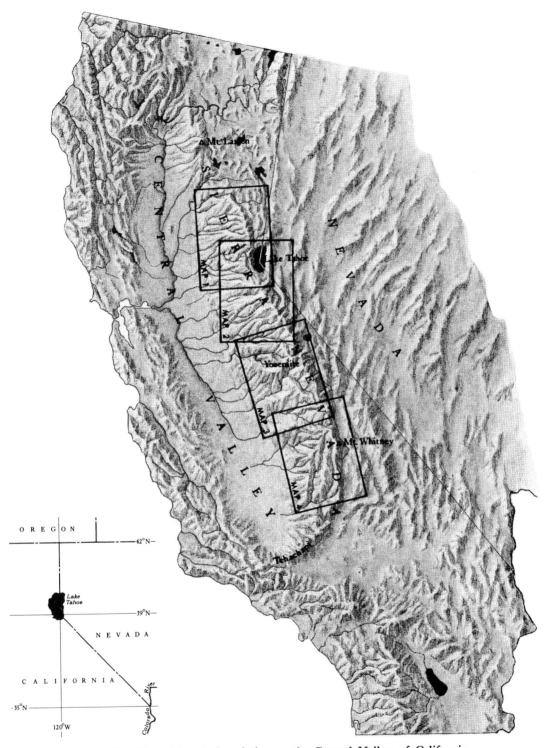

The Sierra Nevada in relation to the Central Valley of California.

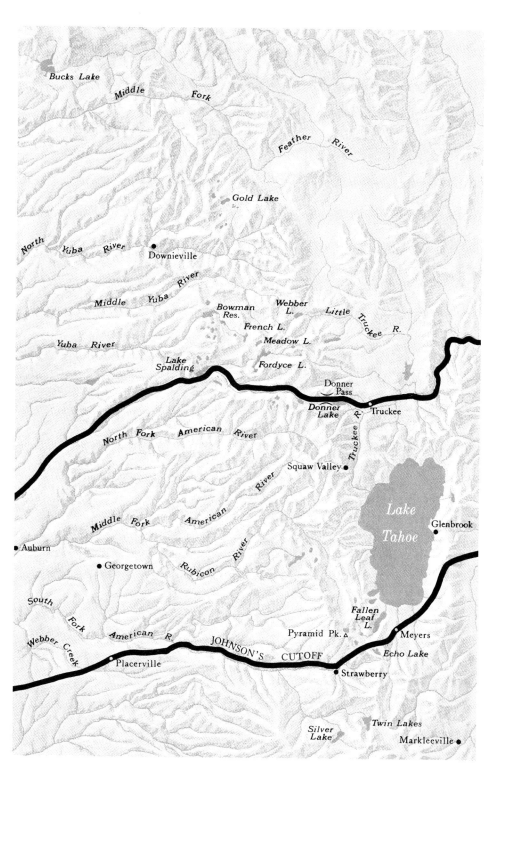

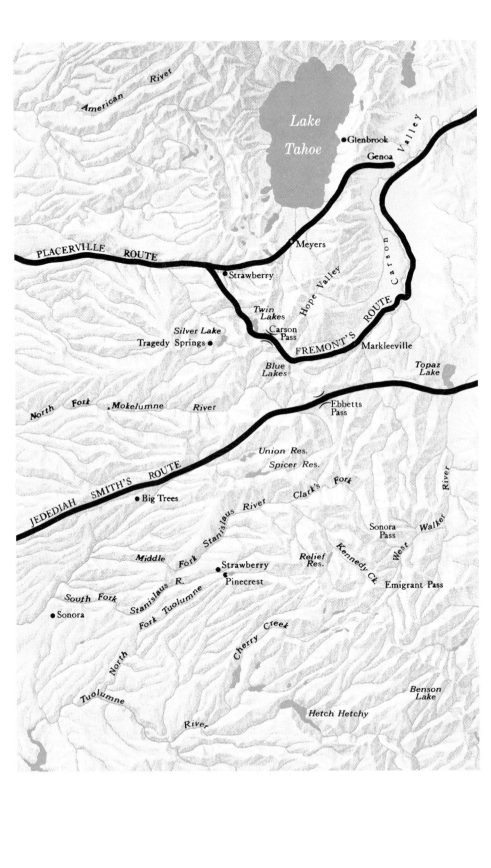

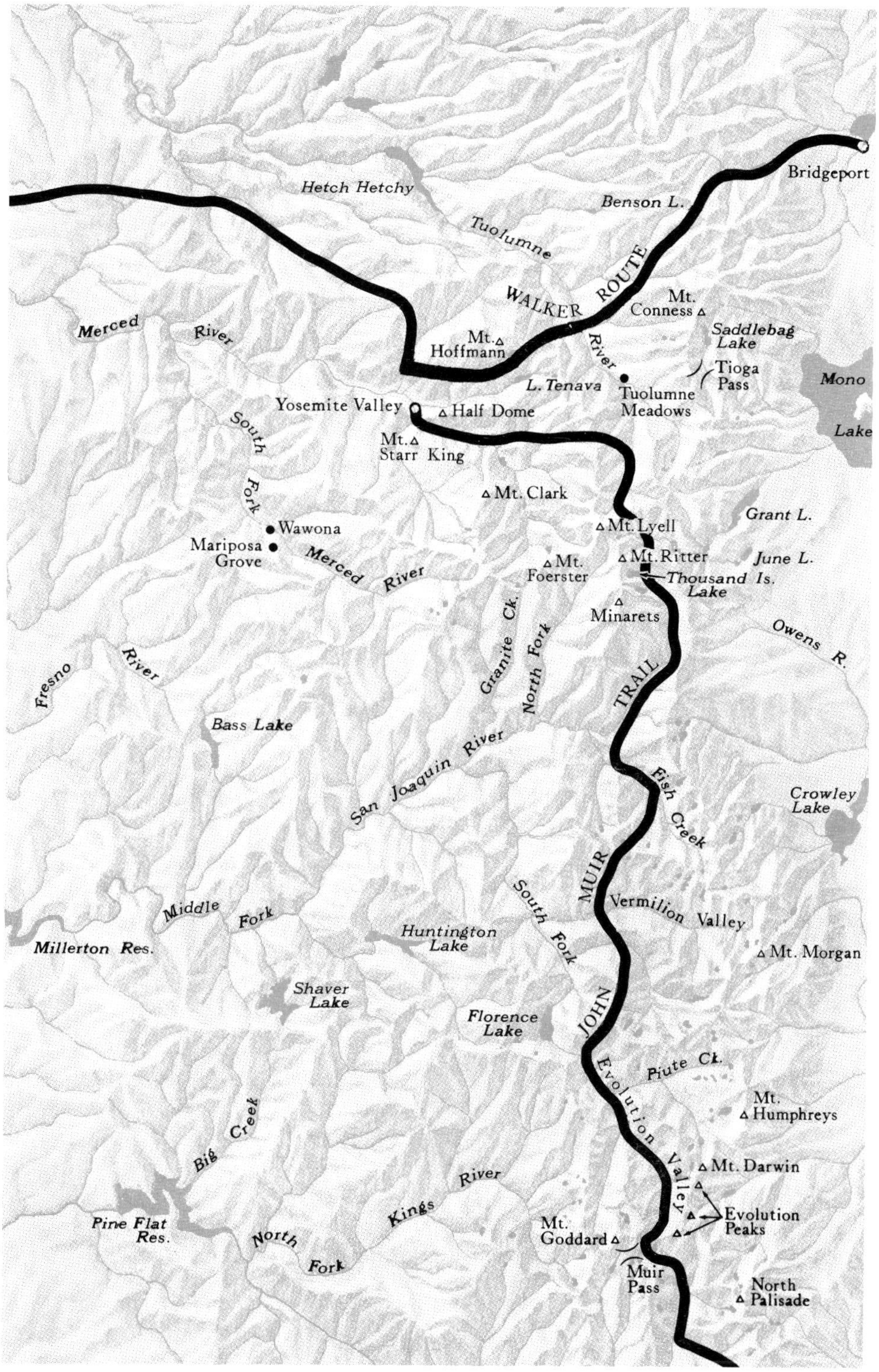
Bridgeport
Hetch Hetchy
Benson L.
Tuolumne
WALKER ROUTE
Mt. Conness
Merced
River
Mt. Hoffmann
Saddlebag Lake
River
Tioga Pass
L. Tenava
Tuolumne Meadows
Mono Lake
Yosemite Valley
Half Dome
South Fork
Mt. Starr King
Mt. Clark
Wawona
Mariposa Grove
Merced River
Mt. Lyell
Grant L.
Mt. Ritter
June L.
Mt. Foerster
Thousand Is. Lake
Minarets
Owens R.
Fresno
River
Granite Ck.
North Fork
TRAIL
Bass Lake
San Joaquin River
Fish Creek
Crowley Lake
MUIR
South Fork
Vermilion Valley
Middle Fork
Millerton Res.
Huntington Lake
Mt. Morgan
Shaver Lake
Florence Lake
JOHN
Evolution Valley
Piute Ck.
Mt. Humphreys
Big Creek
Mt. Darwin
River
Kings
Evolution Peaks
Pine Flat Res.
North Fork
Mt. Goddard
Muir Pass
North Palisade

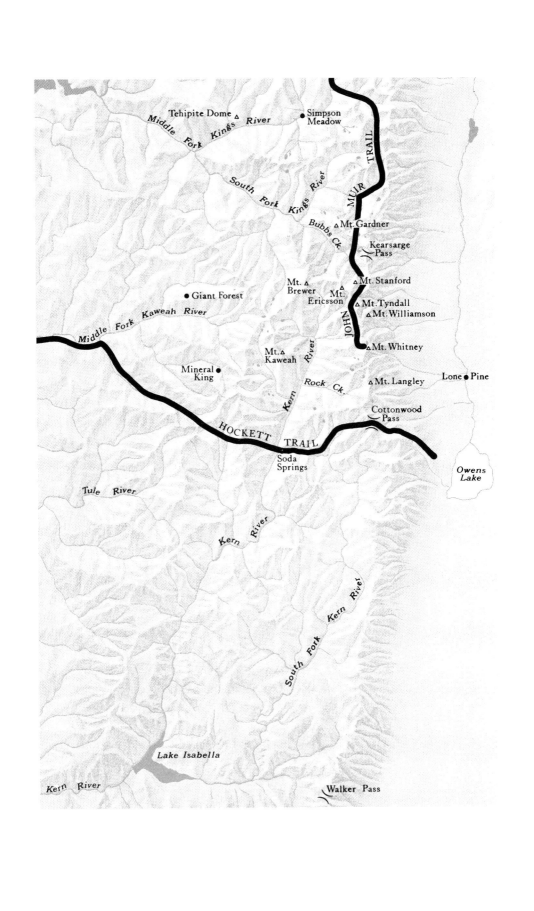

INDEX